Medieval Philosophy

Medieval Philosophy

N Subba Rao

MD Publications Pvt Ltd
New Delhi
www.mdppl.com

Published by :

MD Publications Pvt Ltd
"MD House", 11, Darya Ganj,
New Delhi - 110 002
Phone : +91-11- 45355555
E-mail : contact@mdppl.com
Website: www.mdppl.com

ISBN : 978-81-7533-336-9

Published and Printed by Mr. Pranav Gupta on behalf of **MD Publications Pvt Ltd** at Repro India Limited.

Preface

Medieval philosophy refers to philosophy in Western Europe during the "medieval" period, the so called "Middle Ages." The notion of a "Middle Age" was introduced in the fifteenth century for the period between the decline of classical pagan culture in Western Europe and what was taken to be its rediscovery during the Renaissance. The first known documented use of the expression is from 1469.

The originators of the notion of the Middle Ages were thinking primarily of the so called "Latin West," the area, roughly speaking, of Roman Catholicism. While it is true that this region was to some extent a unit, culturally separate from its neighbors, it is also true that medieval philosophy was decisively influenced by ideas from the Greek East, from the Jewish philosophical tradition, and from Islam. If one takes medieval philosophy to include the Patristic period, as the present author prefers to do, then the area must be expanded to include, at least during the early centuries, Greek-speaking eastern Europe, as well as North Africa and parts of Asia Minor.

The chronological limits of medieval philosophy are equally imprecise. Henry takes it to begin with St. Augustine (354–430), as in effect do MacDonald and Kretzmann. On the other hand, Copleston and Gilson include the earlier Patristic period as well. At the other end of the period, things are even more imprecise. Robinson amusingly summarizes the situation:

> *Scholars have advocated many different termini for our period, and there seems to be little agreement and indeed little basis for reasoned argument on these points. The Middle Ages begin, we are told, with the death of Theodosius in 395, or with the settlement of Germanic tribes in the Roman Empire, or with the sack of Rome in 410, or with the fall of the Western Roman Empire, or even as late as the Moslem occupation of the Mediterranean. It ends with*

> *the fall of Constantinople, or with the invention of printing, or with the discovery of America, or with the beginning of the Italian wars, or with the Lutheran Reformation, or with the election of Charles V. Several reference works I have consulted simply assert that the Middle Ages ended in 1500, presumably on New Year's Eve. Yet another terminus often given for the Middle Ages is the so-called "Revival of Learning," that marvelous era when Humanist scholars "discovered" classical texts and restored them to mankind after the long Gothic night. Medievalists must always smile a little over these "discoveries," for we know where the Humanists discovered those classical texts namely, in medieval manuscripts, where medieval scribes had been carefully preserving them for mankind over the centuries. In view of all this disagreement over the duration of the Middle Ages, perhaps we should content ourselves with saying that our period extends from the close of the classical period to the beginning of the Renaissance. If classicists and Renaissance scholars don't know when their periods begin and end, then that is their problem.*

Still, it is perhaps most useful not to think of medieval philosophy as defined by the chronological boundaries of its adjacent philosophical periods, but as beginning when thinkers first started to measure their philosophical speculations against the requirements of Christian doctrine and as ending when this was no longer the predominant practice. This view allows late ancient and early medieval philosophy to overlap during the Patristic period; thus Proclus belongs to the story of ancient philosophy, even though he is later than Saint Augustine. Again, this view accommodates the fact that late scholasticism survived and flourished even in the Renaissance. Thus Francisco Suarez, who can arguably be regarded as the last chapter in the history of medieval philosophy, was contemporary with Francis Bacon. Nevertheless by c. 1450, at the latest, radically new ways of doing philosophy were clearly emerging.

This perhaps generous interpretation of the chronological limits of medieval philosophy implies that it lasted at least from the Greek patristic author Justin Martyr until well into the fifteenth century more than half the entire history of philosophy generally.

N Subba Rao

Contents

Contents

1

Medieval Philosophy
Beginnings to Avicenna

Introduction

For two centuries, Christians had been employed to translate Greek works into Syriac, a type of Aramaic that had been developed into a literary language. In this way there began, even before the birth of Islam, the great enterprise of translation which would provide the opportunity for the first works of Arabic philosophy and the results of which would provide its subject-matter and foundation. The history of this movement, especially its earliest stage, has not yet been written in full. We can say, however, that between the fifth and seventh centuries AD translations were made from Greek into Syriac, particularly translations of medical works and, even more, of logical works. The first books of Aristotle's *Organon* were, then, not merely translated but received a number of commentaries. The majority of the translators were Nestorians, but they also included Jacobites. At the end of the first/seventh century, the Muslims took over the Fertile Crescent and the Umayyad caliph 'Abd al-Malik decided that Arabic would be the official language of the empire. The work of the translators was enlarged. Translation from Greek to Syriac continued to be their main task, but there were also translations made from Greek into Arabic and from Syriac into Arabic. This third route was used only in the fourth/tenth century when even the educated no longer knew Greek, and when in any case the translation movement came to a halt.

Not only was there a change in the languages from which, and to which, translations were made; there was variation over time in the method and type of translation. Translators into Syriac changed from giving paraphrases to making literal versions. The greatest of them were the two Christian Nestorians Unayn ibn Isâq and his son Isâq ibn Unayn, whose work in Syriac and Arabic dates from the third/ninth century. Acute in establishing their texts and rigorously accurate in translating from one language to another, Unayn and his son ended by creating 'a technical Arabic Capable of closely reflecting the structure of the Greek' ([2.27]). There were many other translators too in their century and the one before, some of them very fine. Rather than list them, it is more useful to step back in time and mention the names of 'Abd Allâh ibn al-Muqaffa and of the Syrian Ibn Bahrîz, who lived at the time of the caliph al-Ma'mun. Both wrote epitomes of logical works.

In this way an enormous library of philosophical and scientific works was built up and revealed to the curiosity and interests of new readers. The last Umayyad caliphs and the first of the 'Abbâsids were especially strong in their support for this work of translation. In the case of the Abbâssids, this enthusiasm was motivated in part by a political motive, since Greek philosophy and science provided a cultural counterbalance to the theology of the Islamic Arabs and to the ancient heritage of the Persians. The intellectual (and, particularly, philosophical) market-place was thus stocked with a complex mixture of goods: an Arabic Plato (the details of which still remain unclear), an Arabic Plotinus attributed to other authors, collections of philosophical comments and aphorisms in which authentic pronouncements mingle with apocrypha, and above all the complete works of Aristotle, without the *Politics* but with various, especially Neoplatonic, pseudepigrapha. This Aristotle is omnipresent in Arabic philosophy, yet its presence was the result in the main of a choice made several centuries earlier by the Syriac translators: 'it was not the Arabs who chose Aristotle, but the Syriacs who imposed [him on them]'.

Al-Kindi

Arabic philosophers drew extensively, then, on Aristotle's work and thought. Yet they were not Aristotelians in the strict sense of the word. This is already clear in the work of the first of them, Abû Yûsuf Ya'qûb ibn Isaq al-Kindi. Al-Kindî was a philosopher, no doubt; but he was primarily a wide-ranging scholar and scientist (and it was just as such that, half a thousand years later, Ibn Khaldûn would remember him). The biographer and bibliographer Ibn al-Nadîm (fourth/tenth century) provides a *catalogue raisonné* of his works: almost 250 of them in all, of which only about a tenth survive. Ibn al-Nadîm divides them into seventeen categories. Classifying them, rather, by subject areas, we find that al-Kindî devoted about 50 treatises to philosophy and logic, but nearly a hundred to the various branches of mathematics (including astrology), and 35 to medicine and the natural sciences. The others do not concern us here. His scholarly and scientific work was thus extensive and varied; we might mention, for instance, in passing his contributions to optics and pharmacology. As a philosopher, he quotes by name hardly any authors besides Plato and Aristotle. We do not know precisely how great his knowledge was of Plato, but he wrote a treatise listing the works of Aristotle. Of the major works only the *Politics* is, as we should expect, absent. The list includes two apocrypha *(On Plants, On Minerals),* but not the *Theology of Aristotle,* a work by an unknown author, probably Porphyry, consisting of considerably adapted extracts from Plotinus' later *Enneads.* Its absence is all the more striking because al-Kindî had corrected an Arabic translation of it made by Ibn Nâ'ima for the son of the caliph al-Mu'taim. And indeed al-Kindî's philosophy is a branch of Neoplatonism, but not one which is disguised by being based on Aristotelian apocrypha of Neoplatonic origin.

Among the handful of philosophical works of al-Kindî's which have survived, the most important is the *Book of First Philosophy*; note how the Greek *philosophia* is transcribed as *falsafah;* similarly *philosophas* becomes *faylasûf,* plural *falâsifah*). Of this book with its Aristotelian title we have only the first part (divided into four chapters). It is a Neoplatonic work in the sense that the main concepts of Aristotelianism (the categories, the predicables, causes) are made part of a theory of the one, into which al-Kindî's ontology is absorbed. In this rich discussion, new ideas and new methods are found in every chapter. We shall consider merely a few significant themes of various sorts. Al-Kindî provides an apologia for philosophy which, he says, has been formed over the course of centuries. We must gather what remains and bring it to fruition. It matters little, he says, that it comes from elsewhere. We must adapt it into our own language and to our own traditions, since it does not differ in content from the messages of the prophets: it is knowledge of God's unity and sovereignty, of virtue and of what in general we should seek and avoid. Using the method of geometry, he shows that the body of the world, movement and time can exist only if they are simultaneous with each other.

It is an important work, which shows how al-Kindî fits together the major systems of Greek philosophy, especially Neoplatonism. The concepts of the one and of transcendence are, in particular, common to this philosophical school and to Muslim theology. The Mu'tazilites especially would make it one of their main themes, and there is independent evidence that al-Kindî was close to them.

The doctrinal themes of the *First Philosophy* can be compared to those contained in other works by al-Kindî: explicitly or implicitly, the main aspects of his thought are to be found in this central work. First, the idea of the underlying harmony between revelation and prophecy is also found in the main discussion of the *Letter on the Number of*

Aristotle's Bodies: the 'divine knowledge' which God gives, from his free choice, to the prophets opens to them the knowledge of visible and invisible substances, whereas men usually have to labour long and hard, using logic and mathematics, to gain it. Thus the final verses of sourate 36 provide illuminating teaching on creation, the sequence of life and death and on contraries in general. Al-Kindî expounds at length the philosophical content of what divine revelation condenses into a few words. Second, as has already been explained, knowledge is gained through science and mathematics. Elsewhere too al-Kindî's arguments often have a rigorous, detailed structure based on the mathematical method. Third, the cosmological theme is developed by the same method in the *Letter on the Prostration of the Farthest Body,* which takes a text from the Koran 'The star and the tree prostrate themselves' as its point of departure. Al-Kindî begins with a semantic analysis of the words 'prostration' and 'obedience', which he says mean the same in this context. Then he explains in detail how God's will works in the world, which he envisages according to Greek cosmology and Aristotle's physics (except that he does not consider it eternal); once they have been created, the heavens are put into motion, and from this there comes about time and then coming-to-be. The heavens live, think and are the agent cause of all coming-to-be. The *Letter on the True, First and Perfect Agent Cause, and the Imperfect Agent Cause [which is called agent] by Extension* explains that true agency is reserved for God alone, who creates the first sphere of the heavens and puts it into motion and, through it, puts all the other spheres into motion: but what comes to be from it is not action, but being-acted-upon.

We should also mention two topics which are implied in the *First Philosophy* but not discussed there. One of these is the soul, the subject of a metaphysical, exhortatory treatise, which gathers together ideas from various sources, in particular ones taken from Platonism, Neoplatonism and Hermeticism. Another is intellectual knowledge, treated in the *Letter on the Intellect,* one of the few works by al-Kindî translated into Latin (twelfth century). Here al-Kindî differentiates four types or levels of the intellect, according to the reinterpretation of Aristotle's theory of intellectual knowledge by the early Neoplatonic school (Porphyry) and John Philoponus. Finally, the *Letter on How to Dispel Sadness* is a lengthy moral exhortation which includes spiritual advice, written in the common philosophical style of the first centuries AD. In this work al-Kindî shows much less of his characteristic turn of mind than elsewhere, where he subjects what he has gathered from the Greek philosophers to his own treatment.

Al-râzî And Al-fârâbî

The most idiosyncratic figure in the history of Arabic philosophy is, without question, that of Abû Bakr Muammad ibn Zakariyya al-Razi, who was also an outstanding writer on medicine. The most important of his many medical works, *al-Hâwî* (known in Latin as *Continens*) has a significant place in the history of medicine, in Christian Europe as well as in Islam, and it was translated into Latin twice (end of thirteenth century and in the sixteenth century). He took his inspiration as a philosopher more closely and constantly from the Greeks than from other sources. He looked to Socrates as the master of all philosophers in his way of life; he knew and quoted Plato, Aristotle, Porphyry, John Philoponus and others. He did not think that philosophy always remains one and the same. It progresses through the very differences between those who follow it, and to be a philosopher does not, he believed, mean to have the truth but to try to reach it a view of intellectual history entirely other than al-Kindi's. The basis of al-Razi's ethics is reason and its aim is the ordering of conduct and the subjugation of the passions. His theology is explicitly philosophical. The world is an emanation from God; and not only God, but also the world soul, prime matter, space and time are eternal. Al-Râzî believed in the transmigration of souls, which could rise to higher moral and metaphysical levels in successive reincarnations. And he denied that there was such a thing as prophecy. God inspires all men equally, but they are not all equal in taking advantage of it. Clearly, these views were not acceptable to the Islamic faithful. Only a few rather short treatises of al-Razi survive, and the work where he denies the existence of prophecy is known only through the quotes made in order to attack it by his contemporary and compatriot, the Ismailite missionary, Abu Atim al-Razi. Despite the controversial nature of his philosophical ideas, al-Râzî was allowed to be the doctor in charge of the hospital at Baghdad.

Abu Bakr al-Razi's place in the history of *falsafah* is therefore a strange one, the very opposite of that held by al-Kindî, another Neoplatonist. Different again is that held by Abû Nar Muammad ibn Muammad al-Fârâbî, who was born at about the same time as al-Kindi died and who lived until 339/950. He maintained the same high level of philosophical thinking as his great predecessor, but he moved it definitely into a new direction, opening up a fresh path for its development. One feature of his work was his great interest and ability in logic. Here he was the beneficiary of the work done by the translators and commentators (most of them Christians), such as Abû Bishr Mattâ and Yuannâ ibn aylân, his masters at the Aristotelian school at Baghdad, whom he considered to belong to the tradition of the Greek commentators. But he went further, especially in the attention he gave to the structure of reasoning and the types of argument. Among his works of logic are books based on, or commenting on (often very freely), all the books of the *Organon,* as well as Porphyry's *Isagoge* and in accord with the practice of the School of Alexandria, the *Rhetoric* (though not, like them, the *Poetics,* which remained on the edges of the Arab philosophical tradition). He also wrote introductory logical works and, more interestingly, a *Little Book of Reasoning according to the methods of the mutakallimûn and the fuqahâ,* which examines critically, according to logical criteria alone, the methods of argument used by the theologians and the lawyers. Al-Fârâbî begins with a systematic exposition of Aristotle's logic. In his prologue, al-Fârâbî explains that he will use 'terms known to those who speak Arabic and examples familiar to our contemporaries'. This method might be taken as one especially designed for teaching, but it might also be seen in terms of a more far-reaching principle of logico-grammatical analysis. Before giving a complete survey of logic and placing it within the whole domain of knowledge, the *Book of Terms Used in Logic* lists the words which are joined to nouns, to verbs and to noun-verb combinations: that is to say, tool-words. In this list are found purely logical terms (such as quantifiers) but especially invariable words, some of which correspond to terms in Greek, others of which have a place only in Arabic. There is, then, here a ţension between the universality implied by the return to Greek philosophy, and the particularity of the language of *faylasuf.*

Here we see the deep structure of al-Fârâbî's thought: more emphatically than al-Kindî's, it is based on the attempt to combine ideas of different sorts Greek and Arabic, philosophical and religious into a whole which is both systematic and historical. Another witness to this way of thinking and writing is the strange *Book of Letters*. 'Letters' has two different (but compatible) meanings here. It provides the work's title first because the book is a set of loose variations, in al-Farabi's usual manner, on Aristotle's *Metaphysics,* which was sometimes called in Arabic *Kitab al-urûf* (from the fact that its books are each designated by a Greek letter). But, second, the title refers to the fact that, just like the *Book of Terms Used in Logic,* this treatise contains a study of various tool-words; and these are what grammarians call *uruf,* 'letters'. Here, however, the list is occupied mainly by terms which are used in philosophy, whether words like 'when' and 'how' or the names of the categories, predicables and so on. In this context, al-Farabi examines the copula in attributive propositions which, in Arabic, poses problems unknown to Greek logicians. (It is wrong, however, to draw as has been done the conclusion that this difference in the way being is expressed caused a radical separation between 'Arab thought' and 'Greek thought'. The Greek attributive proposition can easily do without the copula, and Arabic philosophers were perfectly comfortable in ontology.) This treatise also dwells on, among other things, the relation between philosophy, religion, language and the whole course of civilization, considered in the most general way. Altogether, it examines in depth concepts and themes from the whole field of philosophy: the status of concepts, the categories, the vocabulary of being, epistemology and scientific method. In one way or another it includes the subject-matter of various Aristotelian works along with subjects such as the history of culture and the theory of religion which Aristotle did not consider systematically. Here perhaps is a third reason for its title.

In logic, then, al-Farabi's project was to found the Greek on the Arab and the Arab on the Greek. In political philosophy, his second main interest, his procedure is the same, although it involves more material that is rooted in cultural particularities. Political philosophy includes consideration of the relations between philosophy and religion, which for al-Fârâbî meant the defence of philosophy. A number of his works fit into this class. *The Enumeration of the Sciences* surveys the encyclopaedia of scientific knowledge which the Arabs have built up through their philology, their translations from the Greek and their own creative work: grammar and linguistics, logic, mathematics (in the broad sense of the quadrivium along with mechanics), physics, metaphysics, politics and two exclusively Islamic branches of knowledge: *fiqh* or jurisprudence and *kalâm,* defensive or polemical theology. Although the chapters on these two Islamic subjects seem not to fit in with the rest of the work, al-Fârâbî had promised, in his prologue, to deal with the branches of knowledge 'which are being followed at the present time', a qualification which now is seen to have its rationale. *The Agreement of the Two Sages* is intended to show that, despite appearances to the contrary, Plato and Aristotle do not contradict each other. This subtle, at times even enigmatic work, is at least clear in its aim. Starting from a definition and analysis of the content of philosophy, it attempts to reveal a deep unity among the main doctrines which make it up and so to assert its value against those who attack it, and guarantee its place in the field of knowledge and thought.

During the course of his life, al-Fârâbî was able to observe the crumbling of the Abbâssid caliphate's power. In every part of the empire minor, practically independent princely dynasties sprang up. During al-Muqtadir's caliphate there were thirteen vizirs, amd two rival caliphates were formed: the Fatimid in Egypt and the Umayyad in Spain. Between al-Muqtadir's death and al-Farabî's own, four caliphs were overthrown or assassinated. Not unexpectedly, then, al-Farabi was aware of the importance of politics and the philosophical problems posed by it. They formed the subject of many of his works, and were emphasized even in books of his which also dealt with other areas. His most extensive political work is called *Principles of the Opinions of the Citizens of the Best City.* Here al-Farabi considers the city and its government by placing it within a wider scheme of macrocosm and microcosm, in which the structure of the greater and lesser worlds is seen to be similar at every level. This structure is hierarchical: its elements (the celestial spheres, the faculties of the soul, the bodily organs, the inhabitants of cities) are each seen to depend on something superior, which is the basis for their initial and continuing existence. Al-Fârâbî gives a clear description of the emanation of the celestial intelligences and their spheres, one which Avicenna will copy and fill out in detail. The city should be organized and run by a legislator who combines being 'wise, prudent and a philosopher'. From the agent Intellect there come into the legislator's potential intellect the intelligible forms which make up his knowledge, whilst also putting his imagination to work so that he becomes an 'annunciatory prophet', who can inculcate the best laws in the people through persuasion and thus achieve the aim of political science: to establish the happiness of the city. The legislator will, then, be both philosopher and prophet: he will combine philosophy and religion. Especially in the *Book of Letters* and the *Book of Religion,* al-Fârâbî asserts the priority of philosophy to religion, which 'follows' it: 'good religious laws are subordinate to the universal principles of practical philosophy'. Religion is subordinate to philosophy in the way that imagination is to the intellect, and persuasive discourse to demonstration. These ideas are linked to various ancient philosophical themes: Platonic (the role of the legislator) and Aristotelian (the position of rhetoric). Al-Farabi is certainly nearer than al-Razi to the Islamic view of religion and the state, in that he accepts the existence of prophets and gives a rational explanation for it. But, by sharp contrast with al-Kindî, his doctrine is laicized: it keeps the form of Islam but subverts its content. The philosophical religion about which he theorizes ends by placing the philosophical theology of the Greek philosophers above the teaching of God's messengers.

This is not the place for a history of Islamic theology (the *kalâm*), nor even a sketch of it. This kind of speculative theology began even before the end of the first century, the product of the need to express and defend in formal language the truths first formulated in the Qu'rân. Its main themes included the structure of created being, the relation of human actions to God's absolute power and how God should be conceived. Only the Mu'tazilite school, which began in the second century, need be mentioned here, since it was the first to deal with the central points of theology and arrange them into a doctrinal whole; and since, moreover, its exponents were accused of being close to the *falasifah*. The Mu'tazilites who differed between themselves on many matters were agreed that the good can be known by reason, apart from revelation; that man creates his own acts. They emphasized the absolute unity of God: his names are many, but not his attributes. And some of them engaged in profound speculations about the status of non-existing things (for instance, things before God created them, or those things which God knows will never exist). These are genuinely philosophical themes, and it is legitimate to speak of a metaphysics or physics of the *kalam* but one which has a characteristic vocabulary, set of concepts and structure different from those of *falsafah*. Their paths are different but, quite often, they intersect. Without some knowledge of the *kalâm,* there are important features of Arabic philosophy which will not be properly understood.

At the same period there were other writers connected in one way or another with the central tradition of *falasfah*. First, the collective work of the Ikhwân al-afâ' (Brothers of Purity) should be mentioned. It was produced throughout the tenth century AD. It consists of fifty-two letters, written in a style which is more accessible and persuasive than that of the philosophers and theologians. Taken together, the letters make up an encyclopaedia which is Neoplatonic in its arrangement and concepts, spiritual in content and religious in its basis. The Ikhwân should be placed within Shi'ism or, rather, on its edges, since they were Ismailites. Theirs was an hierarchical organization of initiates. Although they therefore have a rather special place within Islam as a whole, their method of speculation illustrates how the Shi'ites accepted far more readily than the Sunnis the connection between philosophy and religion. Like the Mu'tazilites, the Ikhwân held that truth was originally given in a divine revelation witnessed by the philosophical sages as well as the prophets. Whilst it is just to compare this idea to late Neoplatonism, it also has a precise place in the intellectual and spiritual history of Islam in this particular period. On the one hand, it provided a way to recognize the value of ancient traditions, especially those in what was now the eastern part of the empire, which seemed to pre-date Islam. On the other hand, it was a means of legitimating the philosophy derived from the Greeks, following the path opened by al-Kindî but with greater historical precision. As a result the sages of antiquity (Empedocles and Pythagoras were thought the most venerable) were considered to have lived at the same period as David and Solomon and to have profited from their wisdom; this wisdom, which emanated from 'the tabernacle of prophecy' was successively passed to Socrates, then to Plato and even went as far as Aristotle. The heyday of this historico-ideological doctrine was the second half of the tenth century AD, a time when several emirs of the Shi'ite Buyid dynasty, with its capital at Shiraz, acted as patrons of learning and science. There is a certain uniformity to the philosophy of this period. Ancient philosophy was well and accurately known, but it did not stimulate any really creative thought. Rather, it was linked to a taste for learning and for expounding the stock of ancient wisdom. Writers of this sort include Abu Sulaymân al-Sijistani (died *c.* 990), Abû Ayyan al-Tawidi (died in 399/1099) and Ibn Fâtik al-Mubashshir, all of them men of great learning. Among the works typical of this tendency is the *Eternal Wisdom* of Abû 'Alî Amad ibn Miskawayh, chancellor of the Buyid emir, 'A ud al-Dawla.

This work claims to be a translation of an old Persian book and collects pronouncements attributed to ancient Persian, Indian, Arab and Greek sages. For the exponents of this current of thought, the truth has been available ever since its original revelation. Such a conception comes down to applying to philosophers the principle by which the prophets all transmit the same revelation; but, for this reason, philosophy, having been made sacred, becomes merely a matter of retrospection. Al-Kindî's explicit view was very different, but his idea of a deep agreement between philosophers and prophets left the way open for the notion of eternal wisdom and so may have perhaps contradicted his own theory of progress.

Avicenna

The traditional (perhaps not completely exact) date for the birth, near Bukhara (in present day Uzbekistan) of Abû 'Alî al-usayn ibn 'Abdallah ibn Sina is 370/980. Ibn Sina, known as 'Avicenna' in the West through the twelfth-century Latin translations, is a giant in the history of thought. A polymath, he was in particular an outstanding physician, and it was in this capacity or as a vizier that he served various princes in the eastern parts of Islam. His life was thus far from calm and, at times, it was dramatic. He died at Hamadân in 429/1037 as a result of taking a wrongly made-up medicine. Some of his works have been lost, but what remains is still substantial. It includes treatises on various subjects, especially medicine; writings in which he wraps philosophical views in fiction, in a way reminiscent of Plato's myths; and a set of encyclopaedias, some of which are more or less schematic, whilst others are fairly or extremely detailed. The detailed, lengthier encyclopaedias are *The Direction (al-Hidâya), The Cure (al-Shifâ')*—by far the longest of them, *The Salvation (al-Najât)* and *Instructions and Remarks (al-Ishârât wa-l-tanbîhât).* These are all in Arabic, whilst a fifth large encyclopaedia, the *Book of Knowledge (Dânesh-nâme)* is in Persian. Two rules of method guide the composition of these works. First, they follow in general the scheme of the branches of knowledge traditionally recognized in Aristotelianism: logic, physics, mathematics, and theology or metaphysics. This does not mean that all Ibn Sînâ's encyclopaedias follow exactly this order. For instance, the *Book of Knowledge,* as well as another work in Persian, the *Philosophy for 'Alâ' al-Dawla,* places metaphysics before physics, in accord with the idea of metaphysics as the study of the general properties of being. Avicenna's other encyclopaedias place metaphysics after physics, which prepares the ground for understanding it. The second rule is what follows from the progress of knowledge and Ibn Sînâ's own decisions on theoretical questions. The result of these two principles is that Ibn Sînâ expounds his own views, following Aristotle but not repeating him; thus in the *Shifâ* the material of the *Meteorologica* is differently arranged among different books, and the *Metaphysics* follows Aristotle's plan only distantly. The only works on which he actually wrote commentaries are Aristotle's *Metaphysics* Ë and *On the Soul,* and also the apocryphal *Theology of Aristotle.* These commentaries belonged to the *Book of Right Judgement,* which survives only in fragments (the complete text was lost when the prince whom Ibn Sînâ served as physician and vizier was defeated in battle). In this way there disappeared almost the whole of what has been taken as Ibn Sînâ's last philosophy, what he called an 'Eastern philosophy', distinct from that of 'Westerners'. There has been much speculation about the nature of this 'Eastern philosophy'. Some have seen it as a definite turning towards what would later be called 'philosophy of illumination'. Others point out that a treatise which Ibn Sînâ actually calls *Logic of the Easterners* is not particularly different from his other writings. They consider that the term 'Easterners' refers to an Aristotelian school at Khurâsân. Moreover, in the *Instructions,* which are later than the lost *Book of Right Judgement,* there is no mention of 'Eastern philosophy'.

As a young man, Ibn Sînâ read and learnt everything there was to read and learn. But for the formation of his thought the most important of all the books he read were the *Letters* of the Ikhwân al-afâ', and the works of al-Fârâbî, which were particularly important in allowing him to grasp the point of Aristotle's *Metaphysics* by showing him the deep connection between the theology and the ontology of forms which this text brings together. His interest in the Ikhwân is understandable in the light of his spiritual sympathy (perhaps even adherence) to Isma'ilism; his father was himself an Ismaili. With regard to al-Fârâbî, there is no difficulty in drawing up a list of parallels with Ibn Sînâ's views. The two thinkers shared a universal vision of a hierarchy of being with God at the head of it, and (following the accumulated teaching of the Aristotelian commentators and of al-Kindî) an analysis of the intellect which, using the notions of act and potency, divides it into several ontologically distinct levels. To this, they both linked a doctrine of prophecy; and they also shared an interest in logic. But Ibn Sînâ treated these traditions as he did Aristotle: he handled their various features in his own personal way. A fuller study would need to take these differences into account, listing and analysing them. For instance, in logic Ibn Sînâ combined the rules for attributive propositions and those for hypothetical ones into a more complete synthesis than had been previously achieved.

Similarly, Ibn Sînâ's thinking about the origin of things goes further than al-Fârâbî's. According to Ibn Sînâ 'the Being which is necessary by its essence' is an Intelligence which thinks itself and so is at once thinking and thought. The thought which it has of itself is productive of being. The first being produced in this way therefore exists necessarily and yet, in its own essence, it is contingent. It too is an Intelligence (the First Intelligence) which (1) thinks Necessary in itself and also thinks itself in its two aspects; (2) in its own necessary existence; and (3) in its contingent essence. From Thought (1) there emanates a second Intelligence placed directly below this first Intelligence; whilst from Thought (2) there emanates a form, and from Thought (3) matter, which are respectively the soul and body of the first Intelligence's sphere. The second Intelligence produces the soul and body of its own sphere, and the third Intelligence; and this process continues down to the last Intelligence, that of the sphere of the moon. From it there emanate into the sublunary world the forms which human intellects receive in different ways and the matter which is 'prepared' to receive these forms. The ideas implied by this scheme of cosmic emanation are at the very heart of Avicenna's metaphysics none more so than the correlated notions of necessity and contingency.

Aristotle had established the existence of a pure Act, the First Mover 'on which depend the heavens and all nature'; al-Kindî that of a True One, the 'cause of unity' and so of the existence of 'all beings which are unitary'. Ibn Sînâ bases his own argument on a division of being according to logical modality. All beings of whose existence we are aware are contingent by their very essence, since it includes no necessity; they can without contradiction be conceived as not-existing. Moreover, their existence is ultimately linked by causal relations to the celestial spheres which are themselves also contingent in essence. But it is impossible that a chain of causes should go on forever from one contingent thing to another, since what is contingent is, by definition, something which can equally be or not be; contingent existence tends in itself towards non-existence in so far as it is not founded on something which exists necessarily. There is, therefore, a first term in the causal chain which is necessary in its very essence that is to say, whose essence includes that mark of necessity which is lacking in all other things and which can also be expressed as the identity in it of essence and existence. In this way, the cosmogony sketched above is given a philosophical basis. Just as the whole system of the world comes about from the thought which the Necessary Being has of itself, so this being, in thinking itself at the same time thinks everything in the universe: it thinks 'the higher (that is, heavenly) beings, each in its individuality, and the being of the sublunary world in the universals under which they are classified'.

The distinction between essence and existence is another feature of Ibn Sînâ's thought which is his own; he did not take it from al-Fârâbî, as was long thought because of the misattribution of a short treatise (*Fu û al- ikam,* which might be translated as *Precious Aphorisms*) which continues Ibn Sînâ's own formulation of the distinction. In all contingent things, Ibn Sînâ differentiates, on the one hand, the fact of having a certain quiddity (*mâhiyyah: mâ* is translated into Latin as *quid,* thus producing the word *quidditas*) or, as he is also willing to say, a *aqîqah,* meaning 'truth' what this thing which exists really is; and, on the other hand, the very fact that it exists, its *wujûd* or *huwiyya.* (The word *huwiyya* is made up from the pronoun *huwa* which means 'him' but also acts as the copula in attributive propositions; al-Kindî, who also uses *wujûd,* had already used *huwa* as the basis for another word, *tahwid,* as noted above.) The standard contrast essence and existence in Western philosophy is, then, a good rendering of Ibn Sînâ's distinction between *mâhiyya* and *wujûd.* In existing things essence does not imply existence, otherwise they would exist necessarily. The one exception, as we have seen, is God, and this structural distinction has its place at the level of the ultimate origin of things. But it also gives rise to an idea relevant to the ontology of forms. What sort of being does essence have? It has no effect on existence as such, but essence determines its status in each existing thing. In itself, essence is neither universal nor particular, neither singular nor plural, neither present in existence nor just a concept in the mind; but it can be any of these. To use Ibn Sînâ's own example: the universal 'horse' signifies something which is distinct from its universality: 'horseliness' (*equinitas* in the Latin translations) or 'just horseliness' *(equinitas tantum).* This horseliness can be attached to the 'conditions' of existence in actual horses, or not; in itself, it is removed from any condition and only a 'divine being' can be attributed to it, as Ibn Sînâ says in an enigmatic comment which should certainly be linked to what he says about the origin of the world in God's thought. Methodologically, this doctrine of being supports one of Ibn Sînâ's favourite procedures. He engages in an imaginary experimentation with combinations of forms, an inspection of the 'thingness' (his word too) of a given object, from which one can see what is or is not compatible with its nature and so what should be thought about it. In this theory of essence, Ibn Sînâ can be seen to be following on from the theological speculations about non-existing things mentioned above in connection with the Mu'tazilites.

There remains one area where Ibn Sînâ is close to al-Fârâbî: the theory of prophecy, its nature and function. Prophetic revelation is an outstanding example of the joining of the human soul with the separated Intelligences. Intellectual understanding is the most common instance of this joining, but whereas ordinary men proceed through discursive thought, the prophet is, he said, 'informed of what is invisible; an angel speaks to him'. The function of prophecy is to ensure the social ties which are necessary for men by giving them laws and laying down religious obligations. But it can only inculcate the truth which it contains through symbols which are accessible to simple minds. It is not a matter of the prophets' hiding the truth but of expressing it in another language. Thus the descriptions of the happiness of heaven are allegories of the spiritual pleasures of the separated soul. Besides its use in interpreting prophecies, Ibn Sînâ uses his idea of symbolic expression in two ways. Sometimes he employs it to give philosophical readings of verses from the Qur'ân: for instance, in *Instructions and Remarks* he interprets the famous verse about light as an imagistic description of the intellectual faculties of the soul and their hierarchy, from the material intelligence up to the intelligence in act which is in contact with the Agent Intellect. In the same work, Ibn Sînâ refers to the *Story of Salâmân and Absâl* (about which he also wrote a letter): they are two figures, he says, who represent the soul of man ('yourself') and its level of mystical knowledge, a subject treated in detail in the *Instructions*. Or again this is the second way in which he treats symbols he himself composes stories which put into the form of images the adventures of the soul desiring 'light' *(ayy ibn Yaq ân)* and in search of truth.

Summary

The most widely known of the great Eastern *falâsifah,* because of the extent of his work and the variety of fields, including medicine and literary composition, in which he excelled. Knowledge of al-Kindî and al-Farabi is more restricted to specialist historians of philosophy, but it would be unjust not to recognize al-Kindî's pioneer role and his genius as a scholar and philosopher, or al-Fârâbî's penetration and power of synthesis. Not, of course, that there is any question of drawing up an order of merit. The task of these concluding remarks is, rather, to give a general picture of this period of *falsafah*. It was a lively, creative period, and many lesser but highly able authors, unmentioned in this account, were active. Its central problems resulted from the interplay between two different oppositions. On the one hand, there was the opposition between the Prophet of Islam's revelation and a body of teaching originating in another language and a different spiritual atmosphere. On the other hand, there was the opposition between tradition and progress, which in some ways repeats the first opposition, but in others suppresses it by looking to a wisdom which has always been the same. Leaving aside this illusory solution, there are two different ways in which the main opposition between religion and philosophy was resolved. One way was to reconcile their differences in some way or other. This was al-Kindî's procedure (although his historical view of philosophy did not fully resolve the tension between the terms of the second opposition, tradition and progress). Ibn Sînâ, too, proceeded in this way. He combined a theology which was philosophical in a highly technical way with exegetical and mystical meditations. The other way involved subordinating religion and making the philosophical tradition the solid basis for progress. Al-Râzî went the furthest in this direction; al-Fârâbî tried to have the best of both worlds, but his philosophy of religion has philosophy of mind and political science, rather than the Koran, as its main constituents.

These, then, were the main themes and tensions in the first period of *falsafah:* the first period because, after Ibn Sînâ, Arab and Islamic philosophical and religious thought took on a new configuration. During the fifth/eleventh century, the Seljuk Turks conquered Iran bit by bit, moving from East to West, and they entered Baghdad in 447/1055. They did not suppress the caliphate which had long been in decline, but they put it beneath their authority and presented themselves as its defenders against the various Shi'ite regimes of the Near East and Egypt. As a necessary accompaniment to this military/religious programme, there was ideological reform. Its outstanding exponent was Abû âmid al-Ghazzali. His work took many forms (theoretical, mystical, political), but here we need note merely his hostility to *falsafah.* His main work in this area is the *Incoherence of the Philosophers (Tahâfut al-falâsifah),* in which he refutes twenty theses held by al-Fârâbî and Ibn Sînâ. These theses, he says, express in one way or another three points of view which are directly opposed to the faith: that the world has existed for eternity; that God knows only universals; and that bodies will not be resurrected. Physics and metaphysics are thus to be rejected; the only valuable parts of philosophy left are mathematics and logic. Al-Ghazâlî's attack, which took place in a political climate hostile to whatever fell outside strict theological and juridical tradition, put an end to three centuries of vigour in the *falsafah* of the Near East. *Falsafah* would go on as such for a while in the extreme West of Islam, the Maghreb and Spain, where there was already a well-established scientific and philosophical tradition. And, in the East, the legacy of Ibn Sînâ would continue, but in a way where its mystical tendencies were emphasized. There followed a brilliant line of philosophers whose doctrines brought together a profound metaphysics, religious speculations characteristic of Shi'ism and traditions attributed to the great figures of ancient Persia (such as Zoroaster) or to a mythical past (Hermes). It is difficult not to recall here Neoplatonism at the end of antiquity, in which poems attributed to Orpheus and the *Chaldaean Oracles* were made the subject of commentary and were the goal for pupils who would already have studied Plato and Aristotle. This new Islamic philosophy thus marks the return, though with a different content, of a stimulating structure of thought able to unify different religious traditions. The ideas about 'eternal wisdom' of the fourth and fifth (tenth and eleventh) centuries were a more restricted development of the same way of thought.

Medieval philosophy is the philosophy of Europe in the era now known as medieval or the Middle Ages, the period roughly extending from the fall of the Roman Empire in the fifth century A.D. to the Renaissance in the sixteenth century. It is defined partly by the process of rediscovering the ancient culture developed in Greece and Rome in the classical period, and partly by the need to address theological problems and to integrate sacred doctrine with secular learning.

The history of medieval philosophy is traditionally divided into three main periods: the period in the Latin West following the Early Middle Ages until the twelfth century, when the works of Aristotle and Plato were preserved and cultivated; and the 'golden age' of the twelfth, thirteenth and fourteenth centuries in the Latin West, which witnessed the culmination of the recovery of ancient philosophy, and significant developments in the field of Philosophy of religion, Logic and Metaphysics.

The medieval era was disparagingly treated by the Renaissance humanists, who saw it as a barbaric 'middle' period between the classical age of Greek and Roman culture, and the 'rebirth' or renaissance of classical culture. Yet this period of nearly a thousand years was the longest period of philosophical development in Europe, and possibly the richest. Jorge Gracia has argued that 'in intensity, sophistication, and achievement, the philosophical flowering in the thirteenth century could be rightly said to rival the golden age of Greek philosophy in the fourth century B.C.'

The problems discussed throughout this period are the relation of faith to reason, the existence and simplicity of God, the purpose of theology and metaphysics, and the problems of knowledge, of universals, and of individuation.

Medieval philosophy is characteristically theological: with the possible exceptions of Avicenna and Averroes, medieval thinkers did not consider themselves philosophers at all. Their concerns are theological: for them, the philosophers were the ancient pagan writers such as Plato and Aristotle. However, the theological works of medieval writers use the ideas and logical techniques of the ancient philosophers to address difficult theological questions, and points of doctrine. Thomas Aquinas, following Peter Damian, argued that philosophy is the handmaiden of theology.

The three principles that underlie all their work are the use of logic, dialectic and analysis to discover the truth, known as ratio, respect for the insights of ancient philosophers, particularly Aristotle, and deference to their authority (auctoritas); and the obligation to co-ordinate the insights of philosophy with theological teaching and revelation (concordia).

One of the most heavily debated topics of the period was that of faith versus reason. Avicenna and Averroes both leaned more on the side of reason. Augustine said that he would never allow his philosophical investigations to go beyond the authority of God and Anselm attempted to defend against what he saw as partly an assault on faith, with an approach allowing for both faith and reason. The Augustinian solution to the faith/reason problem is to (1) believe, and then (2) seek to understand.

2

Fieldwork and Taxonomy of Twentieth Century Philosophy

Introduction

It was an interesting time for watching schemes of classification develop simultaneously in various fields; and the schemes tended to be very much the same. Historically, I think the same thing holds. Philosophers begin with two-way oppositions, stringent dualisms; they then compromise on triads, with themselves mediating in the center; and finally, in order to accommodate intrusive but leftover major achievements or phenomena, a four-way scheme is conceded to be better. The development we saw was like Hesse's game with glass pearls. In that game, a thematic pattern was given; each new move had to match it in another area a mathematical equation, then a musical fugue, then a rhythmically unrolling scroll painting, and so on. Hesse's players would have had our full sympathy, though we expected more than cultural elegance from our collection. We were both Platonists, and this in spite of the best efforts of Chicago teachers. I was particularly interested at the time in mathematical metaphor, symbolic logic, and metaphysics; my wife's interests centered more on literature and an interest in people, their types and idiosyncracies (like Jane Austen or Plato in his myths).

A difference between Platonic and Aristotelian logic arises over the question of whether types and kinds are generalizations from sets of particulars, or particulars are as they are because they instantiate general kinds or types. The alternatives make a difference when one wonders, as my wife and I did earlier on, whether life-styles match metaphysical systems for sociological reasons, the systems being abstracted somehow from superimposed individual styles, or whether systems, presupposed but still operative, dominate life-styles dictating consistency even down to fine details.

If one chooses the systems view, how many should there be, and what are they? What do they look like in concrete incarnation and interaction? And how does the leisure-time observation of colleagues, friends, and neighbors match the professional work of literary criticism or study of metaphysical structure? Do pure forms still survive the admixture of feeling, time, and texture, with intact architectures? Do the systems that metaphysicians outline, so sharply that they cut their fingers on the concepts and distinctions, find echoes in the less abstract classifications of kinds of personality, physique, society, sense of spatial form, and housing design that appear in the more concrete fields of literary criticism, anthropology, psychiatry, and educational theory? And are these outlines of the same basic forms, or fragmented and alternative?

Our assumption as a starting point was one with which philosophers are familiar. We thought that every action was guided by presupposed and (usually unconscious) philosophy. What passes for bad luck, if this is true, or for bad judgment, may come from bad metaphysics instead. I still believe this firmly; but like Plato's conviction that applying dialectic could be done systematically and pedagogically, I find the conviction more and more complicated to defend as I grow older.

It was with questions such as these, in our spare time, that my wife and I carried on what I suppose could be described as experiments in applied metaphysics. It was done for leisure, not solemn professional work; for that, I took my systems from the empty austerities of formal logic and the solemn mysteries of major texts, while my wife chose the disciplines of literary and musical formalism.

Systems do seem to behave Platonically. Yet they take on new life when they delineate something in the flow of becoming; there they take on added interest, and in turn the currents of feeling and the subtleties of texture lead back to restyling of their conceptual principles, to tolerance for mixtures, to emergence of new articulations of contrast not caught by the law of contradiction or the disjunction of dichotomous division.

In any case, this history begins with a shared inquiry into systems in space and time, outside the library or laboratory; it moves to an interesting formal discovery that a common basic structure is shared by the main metaphysical schemes of Western philosophy; it takes that insight as justification for expecting mutual appreciation and even adaptation if we can return to the *Symposium*'s Platonic dialogue as model for philosophic form again.

The movement of the story is made up of the inductive discovery that four structures cast their shadows in becoming, the added finding that these shadowcasting structures are transformations of one another, and the deductive projection of this finding to correct an evolved, once useful but unrealistic fondness for analysis by intelligence.

But my induction takes in the history of philosophy, as well as the wider, more casual observations with which it began, and writes the history of pure reason that Kant thought someone ought to write someday. It turns out, as I write it, that Kant was correct when he thought this could be brief. In fact, my version ends in 322 B.C., except for episode, and so is even briefer than Kant had thought. We have added almost an infinity of factual content and textural variation to the bare system forms that rose in ancient Greece like structural steel towers reaching into eternity; ours are warmer, better furnished, more humane, and we light them for display at night. The metaphor of towers fails, however; it must be worlds instead; for once we compare master plans, the up-and-down, front-and-back coordinates reverse or take off at right angles as we move from one of these grand monuments into another. Taking along one's own atlas to another world is more of a confusion than a help.

Richard McKeon had begun his seminars both in classical philosophy and in literary criticism with a grand distinction of systems into two types, "holoscopic" and "meroscopic." The first of these was defined by its method of combination of parts into wholes, and Plato's dialectic was the paradigm. (The "whole" comes out, in these systems, on a level logically different from the parts it combines, so that a simple extensional analysis misses the point.) Aristotle was the prime example of the meroscopic method, investigation by analysis into parts (but into *proximate* parts; anatomical dissection rather than high-speed centrifuging in solution). Aristotle was becoming increasingly visible; we had encountered him via Robert Maynard Hutchins, Mortimer Adler, and Richard McKeon; and oddly enough it was my study with his admirers that led to my appointment as an expert in "subject matter" over against "method" at Teachers College in 1940.

McKeon later added a third system (by 1946) called "logistic," which included a whole range of schemes from Hobbes to Carnap. What led to it was, I think, that many types of scientific and philosophic investigation did not respect either Plato's rule that levels of a hierarchy differ in type or Aristotle's axiom that "proximate causes are more explanatory than remote causes." The logistical systems had no use for either Platonic forms or Aristotelian species but concentrated instead on processes and elements.

We ourselves thought we needed a third system, but we took as our paradigm Bergson rather than Hobbes or Russell. We wanted some place to put philosophies, literary works, and creative personalities that were evolutionary, romantic, and suspicious of literal repetition. Given this orientation, triads that illustrated our scheme of Platonic-Aristotelian-Bergsonian constantly came into view. (For consistency, we should, I suppose, have called the third scheme "Anaxagorean" or "Heraclitean.") Interestingly enough, the three-way scheme of systems of ideas was not suggested by the formal philosophy work in the department. That concentrated on the shifting orientation among things, thoughts, and words; this was the ultimate trichotomy, and within it history displayed an erudition of specimens, each of which we treated separately.

It was rather the "typical biographies" of an anthropologist that suggested a different three-way classification. Wilmon H. Sheldon, in his studies of human physique and temperament, gave a very perceptive account of three life-styles, each with its own conceptual outlook, which he associated with varieties of physique. Without commitment to that association whether it was random, or above average in correlation, for example the three styles certainly did match three tendencies we found in historical systems of philosophy. They were ways of organizing subject matter, of paying selective attention, and of arranging ideas in time that seemed to be contrasting and recurrent themes. The things-thoughts-words trichotomy seemed to lead nowhere. If it could not be bridged, choice of standpoint seemed arbitrary; if it could, differences would go back to ontology (the conceptual referents of words, the *denotata* and *designata* of concepts).

It is only much more recently that Ben Ami Scharfstein has suggested that all philosophers fall into a distinctive, somewhat abnormal, human type; this may be true, but even if it is, Sheldon's three species occur as crossclassifications within Scharfstein's category. Charles Morris extended Sheldon's temperament scheme to a classification of the world's major religions. His venture brought out interesting correlations as a first approximation. (Each religion had a prophet who was its paradigm, and each represented a distinct physical and temperamental type; Buddha was endomorphic, Mohammed Mesomorphic, Jesus Ectomorphic [though styles of representation changed in different periods of the Western religions]. No one likes to be put into a category of someone else's construction; and so no religious group has ever liked Morris' book; in any case, only philosophers in divinity schools cared much about religion when his study came out.)

A further anthropological work that seemed to match our systems in its scheme of classification was Ruth Benedict *Patterns of Culture*. This was oriented around her set of three "value constellations" that could be chosen out of the indefinite range of cultural possibility, each abstract type illustrated by an ethnographic study (of the Dobu, Zuni, and Kwakiutl). It may well be that the ethnography was selective, but the three culture patterns were certainly possible and their approximate fit recognizable, and they nicely matched our three-way plan. (Except that the Platonists Sheldon's ectomorphs, Morris' Christians came out in reverse. One feature of this type was its highly developed inhibitory function of stopping before acting, and sometimes of ruining action by inhibition where it didn't belong. Another was its asceticism, translated into an example of virtue. Now, the Dobu culture certainly stopped, but not to think, and was ascetic, but for the sake of malice, not virtue or contemplation.)

Robert Janes, one of our Chicago group, published an article in 1945 pointing out the correlation of Sheldon's work and Benedict's, suggesting that it could be extended to sociology.

Even in the world of educational theory, schools were also split three ways. There were the "discipline" Aristotelians of Chicago (with their "great books" canon); the "methods" pragmatists of Teachers College; and the "scientific" tests and measurements workers whose techniques dominated the field of "educational research" generally (stressing statistical methods and objective measurements).

Plato's idealism was not represented in this three-way set. (Given that, an odd thing was that when I asked my seminar in practice teaching what they would like to discuss in good pragmatist fashion their choices were Platonic questions.)

I think that though our own observations were casual, the trend we noted was there: that dualisms were being replaced by three-way classificatory schemes in all sorts of taxonomies. Hegelians and Marxists, of course, had always had the three-way scheme; and the pragmatists I knew, because they based their cause on mediating past dualism, also used triads.

But our scheme didn't fit entirely well when we looked at its immediate social applications in everyday situations. Where the three systems we had set up were mutually intelligible but each judged the other two wrong, we ran into actual cases where personal interactions could only be described as "crossed monologues." That is, there would be a whole evening of conversation and argument between parties, neither of whom ever grasped the other's point. This was not disagreement but failure of communication. One could from outside of the argument almost work out a table of the contrary assumptions that were part of the confusion. For example, there could be an argument about the role of information in education. Should there be special programs to ensure that a child's mind was stocked with an adequate inventory of "ideas" or "items of cultural literacy"? This makes excellent sense on a logistical model, such as Locke's, of learning as the storing and retrieval of units of information. It makes no sense at all to a theory such as Plato's where insight is the way to learning, and it is the relations of ideas, not the number, that offer a key to answering important questions. The former view sees no great problem in what to do with ideas once we have them; the latter sees no point in having them without an education aimed at using them. The debate could easily move over to the question of how one measures effective education; each party, trying to be simple and concrete, would choose the opposite course between objective tests and essay questions. And, worst of all, one party would assume that theories dictate what facts can be observed (an extension of Platonism, but a consistent one); the other would argue that what theories can be formulated depends on observed facts (abstraction being simply an additive operation; good Humean probability).

My wife pointed out that to include these cases, we really needed four systems, not just the three we had been working with, and we set them up in a square.

Platonists	Aristotelians
Bergsonians	Atomists

What we liked best about our scheme was that it now pretty well included the people we knew and their reactions. I could have been more academic in this account and claimed that it was the reactions of philosophers to one another that forced one to go to four rather than three possibilities. That study would begin with the classical period and the standing question of why Plato says nothing about Democritus. But rather than working through this systematically, I simply ask any teacher or lecturer to recall cases where someone kept asking a question and could neither accept nor disagree with the answer, but just asked it again. (In our scheme, diagonally separated positions are the pairs that don't have mutual comprehension; adjacent ones are mutually intelligible but disagree. Our fourth component accounted for the fact that Sheldon had been unable to locate about a fourth of his subjects in his patterned types, assuming that there was some analogy between our scheme and his.) Of course, the great advantage, which we should have seen from the start, was that this now separated "process" from "atomic" nonformalist philosophies. Logical positivism could have a compartment of its own, while process theology fell in quite another.

The coordinates specified a method of explanation along the *x*-axis (from McKeon's holoscopic to his meroscopic types), and a direction of explanation from form to flow, or vice versa, oriented the *y*-axis (this was inspired, probably, by Bergson's description of his philosophy as "inverted Platonism"). On the whole, our earlier triads also fit the new scheme well, and we even had places for some of Sheldon's eccentrics and possibly for Morris' fourth religion. But those were fanciful. Our preliminary chart came out:

Plato	Aristotle
Bergson	Democritus

Sheldon and Benedict had suggested:

Ectomorph	Mesomorph

Dobu Kwakiutl

Endomorph

Zuni

Other analogies fit in even better than they had before. For example, we were taken by the match of a technique for scoring Rorschach test responses (Klopfer and Kelley): They cross-classified the projected pictures seen in indeterminate ink blots as static or dynamic, and as response to parts or to the blot as a whole. This we added to our collection, but we assumed that these responses showed sensitivity to types of form; not simply projection, but reception. Given actual forms as stimuli, one would expect such predispositions to stand out more in the attention patterns:

Static

F : *fff*

:

Whole Part

M : *mmm*

:

Dynamic

F represents a whole seen as static (and so, usually, inorganic); typically the blot is seen as a single piece of architecture. *fff* are subordinate wholes, more loosely connected in the total scheme; there is, usually, a tighter fit with detail but less of a total unifying theme. A city street rather than a single cathedral facade would be a typical response here; or a gallery of statues. *M* is a dynamic (and usually living) figure seen in the whole. Faces with varying expressions are perhaps most typical responses of this type. *mmm*, finally, sees the blot as fragmented independent parts, in dynamic sets. Mice running to the corners or flames in spurts were the authors' examples of typical *mmm* responses.

In literature, we tried to isolate four types of development, correlated with structures of time that would match our systems and spatial form senses; there were plenty of matches, but finally we found what seemed a particularly close set. The paradigmatic works we finally chose were;

The Castle	:	*Oedipus Rex*
Kafka	:	Sophocles
The Magic Mountain	:	*Remembrance of Things Past*
Mann	:	Proust

Later, in 1952, Newton Stallknecht defined philosophy as the study of being (quite aware that this had been suggested several times before) and then divided it according to four senses of *is* (in the introduction to his and my *Spirit of Western Philosophy*). It was one way of differentiating, or generating, four systems, all of which would be philosophical, and it fit our own archetypal four quite satisfactorily, as well as matching the time sense dominant in each of our literary examples.

This was Stallknecht's scheme:

Eternal	:	Present
present	:	progressive
Future	:	Past
(inceptive)	:	(perfective)

Though it may not be obvious at once, the present progressive correlates with Aristotle's view of time in his "practical science," where options for choice lie just ahead of the agent, and it matches his concept of crisis in tragedy. In fact, a tragedy of repeated crises ought to be particularly effective to an Aristotelian; and Oedipus Rex, just such a play, was Aristotle's favorite example.

We had several ideas that we wanted to develop. One was a result of my work in formal logic. I wanted to show that the four systems were correlated so that they could be related by some sort of transformation (that is, by some rule such as substituting the dot for "and" by the mark for "or" that would turn an atomistic passage into a Platonic one). Ada had an idea that systems related diagonally in our scheme, though they lacked mutual comprehension, might still have a powerful mutual attraction where they seemed "magical" that is, actual though not explicable in each other's frames of reference. And there was our initial belief, now to be tested with a different classification of philosophies, that applied philosophy could deduce practical solutions to problems of more specific kinds. Another fourfold way came from Stephen Pepper's work with "root metaphors," a classification related more to texture than to structure. We had, in fact, been moving in that direction with our discoveries of reflections of key structures in psychology, literature, and time sense. Pepper's scheme neatly complemented our own:

Diagram	:	Organism
Work of art (in the making)	:	Machine

Richard McKeon, having recognized just three systems in his *Freedom and History*, went on to a fourfold scheme in *Thought, Action, and Passion.* Paul Weiss worked with the interaction of four complementary "modes" in his *Modes of Being.* Mortimer Adler, classifying the variations of great ideas through history, proposed a fourfold set of strands in his *Idea of Freedom.* And, of course, looking for ancestral voices, one could find anticipations of the scheme in Aristotle's history of the four causes, in Plato's account of the "war of the gods and giants" in the metaphysical arena, and in Kant's final chapters on method and history of pure reason in his first critique, *The Critique of Pure Reason.*

The 20th century deals with the upheavals produced by a series of conflicts within philosophical discourse over the basis of knowledge, with classical certainties overthrown, and new social, economic, scientific and logical problems. 20th century philosophy was set for a series of attempts to reform and preserve, and to alter or abolish, older knowledge systems. Seminal figures include Ludwig Wittgenstein, Martin Heidegger, Bertrand Russell, Jean-Paul Sartre, and Edmund Husserl. Epistemology, the theory of knowledge, and its basis was a central concern, as seen from the work of Heidegger, Russell, Karl Popper, and Claude Levi-Strauss. Phenomenologically oriented metaphysics undergirded existentialism (Sartre, Maurice Merleau-Ponty, Albert Camus) and finally poststructuralism. Pragmatist Richard Rorty has argued that these and other schools of 20th-century philosophy, including his own, share an opposition to classical dualism that is both anti-essentialist and antimetaphysical.

The psychoanalytic work of Sigmund Freud, Jacques Lacan, Julia Kristeva, and others has also been influential in contemporary continental philosophy.

A notable phenomenon of the latter half of the century was the rise of popular philosophers who promulgated systems for dealing with the world but were isolated from academic philosophy, such as Ayn Rand, who were radical critics of traditional philosophy and psychology and relied on unorthodox methods. Conversely, some philosophers have attempted to define and rehabilitate older traditions of philosophy. Most notably, Hans-Georg Gadamer and Alasdair MacIntyre have both, albeit in different ways, revived the tradition of Aristotelianism.

3

Philosophy and its Background in the Medieval Period

Introduction

Eriugena and Anselm are, indeed, the two outstanding philosophers of the time, and their thought is discussed in detail in the following chapter. But many of the problems they tackled and methods they used were common to their contemporaries. This chapter is designed to fill in some of this often forgotten background. The names of some of those besides Eriugena and Anselm who considered philosophical questions in the early Middle Ages are known: for instance, Alcuin (the Englishman who became one of Charlemagne's main advisers in the 790s, and Alcuin's pupils Candidus Wizo and Fredegisus of Tours); Ratramnus of Corbie and Gottschalk of Orbais (mid-ninth century); Remigius of Auxerre and Bovo of Corvey (late ninth and early tenth century); Abbo of Fleury, Notker of St Gall and Gerbert of Aurillac (end of tenth century); Berengar, Lanfranc and Peter Damian (eleventh century). Yet much of the material from which a history of philosophy during this time must be constructed is anonymous, and an important part of it consists, not of independent works or even free-standing commentaries, but of glosses written in the margins and between the lines of the manuscripts of ancient or late antique textbooks. Indeed, since a good deal of the philosophical activity of these centuries consisted, not in original speculation, but in absorbing the ideas of ancient texts, the best evidence for it is often not a particular piece of writing, but information as to which centres of learning possessed manuscripts of what philosophical and theological works at which times. For these reasons, the study of manuscripts and their transmission is fundamental to the history of early medieval philosophy.

Libraries, Schools and the Dissemination of Texts

Sometime before 814, Archbishop Leidrad of Lyons presented a comprehensive collection of philosophical treatises to his cathedral library. The manuscript, now in Rome, Casa dei padri maristi A. II. 1, is datable on palaeographical grounds to the late eighth or early ninth century. It contains Porphyry's *Isagoge,* the *Ten Categories* (a paraphrase-cum-commentary of Aristotle's *Categories* wrongly attributed to Augustine), pseudo-Apuleius *Perihermenias* and Boethius' first commentary on Aristotle's *On Interpretation.* It was written for Leidrad and is the oldest surviving collection of works on dialectic. Not only does it contain the ancient texts; it also includes Alcuin's verses dedicating the *Ten Categories* to Charlemagne. In consequence, Bischoff linked this collection to the court library. Similarly, the Frankish royal court in the late eighth century and the cathedral library of Lyons are implicated in the transmission of Plato's *Timaeus* (in the translation by Calcidius). Paris, Bibliothèque Nationale lat. 2164, for example, written in north-east France *c.* 800, can be connected with the group of classical manuscripts in the court library of Charlemagne. Its textual twin Lyons 324 also contains the commentary on the *Timaeus* by Calcidius and may have reached Lyons by the same route as Bishop Leidrad's philosophical and dialectical collection.

That Lyons, famous for its participation in the antique book trade, a notable centre of learning in the seventh century and possessor of many fifth, sixth and seventh-century codices in its libraries, should play a role in the transmission of ancient philosophical texts is certainly credible. Charlemagne's remarkable collection of rare classical texts, moreover, is usually identified as listed on spare leaves in a late eighth-century grammatical collection, Berlin, Deutsche Staatsbibliothek Diez B. Sant. 66, emanating from the court circle. Such texts are now generally regarded as the fruit of an appeal for copies of remarkable or rare books sent out in about 780. In the case of the books associated with Leidrad, and with other classical texts linked with the court, the extant manuscripts are copies made from books sent to the Carolingian court, or, at a further remove, copies of the court transcriptions.

Although not all surviving manuscripts of philosophical and dialectical works have court connections, it is certainly the case that it is from the Carolingian period that our earliest copies of most of the principal works survive. We have in fact very little with which to fill the gap between late antiquity and the Carolingian period as far as any classical texts are concerned. Certainly, knowledge of ancient philosophy was also transmitted through the medium of patristic and Christian writers such as Augustine, Maximus the Confessor and Marius Victorinus, of whose work copies survive from the fifth to eighth centuries in relative abundance. It is from Carolingian copies, however, that most witnesses to classical literature and learning descend. Nevertheless, it would be unwise to assume that no study was made of, or interest shown in, such texts in Italy or Gaul between the sixth and the late eighth centuries. In the eighth and ninth centuries we see classical texts, including those concerned with logic and philosophy, that have gained a sufficient readership and attracted enough interest for a copy or copies to be made of them. A wider intellectual context must therefore be envisaged. We may surmise indeed that Carolingian manuscripts containing philosophical texts reflect not random survival but deliberate preservation. They are the outcome of choices made in the eighth and ninth centuries in relation to distinct intellectual preferences, even if the initial survival of an ancient text beyond the fifth century had an element of chance in it. Thus, as Marenbon has established, the difference in popularity between the *Ten Categories* and Aristotle's *Categories* can be accounted for in that the former accords better with the intellectual preoccupations of thinkers in the ninth and tenth centuries.

Even so, intellectual preferences and an apparent encouragement of this type of intellectual activity and branch of learning cannot be assumed to be the natural outcome of the Germanic groups establishing successor states within the old Roman empire. Why should philosophy and logic have become a focus of scholarly interest within early medieval Western Europe, especially in light of the prevailing scholarly preoccupations with Christian theology and exposition of the Bible? Before attempting to answer this question, let us survey the evidence, in terms of extant manuscript distribution, firstly, that philosophy texts were more widely available throughout the eighth, ninth and tenth centuries, and secondly, that philosophy was studied in the early medieval schools.

In establishing the intellectual context for the study of philosophy in the early Middle Ages principal considerations are what texts were known and available, whether we can document the introduction of particular texts to a wider audience or region, and how ideas could be disseminated. Were particular centres noted for the study of philosophy and how did they come to be in such a position? The principal texts in question are: Plato's *Timaeus;* Boethius' *On the Consolation of Philosophy,* logical writings and the Latin translation of Aristotle's *Categories;* the composite translation of the *Categories* with Boethius' *lemmata;* the early medieval paraphrase of the *Categories* known as the *Ten Categories;* pseudo-Apuleius's *Perihermenias;* Macrobius' commentary on Cicero's *Dream of Scipio;* the *Topics* of Cicero.

If the Lyons philosophical collection and the Lyons *Timaeus* highlight the recognizable role played by the Carolingian royal court in the dissemination of philosophical texts, other centres also played a role, apparently independently of the court. Analysis of the textual tradition of Latin versions of the *Timaeus,* for example, indicates a special role for Ferrières and Corbie for the translation by Cicero, and for Rheims and St Amand for Calcidius's version. Such specialization of book production in terms of types of text copied is an observable phenomenon of the Carolingian period, with classical literary texts concentrated in the Loire, Picardy and Lake Constance regions, mass books particularly associated with St Amand, Bibles and Gospel books of a distinctive format with Tours and a remarkable preoccupation with Augustinian theology at Carolingian Lyons.

The earliest manuscripts of Boethius' translation of the *Categories* of Aristotle, whether complete or in fragmentary form, date from the late tenth and eleventh centuries. They were produced at such centres as Corbie, Fleury, St Gall, Echternach and St Vaast, and were presumably based on earlier exemplars, or, conceivably, one common ancestor. The date of these, whether sixth or ninth century, is a matter for speculation. Three ninth-century manuscripts of the composite translation are extant, apparently from regions as diverse as the Lake Constance area, Picardy and northern Italy. Such distribution suggests either originally widely-dispersed texts or else the consequence of specific contacts between individuals in these areas in the ninth century. The *Ten Categories* survives in no fewer than nineteen ninth and tenth century manuscripts, many of them with extensive glosses. Auxerre is an important centre of production, as is Fleury, but there are examples also from St Gall and Corbie, from as far east as Freising and as far west as Wales, with some French and Italian representatives in the eleventh and twelfth centuries. Examination of the manuscript transmission of other key texts reveals a similar pattern.

Porphyry's *Isagoge* in the translation by Marius Victorinus, for example, survives in fragments, now Munich, Bayerische Staatsbibliothek Clm 6403, written at Freising. In Boethius' translation, on the other hand, it is to be found in many copies of ninth and tenth century date, often coinciding with the *Ten Categories*. It is found, moreover, in such dialectical collections as the Lyons corpus belonging to Leidrad. Marenbon, furthermore, has ascertained that Ratramnus of Corbie, John Scottus Eriugena, Heiric of Auxerre and Remigius of Auxerre knew the *Ten Categories*. Thus Auxerre again figures very prominently, as indeed it does in all branches of intellectual life in the Carolingian world, but representatives of the *Isagoge* and *Ten Categories* are to be found in other cultural centres within the Frankish kingdoms, north and east, some of which had connections with Auxerre. Again a similar pattern emerges when the manuscript tradition of the *Isagoge* and logical collections and Boethius' two commentaries on the *Isagoge* are considered. One ninth century copy of the first commentary (in dialogue form) is extant in BN lat. 12958 of the late ninth or early tenth centuries used at Corbie, though not written there, in order to compile BN lat. 13955. The commentary survives in five tenth century manuscripts whose origins indicate a wide dissemination of the text thereafter, though not necessarily emanating from Corbie itself. Pseudo-Apuleius' *Perihermenias,* too, has a largely Frankish circulation in the early Middle Ages while Auxerre plays a particularly important role in the transmission of Macrobius' commentary on Cicero's *Dream of Scipio*. BN lat. 6370, moreover, although from Tours, has corrections written in the hands of Heiric of Auxerre and Lupus of Ferrières. Other ninth century manuscripts of Macrobius survive also from Tours, Fleury and Corbie with dissemination thereafter into southern Germany and southern Italy. Similarly, work on the 'Leiden corpus' of Cicero's philosophical works has established that Corbie, Ferrières and possibly Rheims in the ninth century as well as Monte Cassino in the eleventh are implicated in the transmission of Cicero's *Topics*.

The textual links among the Carolingian copies of the various philosophical works studied in the early Middle Ages and between these and descendants of later date from elsewhere are sometimes strong, suggesting that individual contacts played a crucial role at some stage in the late tenth and early eleventh centuries, if not earlier. Equally, it is remarkable, within the traditions of the texts, how many independent lines of transmission there are. Although the evidence indicates a group of centres in the early Middle Ages which concentrated much attention on those philosophical texts, there is enough surviving from elsewhere to suggest that study of philosophy was not confined to centres such as Auxerre, Fleury or Corbie but that there were pockets of interest scattered elsewhere, notably in southern Germany. Further, although some of the later centres evincing interest in these texts in the tenth and eleventh centuries are clearly connected with the older Carolingian centres, others are not, and may therefore be the earliest extant witnesses to a far more widespread interest in and study of philosophical texts in Western Europe in the early Middle Ages than the available evidence now permits us to reconstruct.

We may have to envisage, moreover, a considerable survival of late antique exemplars. Traces of their existence can sometimes be deduced, as in the copy of Macrobius owned by Symmachus, whose subscription in his book is transmitted in no less than ten of the later copies. Other examples are the sixth century geographical miscellany which travelled from Ravenna to Gaul and provided the exemplar for the copy made in the circle of Lupus of Ferrières and Heiric of Auxerre; the ancient papyrus codex of Boethius' commentary on the *Topics* of Cicero borrowed by Lupus of Ferrières from Tours, the late antique texts of Terence and the Aratea copied at Rheims and in Lotharingia in the ninth century such as BN lat. 7899 and Leiden Voss. lat. Q79, and the famous Virgil texts thought to have been possessed by St Denis and Lorsch in the Carolingian period. Certainly if one augments the core texts denned in this chapter with texts of related interest and content, as well as the evidence provided by library catalogues of the ninth, tenth and eleventh centuries, the number of centres possessing them is very considerably enhanced. The royal court of the Carolingians, moreover, figures with some prominence.

The *scriptoria* of the monasteries and cathedrals were, therefore, obviously active in the provision of texts. From glosses and commentaries on philosophical texts dating from the ninth century onwards, moreover, it is clear that such provision was clearly related to, and supplied the needs of, libraries and schools. Such specialized book production facilitated study and the intellectual activity of individuals, as is evident from the occasional indications we get of personal libraries, such as that of Gerward of Lorsch or the books added to the library of Murbach by Abbot Iskar. Similarly the requirements of individuals or even institutions stimulated copying activity, in that the network of communications between the various centres established the canon of texts necessary for a particular library to possess as well as furnishing information about where exemplars of desired texts might be obtained. The personal interests of Hadoardus of Corbie, Lupus of Ferrières and Murethach, Haymo, Heiric and Remigius of Auxerre determined to a very considerable degree, the direction of study at the schools and within the groups of scholars with which they were associated.

Other Carolingian masters elsewhere were as active. At Laon, Martin of Laon, as is evident from the number of school texts he annotated, taught script, Greek, law, history, grammar and *computus*. One of his most famous teaching compilations, Laon Bibliothèque Municipale 468, also used by his successors as masters of the school at Laon, Bernard and Adelelm, includes texts on the life of Virgil and commentaries on Virgil, on the liberal arts and 'On philosophers, poets, the sibylls and magicians'. The overriding emphasis of two of Martin's other teaching manuals, Laon Bibliothèque Municipale 444 and 464, is on grammar. At Reichenau, among the many teachers there, one, Walafrid Strabo, reveals his interests to us in his personal compilation of texts. It contains a rich miscellany of grammatical texts, short treatises on metrics and computus, Bede's *On the Nature of Things* and works on time extracts from ecclesiastical histories and an excerpt from a letter by Seneca. If we compare this selection with the school texts listed at the end of the Reichenau library catalogue for 821, there is a similar emphasis on grammar and computus. In very few Carolingian centres, notably Auxerre in the ninth and tenth centuries and Rheims in the tenth century, was philosophy in any sense formally part of the curriculum. Gerbert of Rheims, for example, is said to have taught Porphyry's *Isagoge* in the translations of Marius Victorinus and Boethius, Aristotle's *Categories* and *On Interpretation* and Cicero's *Topics* as well as to have provided instruction in the arts of metrics, rhetoric, arithmetic, geometry and astronomy.

In the tenth century at St Gall it was Notker III Labeo (950-1022) who was the first to translate philosophical texts from the Latin into German vernacular for the sake of his German-speaking pupils at the school of St Gall. According to a letter written to Hugh, bishop of Sitten, Notker translated Boethius, *On the Consolation of Philosophy,* the *Categories* and *On Interpretation* of Aristotle (translated from Boethius' Latin version) and the first two books of Martianus Capella's *On the Marriage of Mercury and Philology* as well as the *Quicumque vult,* the Psalter and the Book of Job. Notker III composed one treatise, *On Music,* in German and wrote a number of others in Latin, such as *On the Art of Rhetoric, On the Parts of Logic, On Disputation* and *Computus,* which were subsequently translated into German. Not all these have survived but among those that are extant are, in the literal translation they provide, invaluable indications of pedagogical methods in an early medieval school, with every assistance being offered to aid understanding of the text, guides to rhetorical figures and dialectical techniques and a wealth of miscellaneous general information about etymology, history, zoology and astronomy. There are, moreover, some fascinating witnesses to the dissemination of texts from Auxerre mentioned above; to these translations, notably of the *On the Consolation of Philosophy* of Boethius and Martianus Capella, were appended commentaries, some of which were based on, if not actually translations of, the expositions of Remigius of Auxerre.

The combination of Notker's texts, as with the range of topics addressed by Walafrid Strabo, Martin of Laon, Gerbert of Rheims and other Carolingian masters, is in fact typical of the different emphases within the school curriculum in the early Middle Ages. It is not feasible to think in terms of philosophy playing a separate role within the school curriciulum in the Carolingian period. Rather, elements of philosophy and the discipline of logic would develop out of the emphasis on the structure of language and grammar and be incorporated into the general teaching of the *artes* as the foundation for a deeper understanding of scripture and the teaching of the fathers. Thus Notker translated texts relating to all aspects of the *trivium* (grammar, dialectic and rhetoric), the *quadrivium* (arithmetic, geometry, astronomy and music) and to the Bible and liturgy.

At other schools in France, Germany and Italy a similarly rich mixture within the school curriculum is to be observed. In the episcopal schools of Germany, such as those of Trier, Augsburg, Eichstätt and Utrecht, Würzburg, Regensburg, Cologne and Liège, and many more, the Carolingian school curriculum was taught, with only occasionally the instruction in philosophy being noted. Ohtrich of Magdeburg, for example, was noted as one of the famous philosophers of his day. Bruno of Cologne, instructed at Utrecht under Bishop Balderich, kept abreast with the newest developments in 'history, rhetoric, poetry and philosophy'. Even at Auxerre, where philosophy is such a major part of the intellectual activity of its leading scholars, it is important to remember that this was also the centre which produced the *Deeds of the Bishops of Auxerre, Miracula,* homiliaries, biblical exegesis of lasting importance, and lives of saints.

Nevertheless it would appear, in fact, that philosophy became a more dominant part of the school curriculum in the course of the tenth century, and became still more important in the schools of the eleventh and twelfth centuries, at least in France. In the later ninth and tenth centuries, moreover, there is a discernible increase in the importance of cathedral schools in both the West and the East Frankish kingdoms, notably, by way of example, at Rheims and Liège and the German episcopal schools mentioned above. The lines of institutional continuity between the cathedral and monastic schools of the East and West Frankish kingdoms in the ninth and tenth centuries to the schools of Paris in the twelfth century are clear [5.60]. It is no surprise that we find in the teaching of the schools of Laon, Chartres and Paris in the eleventh and twelfth century the same mixed curriculum, designed according to a similar structure, and methods of teaching which have their roots in the early Carolingian period. At Chartres, for example, it was possible to study medicine, geometry, computus, music and logic; a manuscript from Fulbert of Chartres' time, Chartres Bibliothèque Municipale 100, was a compilation of familiar texts, namely, the *Isagoge,* the *Categories,* the *Topics* of Cicero and other related texts, including a poem by Fulbert on the difference between rhetoric and dialectic. In the glossing methods employed by Anselm of Laon, of Peter Lombard, or Hugh of St Victor, the development of distinctive layout of text and gloss to accommodate these new developments, and in the philosophical discussion of such authors as Thierry of Chartres, we witness a similar blend of older curriculum and scholarly methods with a response to the new influences in learning and currents of thought, wonderfully elucidated long since by Southern. No doubt this was due in part to the availability of a greater variety of classical texts, especially by Plato and Aristotle but to these should be added the work of the contemporary authors, discussed in the various chapters in this volume. The extant library catalogues of the twelfth century and the reconstruction of twelfth century libraries such as those of Zwiefalten, demonstrate more clearly than any other sources the extent both of the Carolingian foundations of the school curriculum and their intellectual emphases and the innovations of the eleventh and twelfth centuries. Corbie's library, for example, although including a large corpus of philosophical works, with many of Boethius' works, a commentary on Martianus Capella by John Scottus Eriugena, the *Timaeus,* and the philosophical works of William of Conches, and the library of Cluny with its copies of the *Isagoge,* Martianus Capella, the *Categories* of Aristotle,

Boethius' commentary on Cicero's *Topics*, Calcidius and many more, still contain an overwhelming preponderance of patristic texts and biblical exegesis. The primary focus of intellectual endeavour remained the Bible, but philosophy had a secure place in the intellectual activities of many of the leading scholars of Europe.

That learning, including the study of philosophy, enjoyed such a prominent position within the life of the monasteries and cathedrals of Western Europe in the early Middle Ages is a phenomenon to which we have become accustomed, even though the preoccupation with scholarship within a monastic context might appear anomalous. The acceptance of intellectual endeavour as an essential part of a society's activity and the primary focus of its culture is nevertheless a remarkable characteristic of early medieval culture and merits some discussion.

Let us consider, therefore, the role of the royal court signalled at the beginning of this chapter in order to explore, first, the political dimensions of the promotion of education and learning and second, the implications of patronage royal, aristocratic, episcopal and monastic not only in promoting education and the study of philosophy but also in helping to shape particular cultural imperatives that became an accepted part of a society.

Within the Germanic kingdoms Lupus of Ferrières offers a clue, in that he laments, in a letter to Einhard, the passing of Charlemagne:

> *Within your memory there has been a revival of learning, thanks to the efforts of the illustrious emperor Charles to whom letters owe an everlasting debt of gratitude. Learning has indeed lifted up its head to some extent. In these days those who pursue an education are considered a burden to society men have consequently shrunk from this endeavour, some because they do not receive a suitable reward for their knowledge, others because they fear an unworthy reputation.*

Lupus lauded the activities of Charlemagne's grandson Charles the Bald and his support of scholarship in many of his other letters. Further, such authors as Notker Balbulus of St Gall testify to the extent to which the Carolingian rulers actively promoted scholarship. We may add to this the emphasis on correct texts of the Christian liturgy, canon law and the Bible, education and learning in Carolingian legislation and directives from the king to his abbots and bishops, such as the *Admonitio Generalis* of 789 and the *De litteris colendis* of *c.* 800. Although the main aim of such learning was a fuller understanding of the Christian faith, and the provision of an educated administrative class of clerics and lay magnates, sufficient latitude is provided to those responsible for carrying out the wishes of the ruler with respect to teaching and the provision of correct texts for all Christian learning to benefit. Certainly, the subsequent production and dissemination of all kinds of text, apparently in response to the ruler's initiative, is well documented.

What should also be reckoned with is the personal interest of the rulers themselves in matters of higher learning and the degree to which they actively promoted scholarship, the liberal arts and philosophy by means of patronage. From the books associated with the Carolingian rulers it is apparent how they gathered together scribes and artists, not only to produce books which reflect the personal piety and private interests of the king but also as a strategy of royal piety and largesse. As Lupus implies in the extract from his letter to Einhard quoted above, the king's patronage held the promise of material reward. It is clear from the surviving evidence of scholarly activity associated with the court, and the dedications of many works to the king, that many sought such patronage. The essential material support for learning, in other words, was provided by secular rulers as well as by the Church to satisfy particular as well as general goals.

The role of the king in creating the social imperatives that made an exercise of secular patronage in this particular sphere of activity so acceptable is all important. We are not observing merely the consequences of personal intellectual and aesthetic predilections. Certainly the presence of early Carolingian manuscripts with court connections, such as the Lyons dialectical collection or Plato's *Timaeus,* seems to testify to the gathering of rare classical works, and suggests that there are deeper motives in royal patronage to be discerned. What is apparent above all is the sheer organization and determination behind the dissemination of particular texts to do with the Christian faith and learning, and the explicit association of this activity with the exercise of Christian kingship made by the rulers. Thus it is not simply that King Charles the Bald enjoyed his lessons with Walafrid Strabo and derived intellectual pleasure and stimulus from the presence of such scholars as Manno of St Ouen, Lupus of Ferrières or John Scottus Eriugena in his kingdom, or even at his court. Nor is it that scholars who enjoyed royal patronage were thereby able to pursue their intellectual activities; and many had considerable influence on succeeding generations of pupils and scholars. Among them were Alcuin of Tours, Hrabanus Maurus of Fulda and Mainz, John Scottus Eriugena, or Lupus, who was part of the dynamic intellectual milieu focused on Auxerre and Fleury in the mid-ninth century. What is essential is that intellectual activity was recognized to be a fundamental part of the spiritual and cultural goals of all Christians; the king as Christian ruler therefore had a duty to foster this as much as he enlarged the kingdom, promoted the administration of justice and the use of agreed weights and measures or guaranteed the stability and value of the coinage.

The example of the high priority given to intellectual activity and culture set by rulers to future generations, moreover, is not to be underestimated. Of course, the Carolingians were not the first to exercise patronage in this way. Nevertheless, they were arguably the first to take such an effective interest in the correctness of the Christian texts in use in the churches, chapels and monasteries of their kingdoms, and the first whose patronage was more than an occasional interest in benefactions. The Carolingian rulers actually sustained groups of artists, scribes and craftsmen over a long period of time in order to create artefacts or carry out their particular cultural objectives. It was an example, if not actually followed, then certainly emulated by other rulers, and by lay and ecclesiastical magnates. In Anglo-Saxon England, for example, Asser's *Life of King Alfred* recounts the great interest the king took in learning and how he himself translated, as well as commissioning translations from others, many crucial texts, not least Boethius' *On the Consolation of Philosophy*. Cnut is also attested as a patron of some stature. If in the tenth and eleventh centuries on the Continent the Carolingian, Capetian and Saxon kings of the West and East Franks were rather less active in the promotion of scholarship and patronage of learning, the baton fell above all to the bishops. The bishops of Liège, Trier and Hildesheim are cases in ponit. Liège was celebrated for its learning under Bishops Ebrachar and Notker but they were following a tradition established in the time of Bishop Hartgar, who acted as patron and offered a refuge to the Irish scholar Sedulius Scotus. Many manuscripts, ivories and some remarkable pieces of metalwork have been associated with Egbert, bishop of Trier from 977 to 993, and Bernward of Hildesheim, which were produced in ateliers both in their own dioceses and elsewhere. Mayr-Harting has highlighted these bishops' acknowledgement of their reflection of kingly rule, and the way in which they visibly manipulated, or commanded, spiritual power by commissioning book covers and reliquaries wrought in gold and studded with bright jewels, and manuscripts resplendent with fine painting, decorated initials and beautiful script.

The display of wealth that was one obvious outcome of the patronage of culture and learning was also a demonstration of power and might. It is of crucial importance for our understanding of the intellectual culture of the early Middle Ages to see that patronage operated so effectively and constructively in the cultural as well as in the political and military spheres. Indeed, these various activities were seen to interlock and to be many facets of one society. Thus social and political imperatives from the pinnacle of authority, displays of wealth and power, the enhancing of authority, and the incorporation of a further, cultural, dimension within the ideals of political and social leadership had repercussions for the particular cultural preoccupations and intellectual aspirations of early medieval society. Patronage played a crucial role in establishing such preoccupations within the intellectual horizons and educational traditions of Western Europe. We thus observe an essential interplay between political authority, economic resources and intellectual endeavour.

Philosophical Themes

There were three main fields of philosophical activity in the early medieval period: the study of logic, the reading and reaction to ancient and late antique philosophical texts and the analytical discussion of problems about Christian doctrine. The manuscript background to the first two has been explored in the previous section; the following paragraphs offer a quick sketch of some of the main themes in each area.

Logic:

The earliest evidence for medieval interest in and use of logical techniques is found in the *Libri Carolini,* the statement of the Western position on the worship of icons prepared at Charlemagne's court *c.* 790, probably by Theodulf of Orleans. The longest logical passages here borrow material from Boethius and Apuleius on semantics and on the relations between the truth-values of differently quantified sentences. It was Alcuin, who apparently established himself as Charlemagne's leading intellectual in the 790s, who gave early medieval logic its twist towards metaphysical and theological concerns. In his *De dialectica* ('On logic'), the first medieval logical textbook, Alcuin gives pride of place to the doctrine of the ten categories, as expounded in the *Ten Categories,* attributed at this time to Augustine. Aristotle's discussion of the categories is less a piece of logic than an exercise in fundamental metaphysics, an analysis of the different types of entity (universal and particular substances, universal and particular accidents). Augustine had already put the doctrine to theological use in his *On the Trinity,* and Alcuin borrowed and emphasized this theme in his *On the Faith of the Holy Trinity*. The *Ten Categories* became the most eagerly studied logical textbook in the ninth and tenth centuries, and the question of whether God could be fitted into them, already raised by Alcuin, was taken up by his pupils and explored in depth by Eriugena. The glosses to the *Ten Categories,* which vary from manuscript to manuscript, show a definite pattern of development. The late ninth-century glossators tended to use the text as a springboard for Eriugena-inspired metaphysical and theological comments, only loosely related to the logical subject matter. Tenth and eleventh century glossators became less and less interested in such speculation and more concerned to reach an understanding of basic Aristotelian ideas such as the distinctions between substance and accident, and between univocal and equivocal words, or the nature of space and time. Gradually, a translation of Aristotle's own text came to replace the pseudo-Augustinian paraphrase, giving scholars the chance to use Boethius' commentary and, through it, to master the argument of the text and consider the difficult problems about the status of Aristotle's discussion (Is it about words, or things, or what?) which would concern twelfth-century logicians.

The *Isagoge* ('Introduction') by Porphyry, a short guide to the notions of genus, species, differentiating property *(differentia),* distinguishing characteristic *(proprium)* and accident, long regarded as an introduction to Aristotle's *Categories,* was also known from the time of Alcuin. Glosses to the *Isagoge* at least those so far investigated draw heavily on Boethius' commentaries. Porphyry's famous allusion to the disputed status of universals, which became the focus for medieval debates from the twelfth century onwards, seemed to excite no controversy. One of the few early medieval writers to discuss universals, Ratramnus of Corbie, exponent of a somewhat inchoate conceptualism, turned, not to the *Isagoge,* but the first of Boethius' commentaries on it and also to Boethius' *Theological Treatises.* Aristotle's *On Interpretation,* although known, was found forbiddingly difficult by most logicians until the eleventh century; glosses are rare and derivative. But, by about 1000, Abbo of Fleury, Notker of St Gall and Gerbert of Aurillac included it within their teaching, and Abbo compiled his own introduction to syllogistic reasoning, drawing on Boethius' textbooks.

Aside from Anselm's *De grammatico,* there is disappointingly little *direct* evidence for logical studies for most of the eleventh century itself. Material dating from 1100 or just before shows a sophistication in dealing with the *Isagoge, Categories* and *On Interpretation,* and a facility in handling syllogisms and topical inferences which cannot have been suddenly acquired; this is a surmise strongly supported by the confident use in doctrinal controversy and discussion of notions from both the *Categories* (as in the dispute between Lanfranc and Berengar) and *On Interpretation* (as in Anselm's *Cur Deus Homo* and Peter Damian's *Letter on God's Omnipotence*).

Reading Ancient Philosophy

Although some early medieval writers criticized logic as a distraction from religious devotion, no one could claim that the ancient logical textbooks were themselves a challenge to the faith; and, indeed, in his *Theological Treatises* (much read and glossed in these centuries) Boethius had shown how logical techniques could be used against heresy in support of orthodox doctrine. By contrast, Latin texts of ancient philosophy posed what might seem as a direct challenge to Christian belief, by proposing a view at least in some respects incompatible with them. Yet it was not, in fact, any of the three main pagan philosophical books available from the ninth to the eleventh centuries that became the focus of controversy. Plato's *Timaeus* (in Calcidius' partial translation) was found too difficult for sustained discussion; the two introductory books of Martianus Capella, preceding the handbooks to the individual disciplines, were too obviously an allegory to cause problems; and Macrobius' commentary on Cicero's *Dream of Scipio* tended to be looked on as a source of information about natural science, especially astronomy, to which further information of like nature should be appended by glossators. And so, strangely, it was in connection with the work of a Christian author that scholars from the ninth to the eleventh centuries considered most carefully how to react to ancient philosophy. After writing his logical translations, commentaries and translations, and his

Theological Treatises, Boethius, in prison and awaiting execution, wrote his final work, *On the Consolation of Philosophy.* The *Consolation* not only avoids any explicit reference to Christian revelation. It also contains passages which present ancient Platonic ideas which, taken literally, are incompatible with Christianity. In particular, the ninth metrum (or verse passage) of Book III, a prayer incanted at the very climax of the argument, is an epitome of the *Timaeus,* and it refers both to the idea of reincarnation and to that of the World Soul.

What should the Christian reader make of such passages? The most forthright reaction was that of Bovo, a monk of Corvey, who recognized clearly that, although Boethius had written elsewhere on Christian doctrine, he was setting out here to present Platonic and not Christian teaching. Using Macrobius he seems not to have known the *Timaeus* itself he gives a clear explanation of the ideas behind the compressed phrases of Boethius' poem. Although this approach had its followers, it was not the most common one. At much the same time as Bovo, Remigius of Auxerre had composed his commentary, not just to this metrum, but to the whole *Consolation,* drawing on earlier glosses (just as he would do in his extensive commentary on Martianus Capella) but developing them in his own way. His effort was to find an explicitly Christian meaning hidden in the apparently Platonic phrases of Boethius. About a hundred years later, Adalbold of Utrecht pursued a similar Christianizing line in his commentary on Book III, metrum 9, although he allegorized less thoroughly than Remigius and ended with an unintendedly strange amalgam of orthodox Christianity and Platonic teaching. Twelfth-century scholars, especially William of Conches, would follow and sophisticate the approach pioneered by Remigius and Adalbold, applying it to genuinely pagan texts as well as to the *Consolation.*

Problems Raised by Christian Doctrine:

From the twelfth century onwards, much of the best philosophical thinking took place in the context of theology, the systematic investigation of Christian doctrine which would be typified in the universities by the commentaries on the

Sentences of Peter the Lombard. In the ninth to eleventh centuries, it is difficult to talk of 'theology' in this sense. But philosophical discussion still arose in connection with various types of writing concerned primarily with Christian doctrine: sermons and biblical exegesis were inclined to be unargumentative (though Eriugena's are an exception), but other works about doctrine, stimulated by controversy or responding to particular questions, often contain interesting material for the historian of philosophy.

One of the fiercest controversies in the ninth century was instigated by Gottschalk, a monk first of Fulda, then Reichenau, then Orbais. In a series of writings from the 830s onwards, Gottschalk championed the idea, which he claimed (with some justice) to be Augustine's, that God's predestination is dual; of the good to bliss and of the wicked to damnation. He found many well-educated supporters, but others in the Church feared that his teaching would discourage people from trying to act well by making them think that, regardless of anything they did, they were from eternity predestined to hell or to heaven. Two important churchmen Hrabanus Maurus, archbishop of Mainz and prolific scriptural exegete and encyclopaedist, and Hincmar, archbishop of Rheims wrote against Gottschalk; and they also commissioned an attack from a scholar attached to the court of the emperor, Charles the Bald; this would be John Scottus Eriugena's first treatise, his *On Predestination*. Although Hrabanus' and Hincmar's pieces (not, however, John's) amass patristic quotations, all three involve argument and analysis, and together they provide the earliest medieval attempt to explore notions such as free will, evil and punishment.

All three writers challenged Gottschalk's formula of dual predestination by saying that God *predestines* in one way alone the good to salvation but he *foresees* both the salvation of the good and the damnation of the wicked. Only those predestined to salvation can be saved, because for salvation God's grace is needed. Yet God cannot be said to 'predestine' the wicked; rather, he fails to predestine them. Eriugena also adds the argument, based on the Platonic view that evil is not a thing but a deficiency, that God *could* not possibly predestine anyone to a wicked life or to eternal punishment because, as evils and therefore deficiencies, they have no cause. (This last is a particularly silly argument; the emptiness of my glass is just as clearly caused by my having drunk the wine as its fullness was caused by my having poured wine into it from the bottle!) So far all three writers have hardly distanced themselves more than verbally from Gottschalk, since on their view people will still be damned, whatever they do, if God fails to predestine them. Hrabanus and Hincmar are aware of this problem but try to dodge it, stressing God's inscrutability or, in the case of Hincmar, suggesting that God withholds grace from those whose future misuse of their wills he has foreseen. Eriugena does not resolve the central issue. How can an individual human being be held responsible for the evil actions which, without the help of grace, he cannot but perform? Rather, he concentrates on relieving God of any responsibility for unjustly punishing those who are not responsible for their wickedness by an astonishingly bold move. He claims that God does not punish anybody. Sinners are punished (through ignorance, or through the knowledge that they lack beatitude, or through the frustration of their desire to become nothing at all), but not by God, who is merely the framer of just laws.

There were various doctrinal controversies in the two following centuries which stimulated philosophical discussion, most notably the dispute in the mid-eleventh century between Lanfranc and Berengar over the eucharist. But even more interesting for the history of philosophy is a work written at much the same time, as part not of a public controversy but of a private debate. Peter Damian was unwilling to accept Jerome's statement, put to him by a friend, that 'whilst God can do all things, he cannot restore a virgin after she has lost her virginity' and he wrote his *Letter on Divine Omnipotence* to explain why not. Damian is known as an ascetic, contemptuous of pagan philosophy, and historians have often interpreted his rejection of Jerome's position in this light; as an extreme manifestation of his anti-philosophical stance, according to which he claims that God can undo the past, making what has happened not have happened and thus violating the fundamental logical law of non-contradiction. On a careful reading, however, the argument of the letter is seen to be quite different. Damian contends that, by nature, it is impossible to restore her virginity to a virgin who has lost it. By this he means that there is no way of repairing the ruptured membrane. The only way, then, that by nature a non-virgin could become a virgin would be if the past were changed, so that her virginity never had been lost. But, Damian goes on, this changing the past is *impossible* absolutely, even for God and certainly by nature. Making a non-virgin into a virgin by repairing her virginity (not by changing the past) is possible, however, for God, though it is impossible by nature. Here, then, Damian seems to be distinguishing between the physically impossible, which is possible for God, and the logically impossible, which even for God is impossible. But, at one point, he asks whether God could make it that Rome had never existed and answers that God could. He goes on to explain that, since God lives in an eternity which is timeless, to say that God could now make it that Rome never existed is equivalent to saying that God could have from the beginning shaped a providence which did not include the existence of Rome. Damian's position is defensible, though when clarified it becomes less bold than it at first seems. He makes two arguable claims: (1) that God might have chosen a providence other than the one he has in fact chosen—a providence in which, for instance, Rome never existed; (2) that God's choice of providences does not take place at any moment in time, but in timeless eternity. (1) would be accepted by most Christian thinkers; the meaningfulness of (2) can be queried, but the position has had many adherents, from Boethius' time until now. Taken together, (1) and (2) lead to the conclusion that God could make it (tenseless) that Rome never existed. Since God exists timelessly, any verb which is applied to him is timeless; the apparently paradoxical 'God is able to make it that Rome never existed' is no different in meaning from the straightforward 'God was able to make it that Rome never existed'.

Medieval philosophy is the philosophy of Europe in the era now known as medieval or the Middle Ages, the period roughly extending from the fall of the Roman Empire in the fifth century A.D. to the Renaissance in the sixteenth century. It is defined partly by the process of rediscovering the ancient culture developed in Greece and Rome in the classical period, and partly by the need to address theological problems and to integrate sacred doctrine with secular learning.

The history of medieval philosophy is traditionally divided into three main periods; the period in the Latin West following the Early Middle Ages until the twelfth century, when the works of Aristotle and Plato were preserved and cultivated; and the 'golden age' of the twelfth, thirteenth and fourteenth centuries in the Latin West, which witnessed the culmination of the recovery of ancient philosophy, and significant developments in the field of Philosophy of religion, Logic and Metaphysics.

The medieval era was disparagingly treated by the Renaissance humanists, who saw it as a barbaric 'middle' period between the classical age of Greek and Roman culture, and the 'rebirth' or renaissance of classical culture. Yet this period of nearly a thousand years was the longest period of philosophical development in Europe, and possibly the richest. Jorge Gracia has argued that in "intensity, sophistication, and achievement, the philosophical flowering in the thirteenth century could be rightly said to rival the golden age of Greek philosophy in the fourth century B.C."

The problems discussed throughout this period are the relation of faith to reason, the existence and simplicity of God, the purpose of theology and metaphysics, and the problems of knowledge, of universals, and of individuation.

Medieval philosophy is characteristically theological: with the possible exceptions of Avicenna and Averroes, medieval thinkers did not consider themselves philosophers at all. Their concerns are theological; for them, the philosophers were the ancient pagan writers such as Plato and Aristotle. However, the theological works of medieval writers use the ideas and logical techniques of the ancient philosophers to address difficult theological questions, and points of doctrine. Thomas Aquinas, following Peter Damian, argued that philosophy is the handmaiden of theology.

4

History of Pure Reason in Medieval Philosophy

Introduction

In the first place, they centered their interest in ethics on prescriptions for the best way of life. Within that scope, the goals all proposed were negative. The Epicureans, who carried forward the atomic theory, held that the end life was freedom from passion. The Platonic Academy turned skeptical in its metaphysics and took for its ethical aim suspension of judgment freedom from disappointed expectation. Aristotle's Peripatetic School practiced escape through scholarship and freedom from extremes in habits or actions this by way of commentary on the ethical treatises of Aristotle. The Stoics stressed freedom from passion.

The ultimate rejection of a materialistic world and a Roman Empire that seemed intolerable took form in a revolution in the Academy in the second century A.D. The skeptical Academics had held that our only sure knowledge would be a vision of Platonic forms but that these forms remained unknownable. Neoplatonism reversed the argument; claiming that we do have knowledge, it inferred the reality of Platonic forms. But it disconnected the Platonic formal world from nature far more sharply than Plato had done and made the end of life a removed, mystical contemplation of that formal system. Plotinus, the leading spokesman for this new Platonism, makes this attitude clear in his saying, "Action is only an inferior form of contemplation." The world proceeds by "emanation," an outpouring from the One, Plato's Form of the Good, the only thing *completely* real and self-sufficient in the scheme.

As Christianity became the official religion of the Roman Empire, it found in Neoplatonism much of what it needed as a supporting philosophy. In the fifth century A.D., St. Augustine set up a Christian adaptation, in which a Trinitarian God was partially identified with the levels of reality in Plotinus. The Platonic forms became ideas in the mind of this God, who used them as models in his creation of the physical world (which, unlike Plato's Demiurge, the Christian God created out of nothing). Man, with reason and an immortal soul, could share some vision of these ideas, by an insight based on introspection. ("I care for God and the soul and nothing else," St. Augustine wrote.) Cosmology became the religious drama of a world history of creation fall redemption last judgment. Images and analogies were extensively pursued; the philosophy lent itself well to metaphor.

Through a period of eclipse of scholarship in the West until it again reached a high point in the twelfth century, Platonic formalism (with some key distinctions sharpened) was the dominant philosophic system. Where this could lead logically is shown by St. Bonaventure's short essay, "Reduction of All the Arts to Theology."

But shortly after the end of the thirteenth century, the dominant philosophical system of the Latin West had become that of Aristotle. His work, available but untranslated and neglected, came to the attention of Latin scholars through the admiration it received in the Arabic universities of Spain. Presently, in addition to Latin versions based on Arabic, new Latin translations from the Greek text were prepared (by a word-for-word method that makes for difficult reading, but from which we can actually recover the Greek original). St. Thomas Aquinas is the leading figure in the debate that ended with an Aristotelian victory. Certainly one of the most important new ideas that came with this change of authorities was the notion that human knowers must discover forms by observation, not simply inner recollection. So, since "there is nothing in the intellect that was not first in our senses," the created world now became an object of more serious study, along with God and the soul. Theology, based on revelation, was distinguished from philosophy, based on Aristotelian natural reason, and analytical demonstration took the place of analogical dialectic.

Aristotle's world view had a tidy finite cosmos, with the earth in the center, revolving spheres bearing planets and stars revolving about it, and a continuing input of energy from a first moving cause; this suited the Middle Ages well. And the methods of classification and logical proof brought new discipline to the arts and sciences. In this later medieval period, a Latin philosophical vocabulary became standardized, which diffused and carried with it a built-in Aristotelian common sense as it was adopted by the Romance and Germanic languages.

Looking back, I can see several lines of instability that were to lead to a displacement of this system by materialism and mechanism in the seventeenth century. The formalism stressed classification of things by types, though the religion it supported stressed the infinite worth of individuals. The rule that we must *observe* was satisfactory so long as it was taken rather commonsensically. Casual observation does show things running "normally"; closer inspection, though, sharpened by measurement and new instruments, gives a less-reassuring picture. Aristotle's account of change as "the coming into act of a pre-existing potency" was a dangerous temptation to retreat to merely verbal explanations. The pattern can clearly extend quite widely: "Water freezes because its potency for frigidity is becoming actualized." Respect for authority and textbook presentation styles certainly helped create an appetite for change.

The transition from medieval to modern thought actually had four phases. At first, renewed appreciation of classical art and literature brought a revitalized Platonism to the humanities. The new tools and records of observation brought a new model of materialistic precision and of a single type, efficient causality in the natural sciences (as opposed to the Aristotelian four-causal model). At first, only the outer world was supposed to be better explained by mechanistic determinism than by Aristotelian causality. The new interest in Plato of the period suggested that a Platonic psychology might be used as a replacement for that of Aristotle. This unstable compromise could no longer hold after the methods of inquiry used in the sciences were applied to psychology, the mind itself being treated as an organ that could receive, associate, and remember sense impression and ideas. This development made psychology only a branch of physics; but the rejoining of mind and matter along this line came to seem increasingly plausible.

Descartes best represents the second phase of this revolution in systems. His "new method," the subject of his *Discourse on Method*, often taken as the landmark that denotes the beginning of modern philosophy, works differently when he is examining his idea of God and when he is analyzing the world. In the former case, the method returns to traditional Platonic dialectic, seeking truth through introspection; but in the latter case, the method is an analysis of extended particles with volume and momentum, exactly like the classical atomic theory. But in neither case does Descartes trust Aristotle or any other authority; and he encourages his reader to follow this example. It is probably here that a common theme does in fact make Descartes' work stand out as a landmark. Later, Leibniz and Spinoza follow Descartes in building elegant non-Aristotelian metaphysical structures. But in all three, there were such glaring internal inconsistencies that modern thinkers came to be very distrustful of system building in general.

The reaction against Scholasticism illustrates an interesting point; that systems have trouble in being both philosophically consistent and complete. Attention refocuses on experiences, skills, or objects that had not been anticipated in the original taxonomy. The modern systems of the continental rationalists who mark the philosophic break with Scholastic thought achieved greater completeness, but each time at the price of consistency. I think that René Descartes, one of the key transition figures in this story, had a mistaken notion or feeling that there could be only two opposed systems of philosophy. In that case, if Aristotle's was one, and it was wrong, any consistent non-Aristotelian system would be right. The materialistic mathematical physics of a world of qualitatively neutral particles seemed true in physics, as against Aristotle's mixture of four qualitative elements. Also opposed to Aristotle was the Platonic psychology, carried forward by Augustinians, which viewed knowledge as direct recognition of Platonic forms; this view is particularly attractive to mathematicians, and Descartes, a great one, was no exception; he accepted this as his philosophic basis for psychology. The result was that by joining two schemes both opposed to Aristotle he still had a totally different system for mind and for matter and no way of reconciling them. He put the case in a way that shows how revolutions begin as transitions in which many core features stay unchanged. There are, as Descartes puts it, three kinds of substance: mind, matter, and God. Now, there is no need either in psychology or in physics to carry forward the Aristotelian idea of "substance," but this proves hard to displace. Descartes' mind is "a substance, the essence of which is to think." Matter is "a substance, the essence of which is to have extension." Mind is unextended, matter unintelligent. And yet, Descartes admits, we have a clear idea that our minds and bodies act on each other. And given his psychology, what we clearly conceive must be true. The only trouble is that clarity is not enough; we also need a *distinct* idea of *how* there is this causal interaction. And Descartes spent the last years of his life in research in medicine, trying to find a distinct idea of mind-body interaction.

Given the split between the definitions of mental and material substance, it was inevitable that Descartes would fail. Gottfried W. Leibniz' attempt to solve Descartes' problem, which he accepted, was a model of ingenuity. He reduced the world to small substances called "monads," which were like souls. The monads did not experience a non-psychological world directly, but only viewed representations of it internally; so there was no "material" non-ideational substance to contend with. Leibniz thought that there were infinite possible worlds, of which we lived in the only actual one, namely the best. But, as Voltaire cruelly suggested in his novel *Candide*, this "best world" of ours can be a little shop of horrors; the moral facts and Leibniz' blithe metaphysical optimism did not go together. Further, Leibniz' God had created his world from nothing, so that there was not Plato's recourse to limitations of a pre-existent matter open. But metaphysically, if not aesthetically, worse than this, Leibniz' work with mifforlike "representations" as the only content of our knowledge was set up in a way that would make it impossible for us to distinguish possibility from actuality. My colleague Newton Stallknecht reconciled Leibniz and Voltaire in a brilliant and witty fashion: Leibniz may be right, he said, that there is one best of all possible worlds, the others worse; but Voltaire's observation shows that we are not living in it. Instead, we must be creatures in one of the worlds God rejected because of its defects. Stallknecht went on to prove that in Leibniz' system, there was no way for any of us to tell the difference between our representations of an actual world from those of and in a world merely possible. So this attempt to reduce reality to small subjective minds, each in its own theater of representations, was not consistent.

Spinoza took Descartes' third kind of substance, God, and made this constitute both mind and matter. Substance he defined as "that which needs nothing other than itself to exist," and thus subject to no limitations. (The first part of this idea sounds like Aristotle's Prime Mover; but the second is more in keeping with the new science that would have thought of "limitation" in terms of spatial or temporal extension.) By definition, there could be only one substance,

God. But to us, God appears as existing in individual, finite "modes," unreal yet egocentrically voracious. And Spinoza's whole philosophy traces patterns of these modes that are only apparent, and which on his own axiomatic basis ought not to exist at all. His attempted "solution" is rather a universal solvent; and like the mysticism of Parmenides, it lies beyond the frontiers of philosophy.

In England, meanwhile, the mind-body problem also inherited from Descartes took another turn. The British empiricists applied the analytic methods of the new natural science to the traditional subjects of soul and mind. They analyzed the "ideas in minds" that had been the trans-scientific, subjective domain of the Cartesian "thinking substance." But again, this is not the total revolution some historians would make it. For the British group assumed that "ideas" must be "in" some *substantial* subject, namely our minds, where they are open to our inspection. This group also assumed (from the scientific accounts of sensation) that ideas represent atomic, distinct, sensed qualities, shapes, or feelings. These ideas originate, we are told, in impressions acting on our senses from an external world. But on analysis, our idea of such an outside agency is only another mind-contained idea. The analysis of ideas treats universals as incomplete representations, abstraction selecting only a part of the content of impressions. Relations are not included in the inventory of impressions, and this made continuity a special problem. David Hume, who carried this new psychology by analysis to its rigorous conclusion, could finally find no difference between ideas of cause and effect and habits of expecting one thing, given another; he could find no way of access to an objective world that was not an idea; and, worse, he could not even find an impression or idea of a self. This is exactly the result I discussed earlier in connection with the things-thoughts-words trichotomy. If philosophy starts with the patently absurd axiom that all that we can know or feel are our own subjective ideas, it will never reach an objective or interpersonal world, formal or material.

On the other hand, if the objective methods of science are extended to psychology, this does resolve the incorrigible split in the systems of Continental philosophers. Mind can be treated as part of nature. And John Locke, the first of the British trio (our second was Bishop George Berkeley), when he was not being self-consciously analytic (for example, in his tremendously influential writing on education) sounded much like Aristotle.

In the eighteenth century, the new science that had been so dazzlingly successful in astronomy and physics extended its successes, with an explicit recurrence to the atomic theory and an extension of conservation laws to chemical reaction, and began to transform itself into both a general common sense and an intellectual metaphysics.

The collision of Continental rationalism and British empiricism was adjudicated, for the audience able to follow its technicalities, by the philosophy of Immanuel Kant. Kant's critical philosophy repeated Aristotle's distinction of theoretic-practical-productive (this last including aesthetic) domains and built uncrossable barriers between them. What science can understand is the active interpretation of a swarm of minute impacts of sensation, which are organized *by the observer* in space-time, cause-and-effect patterns. The result is a world of *phenomena*, things as they appear when we have edited them, not things in themselves. Kant is looking at the other side of the imperative to observe that science inherited from Scholastic Aristotelianism. The older models had assumed a mind that was passive; Kant argued that a great deal of the order common to human experience was so common because it was the observer's contribution, one that had to be made to derive any intelligibility from the chaotic manifold of sensation at all. On the other hand, what we feel in moral situations is our reason, which issues commands; and this is our property because we are things-in-themselves. Natural law and moral law are thus placed in non-intersecting dimensions, so that neither can transfer to the other. Aesthetics and religion are in yet a third sphere (of beauty and hope), incommensurable with both science and morality.

This argument was carried out by Kant in impressive detail. It had to be if it was to succeed; for Kant had noted that man is a metaphysical animal, reluctant to accept any distinction as a finality. The argument hinged on the inference noted above, that the conditions necessary for any possible experience must be supplied by the experiencer; a contribution, not a discovery.

Kant's critical philosophy may have made science seem less offensive to custom, law, and faith. If so, it played a role in clearing the way for the diffusion of the scientific world view in every other domain, a diffusion that presently co-opted ordinary ways of thought and patterns of imagination. It raised intellectual problems that were insoluble except in Kant's way on the assumptions that Kant made about substance, causality, and time. Among these was the notion that every observer must bring along Aristotelian logic, Euclidean geometry, and Newtonian physics if any consistent science was to be possible.

The impact on professional philosophy of Kant's criticism, which seems somehow a belated Aristotelian intrusion without Aristotle's unifying metaphysics, was great. (And I should probably have compared Kant to Socrates as well as to Aristotle; he brought a touch of both to the European scene.) Merely to follow Kant's argument was such an achievement that, as Stallknecht once said, "No one who has put in the effort to master this system can bear to ask whether it might be wrong!"

The German solutions to Kant's forced distinctions consisted in claiming that, in various ways, human thinkers did have access to things-in-themselves. George Wilhelm Friederich Hegel made this access come by way of reason, Gottlieb Fichte via will, Friederich Schelling by way of imagination. Hegel set out on the particularly suggestive line of thought that the traditional "contradictions" in philosophy were only stages in thought to be resolved with the advance of history. History itself was the thought of an Absolute Mind, reasoning its way from a postulate to the temporal succession of its opposite, and finding a synthesis to resolve that contradiction. This thought moved through time in a rigid dialectical plan by which "spirit" advanced beyond "nature" to realize "freedom."

But on a larger scale, more relevant to my outline history here, Whitehead seems right in discounting the general intellectual effectiveness of Kantian criticism on later metaphysics. The one product that was to have pervasive general and practical impact was the realigning of Hegel's dialectic with the prevalent material direction of type IV systems of thought to produce Marxist "dialectical materialism" in the nineteenth century.

On the whole, the system builders are Continental philosophers. In Britain, generations of empiricists (as opposed to rationalists) Hobbes, then Locke, Berkeley, and Hume avoided a dualism of mind and matter by including the mind in the realm of scientific inquiry. They made an arbitrary mistake in assuming that we can only know our own subjective ideas; this theory of representative perception puts each of us in a private picture-gallery of images in the mind, with no possible way of judging whether they match anything outside or not. But take away that needless restriction, and we have the mindset of the modern "science" that becomes the dominant philosophical force as it is generalized into metaphysics in the eighteenth and nineteenth centuries.

The modern system that came from rejecting Aristotelianism was again Democritean. Whitehead explains its genesis as a piece of selective abstraction overgeneralized. The mathematical laws of nature that were derived work beautifully for the world of "aggregates," extended objects treated in terms of formulas based on force and mass. But the extension of this model to claim itself to be the whole of reality was, says Whitehead, an erroneous overgeneralization. On the other hand and making the philosopher who admires Whitehead uneasy technology based on this kind of thought repeatedly accomplishes things that its critics say cannot be done. The synthesis of organic chemical compounds was one such breakthrough; the chess-playing machine that beats everyone but Karpov will be another.

The Democritean theory is, however, notably limited in its application to questions of ethics and value. I suppose it finds itself somewhat in the position of a Greek Sophist who, having argued that no one ever acts to his or her disadvantage, meets Socrates on his way to his trial. The tension between two domains of science and humanism ended, in the enlightenment, with Imnanuel Kant's critical philosophy. In effect, Kant argued that natural science, ethics, and aesthetics must go their separate ways. Only contradiction can come from trying to include or identify one of these dimensions with another. Laws of nature, ethical imperatives, and religious hopes are different dimensions of reality, with no systematic metaphysics able to bring them together. This belief is in the tradition of Aquinas, who had separated revealed theology from natural philosophy, or of Aristotle, who rejected attractive abstract speculative systems not grounded in observation. Kant recognized that human beings are metaphysical by nature, and that only the most rigid discipline will keep human reason from recombining the dimensions of what I can know, what I ought to do, and what I may hope that his critical philosophy had separated. Kant, too, was a formalist; but his Ideas of reason were forms of which we could never show the reality by argument or experiment. (Perhaps Kant would have been right in his own context. For he thought, optimistically, that Aristotle had completed logic for all time, as Euclid had geometry, and Newton physics and astronomy. This, I must say, reminds me of Aristotle's assignment of labor in his Lyceum: He lectured on the principles he had discovered, while his colleagues wrote historical introductions collecting the errors leading up to, but corrected by, them.)

In any case, philosophy polarized in its response to Kant's attempt to prove his distinctions final. Hegel is the most notable of the post-Kantian idealists who made matter only an idea, science a train of thought in an absolute mind. (Only, as Whitehead noted, the Absolute Mind's thought exactly matched the materialistic science of the time.) Bertrand Russell, among a host of others, was indignant at Hegel's claim that history had progressed from its beginning to its goal in the Prussian state, which was the high point in "spirit's quest for freedom." "Freedom to obey the police," said Russell.

The opposite tack was also tried, the most politically influential form being Marxist dialectical materialism. The laws of matter in motion, with no need for an Absolute Mind to legislate them, guaranteed direction and progress through successive emergence and resolutions of opposition. (One of Marx's admirers, Lasalle, wrote an elaborate and admiring study of Heraclitus.) The dialectical materialist plan, inspired by Hegel, generalized to all reality the patterns of conflict and compromise we observe in the class structure of human societies. It never worked for physics, or for formal logic, or for mathematics.

Nor did the Marxist governments want their scientists to revise disciplines that, orthodox or not, were of immediate military practicality. But plant genetics was remodeled on the pattern of human social classes, and the result was a failed harvest. When linguistics took this turn, the end product had no coherence.

But the main intellectual drive after Kant was toward a generalization of science as the universal arbiter of fact and model of method. A materialistic, analytic style of thought hardened into common sense as well as shaped academic disciplines (particularly in the social sciences, as well as in philosophy). The dialectical idealism of Hegel was a reversal of Kant's analytic ("critical") method, and Marx's dialectical materialism arose by reversing Hegel's explanatory direction. The main stream of thought, following natural science, kept Kant's emphasis on analysis but left no room for the formalism so crucial in his ethics and cosmology.

The opening of the twentieth century was marked by a dualism; a rather milder Platonic idealism in contest with a subtler Democritean analytic materialism. At about this point, the theory of evolution, first biological then cosmological, struck with much of the impact that the heliocentric new astronomy had at the start of the modern era. The ordering of nature in scales of increasing complexity and diversification, which had already been described in that way by Aristotle, was now, with Darwin, explained by natural selection. Man's assumed discontinuity with the rest of creation was challenged by the evidence that we, too, were a continuation of this selective process. Our very rationality, which ever since Aristotle has defined us as unique, could be viewed as an adaptive tool in the evolutionary process. And some philosophers turned to systems that were essentially oriented toward continuous processes, systems that looked to space and even more to time as their directional frames of explanation, and to processes of synthesis, accumulation, and interaction to match the continuity of evolution viewed on a large scale.

The twentieth century, just assimilating Darwin and then stunned by Einstein, opened with a new attention to kinds of process philosophy. This was a drastic change of method, which branched into pragmatism along one line of descent, Bergson's romanticism along another, and Whitehead's "philosophy of organism," as he termed it, a third. An aggressive protest was sharpened by the continuing and cresting wave of logical positivism, carrying the materialistic and analytic traditions forward with more polemical energy than consistency. The process movement was extended by existentialism, with its emphasis on one directional time, freedom, and individual subjectivity. British linguistic philosophy fell somewhere between. Its appeal to ordinary use of language (rather than "ordinary usage," it was always noted) was in effect a return to a hereditary common sense that was Aristotelian. (As we saw earlier, Aristotle's philosophical vocabulary swept into and constituted the technical languages of Europe; and it also spilled over into the "ordinary use" of those languages, as when we ask, "What's the matter?") And in fact Aristotle's philosophy has come back in vogue as a kind of continuation of this strand of British thought.

A paragraph is in order here on one drastic case of revolution to process thought. John Dewey's pragmatism, with its view of intelligence as a tool for modifying the environment and of human life as part of a continuous, evolving cultural process, beautifully corrected the atomistically-oriented "discipline" approach of American education. Here, the idea of learning by doing was peculiarly suited to everyday life in a way that the verbal and conceptual niceties of upper-class British and Continental notions were not. The ideas that school could be pleasant and that "activities" were sometimes better learning experiences than "disciplines" could not have been more welcome or come at a better time. The teachers colleges and departments of education reacted to the new idea with enthusiasm and a feeling of final insight. The release from a system in which, ever since Aristotle, "learning is a painful process" had been an axiom, the idea that something *useful* might displace dead languages even though it wasn't very scholarly, was a real liberation. Unfortunately, the new generation of educators had not applied Dewey (or Hegel or Marx) to their own case. They felt that they had reached the final end of philosophy's bedeviled history. They had the answers, and what academic philosophy departments were teaching and doing research in was escapist, outdated trash. (This is what was felt; it was usually said more tactfully.)

In the second half of our century, as logical positivism fades into more modest analytic styles, the existentialism of post-World War II, pragmatism, and process thought are becoming dominant against a stubborn establishment rearguard action in British and American philosophy. But it is a disorganized action, which has only an outdated common sense as its guide to platitudinous advice for medicine and law, and ponders a Byzantine maze of ethical "dilemmas," wittily phrased.

The history of philosophy in the twentieth century, however, has been marked from midcentury onward by incredible fragmentation as journals and publications have proliferated in response to professional demands for publication. I myself, because I taught introductory courses, felt some need to stay with developments. Between 1970 and 1980, I had articles published in the initial volume of each of a set of new journals that were founded. Then I was lost in the flood; it is only now in the century's last decades that I am again an author in number one of volume one of a new series of papers in philosophy. The one point that most impresses a Platonist at large is the lack of any Platonism. Programs in "ancient philosophy" require philosophic Greek but teach it by textbooks derived from Aristotle. Cosmologists talk admiringly about the importance of "aesthetic qualities" in choosing between hypotheses, but it does not occur to them that this preference implies a metaphysical justification. That value judgments are susceptible to rational discussion is not a popular idea, though plenty of our contemporaries are willing to discuss "what we mean by 'value judgments.'" Systems are out of fashion. Journal articles and notes replace them. However, a professional historian of ideas can, in fact, still detect the direction of the new currents of thought that have been most effective in reshaping common sense and practice in this century.The moral of my two-part history is that dominant systems seem to change either by revolutions in method or by revolutions in direction; we have not yet seen a major case in which both changed at the same time. There is a good reason for this. The radical change would come out with something unintelligible, because it is too different; something must conserve continuity. If systems have transformed in a pattern, as in fact they have, the relation governing that pattern has been alternate revolution in method and direction.Thus, if we take Platonism as a starting point, the following outline shows Western philosophy's subsequent history.

- Fifth C.A.D. Platonism (formal direction, dialectical method)
- Revolution in method
- Thirteenth C.A.D. Aristotelianism (formal direction, analytic method)
- Revolution in direction
- Seventeenth C.A.D. Modern science (material direction, analytic method)
- Revolution in method
- Twentieth C.A.D. Philosophies of process (material direction, dialectical method)
- Revolution in direction

- Twenty-first C.A.D.(?) Platonism (formal direction, dialectical method).

It is not clear whether intellectual history passes at a different rate depending on the dominant philosophical system more slowly as the principles of explanation are more abstract and removed from passing time or whether it is the case that the general rate of social, artistic, and intellectual change accelerates, and accelerates with increasing rate, through human progress.

The pattern, as it continues, should turn to Platonism again, stabilizing process by reversion to non-fluid actual form. Platonism has been lacking particularly in the field of ethics, where aesthetic criteria have been the strongest normative standards available. Process philosophy seems able only to give us ethical norms as possible, not actual; analysis, only as second-intentional, not first-intentional, and not imperative; and the fall back to Aristotle, an analytic conservative reversion now tried out in some quarters, gives us mediocrity as a criterion where excellence would serve better.

There is some reason to expect a resurgence of Platonism in contemporary philosophy. The mathematicians have already moved ahead; a majority today are back to good "realism" as regards the status of their forms. Younger metaphysicians are working with Platonic themes and categories; younger moralists are reviving the early Socratic dialogues as something other than mere diverting conversation or deliberate displays of Socratic sophistry.

Transcendental idealism, advocated by Immanuel Kant, is the view that there are limits on what can be understood, since there is much that cannot be brought under the conditions of objective judgment. Kant wrote his Critique of Pure Reason (1781-1787) in an attempt to reconcile the conflicting approaches of rationalism and empiricism, and to establish a new groundwork for studying metaphysics. Kant's intention with this work was to look at what we know and then consider what must be true about it, as a logical consequence of the way we know it. One major theme was that there are fundamental features of reality that escape our direct knowledge because of the natural limits of the human faculties. Although Kant held that objective knowledge of the world required the mind to impose a conceptual or categorical framework on the stream of pure sensory data a framework including space and time themselves he maintained that things-in-themselves existed independently of our perceptions and judgments; he was therefore not an idealist in any simple sense. Indeed, Kant's account of things-in-themselves is both controversial and highly complex. Continuing his work, Johann Gottlieb Fichte and Friedrich Schelling dispensed with belief in the independent existence of the world, and created a thoroughgoing idealist philosophy.

The Critique of Pure Reason by Immanuel Kant, first published in 1781, second edition 1787, is one of the most influential works in the history of philosophy. Also referred to as Kant's "first critique," it was followed by the Critique of Practical Reason and the Critique of Judgement. In the last section of the introduction Kant states that "... If this Critique itself does not assume the title of transcendental philosophy, it is only because, to be a complete system, it ought to contain a full analysis of all human knowledge a priori.

Before the time of Kant, it was generally held that whatever knowledge was a priori must be of the nature of an analytic judgment, that is, what is stated in the predicate must already be present in the subject and it is therefore, independent of experience (e.g., "An intelligent man is intelligent" or "An intelligent man is a man"). In either case, the judgement is analytic because it is arrived at by analyzing the subject. Before the time of Kant, it was thought that all judgements of which we could be certain a priori were of this kind: that in all of them there was a predicate which was only part of the subject of which it was asserted. If this were so, we would be involved in a contradiction every time we would try to deny anything that could be known a priori (e.g., "An intelligent man is not intelligent" or "An intelligent man is not a man"). Thus according to the philosophers before Kant, the Law of contradiction is sufficient to establish all a priori knowledge.

5

Philosophy Systems and its Working

Introduction

The *Symposium* is in a mood and a dramatic form that Plato never repeated. E. Von Sybel suggested, in the nineteenth century, that this was the author's vision of the working of his projected Academy, and in principle the suggestion is certainly a happy one, and right.

Evidently, because it was pre-Aristotelian, the Academy could not have been modeled on Aristotle's original idea of a university. That was to be departmentalized, with professional specialists as a staff and independent lecture courses as its curriculum. Instead, with Plato, we find a selection of mature gentlemen, all with professional interests and competences, but none narrowly limited by them. They are bound together, for this banquet, by a spirit of friendship amplified by a season and a day for celebration and for warming wine. Agathon is at the peak of his career; Athens on the brink of a disaster still shines at the height of her glory; Plato and his readers appreciate this moment from a romantic past. The conversation is no doubt what

Von Sybel thinks it, a model of the sort of thing that Plato wanted to incorporate in his new building and lands next to the park of Hekademos. The conversation is memorable, as we are shown in its passing from Aristodemus to Apollodorus to Glaucon and Apollodorus' companion, then on to Plato's readers.

To understand love would be to master the key Platonic problem of the relation of being and becoming. When Whitehead contrasts the temporal currents of feeling with their "causal efficacy" to the vision of repeatable form, with its "presentational immediacy," there is a later echo of this same central theme.

The participants in Plato's symposium are chosen to represent the range of special intellectual interests and inspirations which that dramatic time in Athens could provide. Phaedrus is a humanist, a lover of poetry. He is not a philologist like Prodicus, who analyzed linguistically, nor a Protagoras, obsessed by the rhetorical consistency of a text, but a true "lover" of literature. Pausanias is a combination of anthropologist and lawyer. He is like Herodotus in his curiosity about alien cultures; he is like the Sophists in his concern with convention and law; but unlike the Sophists in Plato's other portraits of them, he is capable of loving someone besides himself and of sharing in, not running away with, the dinner conversation. Eryximachus plays a double role. He is a humane doctor of medicine, most noble of the arts, but also a spokesman for natural science and cosmology. His medicine rests on the cosmological philosophy of Empedocles, with its generalization of love and hate to elemental cosmic forces. Aristophanes' fit of hiccups calls special attention to Eryximachus' location in the program of speeches. The physical interruption cured with help of his professional advice causes his move to a position *before* Aristophanes, who sums up the "level of becoming," which is therefore where the "art" of the physician belongs; but, with more insight, Eryximachus might have been the spokesman for the "science of love" on the level of being, a science outlined by Diotima later, instead.

Poets, in this Platonic context, prove collaborators, not

opponents, in creating "philosophy." In fact, the dialogue will end in a closing vignette where Socrates mediates between the drowsy Agathon and drunken Aristophanes. It appears, then, that poets were imagined as included in the fellowship of Plato's educational experiment. In fact, they could come to be philosophers, if only they could combine their insights and imagery.

The interlude between Socrates and Agathon shows us in miniature another side of the proposed Academy. It will, apparently, include Socratic "examination," yet not as a final aim or sole curriculum.

The mysterious Diotima brings Apollo on the scene. His inspiration, transmitted through her to Socrates, makes the "science of love" emerge as a formalist dialectical achievement, mounting from individual bodies to the ideal of beauty. But just at this point, the god of wine enters again with Alcibiades, and Dionysus' spirit dominates until dawn.

A noteworthy thing about this imagined conversation piece is that it is not reductive. The formalist, Apollonian "ladder of love" is balanced by the existentialist, Dionysian moments and speakers, with lawyer, doctor, and Socrates (a mediating *daimon*) in between.

Love is to be understood as a conjunction of a principle of plenitude and one of limitation. Without the bodily incarnation Eryximachus dissects and psychoanalyzes, Eros could never dominate becoming. The existential sense of *time running out*, which Diotima states so well and which echoes in Phaedrus' romantic poetry, may be forgotten for a moment in the vision of a beauty "that has no face, or hands, or body"; yet it is remembered quickly enough. Socrates emerges from the adjoining portico to join the banquet.

The conventions Pausanias has collected share a respect for law and a desire for order. That respect and desire are projected inexactly in the practical domain; the vision that inspires them is hardly recognized or remembered. But without the order of a "good" love, the vision of beauty would not become relevant to societies at all. Anthropology is not made useless when one has a vision of a timeless ideal society; societies must be described and compared and law and custom judged by the proximate effectiveness that they have in moving toward an ideal's realization. (The Academy, as it turned out, took law and constitution writing as a much larger part of its work than is foreshadowed here in Plato's program, just as it did the "sciences" that Eryximachus admired but had not mastered. The sciences, of course, come into the foreground much more in the *Phaedo: Custom and laws must wait for the Republic.*)

What would a symposium be like today, designed as a project for a new university? One thing is clear. Where both our arts and sciences operate objectively and abstractly, carefully keeping at a distance from us, the new approach to philosophy requires *presence*. This it must keep, even in the discussion's most critical moments and skeptical manifestations; but this does not mean that analysis is excluded from the project. Quite the contrary; its aim at clarity is just as relevant as the dialectician's goal of comprehension. But, examples as well as counter examples are needed for its proper functioning in making ideas clear.

A general prescription for future philosophy begins with establishing proper presence and feeling. The feeling must be one of shared direction, and the presence friendly. At first, any advance we make will be focused on specific areas, problems and techniques. But the sharpness of focus is not to be sharply restrained (as it would be in a traditional Aristotelian or atomist frame) to an immediate perimeter insulating us from a continuously widening context. "Philosophy is not a science," wrote Whitehead; the philosophic need for wide context is one reason why that is (for the present state of science and professions) a true observation. When ideas now jump across gaps into other arts and sciences, they emerge as new "paradigms." Some of these are revolutionary, more are obviously strained, still others downright misleading. But the tracks of such ideas in their paradigm crossings are evidences of a philosophic approach at work.

We can say, in outline, that four basic approaches must be represented if our new symposium is to be most effective. The four approaches, even though their views transform, are complementary, not quite the same. And some aspects first appear in their clearest form in one frame, transposing only with some effort to the others.

Suppose, now, that I want to advance the philosophy of education by including insights from Whitehead's post-1922 writings in our currently accepted discussions. It will not be enough to put the titles of five works on some assigned reading list or reserve shelf; when they are to be applied, ideas need an advocate who himself exhibits the application. In the present case, let this begin with a small technical opening. Whitehead criticizes the notion that things are sharply separated from each other by being differently "located" in "insulating" times and spaces. But in fact, he claims, they overlap and interpenetrate. Now our classrooms, textbooks, classroom walls, and exercises have for generations featured political maps on which national boundaries have darker lines than longitude and latitude coordinates. What more effective reinforcement could there be of the "fallacy of simple location" as applied to world society? Metaphors of "sovereign states," "self-determination," "*vital* interest," "cultural purity" are seen as factual, not metaphorical. So for a long time the map *colorings* indicating colonial possession gave a direct presentational immediacy to the notions of colonialism, colonies' dependence, and colonizers' superiority. What lines would it be more causally efficacious, concretely relevant, interesting, or idealistic to darken instead?

The Platonist in our group opens the discussion with a mapping of coordinates locating points in space, which is such an obvious thing to do that no one pays much attention to it. But historically, the substitution of coordinates in a spatial plane for visions conjectured from tales of voyages and cannibals was a major advance in Miletus, sixth century B.C. The atomist at the outset proves a flexible partner. If we can tell him what we want emphasized, he can show it on the map textures, isobars, political boundaries. But there must be facts available to serve as guidelines in this artistry. The Aristotelian is ready with a whole practical inventory of species of mapping. He is a practical thinker, and each factor relevant to prudence can have a map of its own. The set can show political boundaries (not necessarily in the darkest lines), population densities, altitudes, even communication distances, airplane routes, languages; and from the set we can choose a few that will serve as "the best maps in general."

The Platonist thinks that it would be a good idea to have "synoptic" maps. "We could show the relation of things such as climate and population density, for example, by superimposition, with a more complicated color code. I like to see things together when I can." The process philosopher says that he had been thinking along another line. It seemed to him important to map time as well as space, and the Aristotelian serial sets could show historical sequences. Explorations, migration, colonialism, could be visualized historically. And, most important, the sequence could extend to a projected future, with a key to indicate what assumptions about air pollution, population control, the ozone layer are used for the projection. There will be a continuity, he argues, but not a determinate causality, between a present and a projected map. Maps of the future constitute an idea that pleases the atomist; he admits he would not have thought of it himself, and when he thinks about some of the scenarios, it is frightening, but he sees no technical problems in the idea because they can use computers for extrapolation. The atomist wonders about including insets on a different scale for various purposes; the process philosopher is thinking about subjects cuisine, mountains to climb, cultural borders that would catch some special sense of adventure.

The Platonist, who contributed the idea of mapping as synoptic vision, has all along had quite another function in mind for the maps. "I want my students to learn moral lessons," says the Platonist, rather to the surprise of the other three. "I want my maps to show how ideals of nobility and human betterment have changed the facts of the inhabited world: I would like maps showing such histories as the decline of slavery, the advance of women's rights, the futility of warfare. I only wish we could measure some of these things better; the atomist would be happier. Yet on the whole, he can find approximate measures."

"You have forgotten something, though," says the process

philosopher: "your maps all show progress, but history doesn't run in any such neat uphill direction. Fanaticism, massacre, destructions of civilization are real, too, you know; and it is at our own risk that we overlook them. And the uncertainty adds a sense of adventure to our own existence, even if it is mixed with danger."

The atomist sums up their conversation: "I've certainly not learned anything new about my trade as mapmaker; but somehow, I've changed my feeling about the possibilities latent in maps. That extrapolation of population, climate, and resources into the future really frightens me to think of though as a technical project it's just the same as all the rest."

Well, at least we have new ideas here to guide a new "school map" Academy. Has this conversation been cartography, or philosophy, or professionalized visual education? (If it *is* applied philosophy, look at the terrain waiting for us to extend the application!) Does it change each participant's understanding of what "maps" really are, and of the relation of cartographic to other spaces (remember the fallacy of simple location)? Of the way things about our own size, or on a cosmic scale for that matter, are related in their separations and connections?

Plato has other discussions of method later in his writing that spell out what is shown but not explicitly said in the *Symposium*. They range from a demonstration of pure hypothetical-deductive technique in the dazzling abstractions of the *Parmenides* through the minefield of "meanings" that confront the user of language in the *Sophist* to the late autobiographical account of the vision of Platonic forms by insight in the *Seventh Letter*. Except, perhaps, for the two poets who share their Muse with Socrates and with the dialogues' offstage author each perspective in the *Symposium* will find a longer onstage role in Plato's writings. The guess, in the *Republic*, that higher education can teach a science of values in five years to properly prepared students, and that experience can show them how to apply that abstract knowledge in fifteen years more, must be revised as time shows the Academy that the program takes longer; thirty years later, the abstract half had been only locally and sporadically successful if at all and Plato's final application to the concrete took the twelve books of the *Laws* to approximate, yet remained radically incomplete.

When the theme is being or becoming, or love relating them, rather than space-time location, we have purer philosophy. This is the theme of a dialogue between incarnate ideals, indivisible elements, materially instantialized principles, and evolving processes. Its aim is a shared feeling accompanied by shared formal insight. The method should be the transformation that comes from the mutual interaction of real participants that Plato illustrated in his imaginary *Symposium*. There are more specific conditions we need to make this enterprise possible. I have not developed descriptions of *feeling* very far; those rather need to be presented. For *thought*, I believe that I *have* shown that there is no impossibility in cross-system conversation, nor trans system shared insight.

In different historical treatments, the theme of being has been treated as a central focus of different lines of causality, as in Aristotle; as the "ontological principle," the insistence that explanation include reference to concrete "actualities," in Whitehead; as a synoptic form stretching over motion and life in its full extension, in Plato; as families of increasing complexity built from first particles, in atomism. One can create the same dialogue form starting with any of these standpoints, then bringing in the others in such a way that there is genuine emerging alteration as each adapts to include some overlooked specification or unmentioned background generalization contributed by the others. The thing itself, whatever particular being we are talking about, needs longer dialogues in the new form, dialogues that I hope will be written in the philosophy of the next century.

Our human drive towards generalization first finds a stopping point in four very large-scale philosophic system families. But the same natural drive toward greater generalization from which those families arise makes us hope to see only contrast between them, not ultimate exclusion, and to seek some newer synthesis. That synthesis itself must have a new "mixed constitution": For it cannot exclude concreteness in favor of clear yet forceless abstraction, nor do without lines that mark discontinuities of formal and material variation.

It must still show my Platonic preferences that I should take cartography as my example of a subject to look at "synoptically." Yet "maps" admit more variation than our first mental image of a visual plane suggests. Maps, as early as the fourth century B.C., showed contrast in elevation by three-dimensional design, contrasts in terrain by texture; insets can change spatial scale, and design modifications can add temporal sequence to our structure. A Platonist does not confront a map that is a blur of continuities; he specifies good Aristotelian-seeming isobars dividing reality: in fact, two main sets, temporal and structural. Only, these mark off changed degrees against a common backdrop, not map-ending borders that will transmit nothing. The Platonist, like the process thinker, also sees texture and adventure in the becoming charts: the site of Troy, the unexplored Smol River in New Guinea, the isolated evolutionary islet of Tasmania. The atomist is our technologist: Becoming can be compacted into packets by his analysis and wonderful precision of detail reached in his projections. But he is a pointillist; and so even he, as the artist, must sometimes step back and take a different relation to the work from his close up, item-by-item points he inserts as a technician. This is in fact built into his theory, as the converse of his axiom that quality is reducible to quantity: Quantitative elementary points are expandable into qualitative perspectives and adventures. Each of the four participants, whether in mapmaking or in philosophizing, adds some new insight to the others; but only when they are seen and felt in their correct relation. We want our synthesis to yield aesthetic contrast, not the fission of dogmas in collision, not the neutralizing monotony of one orthodox universal solvent homogenizing all the rest. And aesthetic contrast is exactly the relation I have shown to be possible by my scheme of structural transformation, and, in small sample, actual by my brief model of shared topical discussion.

I go back again to Plato's *Symposium*. Socrates leaves his Platonic meditations in the adjoining portico to join the drinking. Agathon removes the last barriers to friendship, the social class distinctions, for the evening: For this night, the diners will be guests of his servants, not their masters. The talk can now be what Plato says philosophic conversation must be in his *Seventh Letter*: "ith friendly questions and answers, devoid of envy."

And at dawn, the patronage of Dionysus comes to an end. Apollo now displaces him, and Plato's Socrates moves on from this daydream of a new Academy. Many years later Plato is to write that though his dream has briefly become real, in his Academy, he can give no rules for its export to another city even if that were a new colony of his own design nor can the insight ever be put into writing. But this doubt of his that philosophy can be written shows that he underrated the power of his own earlier literary creativity; and his doubt of exportability shows that he also underestimated the vitality of the creative impact of his transmitted writing.

6

Jewish Philosophy in Medieval Period

Introduction

In Jewish schools the Torah was studied in Hebrew and, for the believer, the world was built around the revealed text. From the creation, God has guided the course of universal history. The sun and the planets are subject to his will. The God of the Bible is a moral agent who wills and decrees. To man, whom he has created 'in our image and likeness', he gives commandments and issues prohibitions. Humans can grumble to God, plead with him, make him change his mind. Moses speaks to God man to man: there is a dialogue between them. God is free to reply or not, but he is visibly and audibly in the presence of the prophets, appearing as a majestic king or sending his angels.

God has made a pact with the Jewish race. They are the chosen people, especially close to God. Other peoples are God's instruments, whom he uses to punish the people of Israel and bring them back to the right course. God has given his people, through Moses, his Law, the Torah. Even for the later prophets, who considered that God was king over all humanity, it was the Bible which enshrined divine will.

This text, revealed just once in human history contained all God's commands and all his prohibitions. For Jews the Torah, regarded as eternal and complete truth, given once and for all, was the criterion for all other truths. To turn against it would be to turn against God himself.

Philosophy came from outside. It was enshrined in Greek texts, translated into Arabic and, from the twelfth century onwards, into Hebrew. It appears that, at the very start, the Jews made use of doxographies; but the texts of Plato and Aristotle, along with Arabic commentaries, very soon became available to them. Arabic was the language which the Jews in Islamic lands spoke and wrote (sometimes, using Hebrew characters). For the whole of the first period of Jewish philosophy, philosophical texts were written in Arabic. Philosophy also included science and was a requisite for many physicians, astronomers and astrologers. It was not taught in the Jewish schools but by private tutors, and so it was available only to the better off. Yet the majority of philosophers who had a significant influence on Jewish thought in general were also rabbis, talmudic scholars and leaders of their communities. Although they were sometimes attacked for their opinions, the philosophers remained none the less within the Jewish community. This was possible, perhaps, because there are no articles of faith in Judaism. Orthodoxy is based, rather, on the Bible, which is far from monolithic and contains various passages that can be interpreted in more than one way. It is well known that, with regard to the Law, from early times oral teaching gave room for variety, nuance and innovation on the basis of the written text. The teaching was then recorded in writing and itself expounded and glossed until it formed an enormous (and even today still-expanding) body of material. Its importance shows how new problems were resolved without going against the old texts. And this use of allegory and symbolism as tools for interpretation allowed different systems of thought philosophical, kabbalistic or ascetic to remain within Judaism.

Jewish Philosophy in Islamic Lands

Jews in Islamic lands divided into the same philosophical schools as the Muslims: the *kalâm,* Neoplatonism and Aristotelianism. Similarly, the questions which Jewish philosophers set themselves were, to a large extent, the same as those discussed by their Muslim counterparts.

The kalâm

The *kalâm* or, to be precise, the Mu'tazilite school, provided the context for rabbinic thought for a number of generations, and it lasted even longer among the Karaite Jews. Dâwûd ibn Marwân al-Muqammi (ninth century) is the first rationalist Jewish thinker whose work survives. His *'Ishrûn Maqâla (Twenty Chapters)* expounds ideas inspired by the *kalâm* but strongly influenced by Christianity, to which for part of his life he was a convert. His treatise is modelled on treatises of the *kalâm,* except for his vigorous defence of Judaism and his arguments against other religions.

By contrast, other Jewish thinkers adopted only some ideas from the *kalâm,* in particular, the definition of reason as a universal moral law transcending race and religion, which man finds within himself, and which applies to God, assuring us that there exists a good God in whom we can trust. Among the Karaites, Abû Yûsuf Ya'qûb al-Kirkisânî (Jacob al-Kirkisani) gave the fullest theoretical discussion of this doctrine, whilst Japheth ben Ali made a translation of the Bible into Arabic, accompanied by a commentary where these ideas emerge in the reading of the text. Both thinkers lived in the tenth century. Their great contemporary among rabbinic Jews was Saadiah ben Joseph Gaon (882–942), who was born in Egypt and moved to Babylon; there, in 928, he became *Gaon,* the head of the Talmudic academies. He was extremely prolific in every field; as a grammarian and lexicographer, a translator of the Bible into Arabic and commentator on it, as a liturgical poet and compiler of a prayer book, as a Talmudist and a jurist, as a writer on the calendar and chronology. Saadiah philosophized and engaged in polemic to prove the absolute truth of rabbinical Judaism against the claims of the Karaites and dangers posed by other religions, and by the various schools of philosophy and by scepticism in its different forms.

Arguments based on reason are found in most of Saadiah's works, but it is in two of them that they receive a systematic exposition. They are the *Commentary on the Book of Creation (Tafsîr Kitâb al-Mabâdî, Peroush Sefer Yetzira),* which was translated into Hebrew several times and used especially in the eleventh and twelfth centuries; and the *Book of Doctrines and Beliefs,* which still remains today one of the fundamental works of Jewish theology.

In the introduction to his *Amanat,* Saadiah proposes a theory of knowledge. Conviction arises from three sources: external reality, reason (that is to say, knowledge of good and evil) and what reason deduces necessarily from the reality of things and from the knowledge of good and evil. To these three Saadiah adds 'the truthful tradition', that of the Torah (including the oral Torah, the Talmud). The truthfulness of this tradition has been proved, Saadiah says, by signs, prodigies and, in particular, by the miraculous feeding of the Children of Israel with manna during their flight from Egypt. Whereas miracles and prodigies might be illusory or simulated, the miracle of the manna could not have been simulated, since it lasted for forty years and was so public an event that any idea of a carefully contrived lie is implausible. Nor could it have been a natural phenomenon which Moses was able to produce, since the philosophers would also have known about it and made use of the technique themselves. The 'truthful tradition', the fourth source of knowledge, is therefore based on the historical experience of the Jewish people. And Saadiah's argument gains added strength since none of the other religions questions the historical reality of the exodus from Egypt and the Jews' wanderings in the desert.

The Torah itself asks us to seek to understand the teachings it transmits. It does so for two reasons: first, so that the knowledge transmitted by tradition becomes firmly fixed in the intellect; and, second, so that we can reply to those who call the Law into question. Now, the knowledge which rational, scientific investigation uncovers turns out in fact to conform to traditional knowledge. Saadiah was thus able to represent the Torah and scientific knowledge as two twigs from the same branch. They can in no way contradict one another. Any apparent contradictions are the result either of mistakes in our reasoning, or of our failure to interpret Scripture correctly.

The structure of the *Amanat* reflects this identity between tradition and reason. Each chapter begins with an introduction to the problem. Then follows an examination of biblical texts which confirm the thesis and, finally, there is a rational analysis of the problem and a refutation of opposing theses.

Saadiah begins by setting out the way in which this enquiry should be pursued. Here the senses cannot be of any help. Only rational arguments can be used. Whatever the hypothesis the eternity of the world, the eternity of matter, and so on an attempt must be made to establish it by reason.

Saadiah's deep intuition is that the world is limited and changing. Only the infinite action of God can sustain and explain this constant change, the perceptual generation of a world both spatially and temporally finite. The world and man, limited and imperfect, bear witness to a perfect and infinite being and lead us to a rational knowledge of the one God, creator of the world. In the introduction to the chapter on the unity of God, Saadiah lists all the objections which were made in his time to this rational way of thought and refutes them all.

Our Lord (be He exalted and glorified) has informed us through the words of His prophets that He is One, Living, Powerful and Wise, and that nothing can be compared unto Him or unto His works. They established this by signs and miracles, and we accepted it immediately. Later, speculation led us to the same result. In regard to His Unity, it is said, 'Hear O Israel, the Lord our God, the Lord is One'.

God, the creator of the world, is therefore one; but who is

he? And, when we say of him that he is one, about what unity are we speaking? What is the knowledge he possesses, on account of which we say he is knowing, and what are the actions which are attributed to him, on account of which we say that he acts? The rabbinical Jews replied to these questions with verses from the Bible which often use in connection with God not only such adjectives as 'powerful', 'good and merciful', 'jealous', but also attribute to him bodily movements 'God rises', 'God comes down' and even parts of the body 'God's arm', 'God's hand'. But Saadiah strongly opposes any notion of divine corporeality. One of the central aims in his thought is to purify the idea of God and demonstrate that God is incorporeal and transcendent. Everything in our world can be defined according to the Aristotelian categories. Even the soul and 'divine Glory' are definable substances and so more or less corporeal, because for Saadiah body and substance are one and the same thing. God, however, cannot be defined by any of the Aristotelian categories. He transcends them all; and there is nothing in common between finite, composite bodies, which are subject to change, and God, who is immaterial and always remains exactly what he is. Whilst his attributes, power and knowledge, signify that God is not lacking in power or knowledge, power and knowledge such as they are found in man cannot be applied to God because, in God, attributes are identical to essence. Men gain knowledge by learning over a period of time; it comes to be where it was not previously, and in old age it decreases, at death it disappears. But God has knowledge for all eternity. When we talk about God using positive attributes, in reality we are talking about 'something other', about which we can only form a vague notion and of which we know only that it does not resemble what exists here below. God's attributes are identical to his essence (or quiddity), and none is outside his essence. God is absolute unity. Since we can arrive by reasoning at a refined and exact knowledge of God, why was it necessary to send the prophets? According to Saadiah, God, in his supreme knowledge, has acted 'for the good'. He does nothing in vain. The 'justice of

God', as conceived in the second of the Mu'tazilites' theses, shows why the very nature of God makes prophecy legitimate. Saadiah then goes on to explain why revelation was necessary for mankind. First, it sets out the actions which allow the very general moral laws, dictated by reason, best to be put into practice. Second, it includes other commandments, which are of value and which reason does not teach. Third, it allows people to act immediately, whereas reason, although based on the same principles, takes time to arrive at its conclusions. Moreover, some men never reach the level of rational knowledge, because of their imperfection or their disinclination to study, or because of the doubts which trouble them. The Bible, however, is often written in anthropomorphic terms, which contradict what reason teaches us; that God is one and incorporeal. Yet tradition is drawn from the same source as rational knowledge and so it cannot be contrary to reason. A rational explanation must therefore be given for the whole of scriptural revelation, and especially for the visions of the prophets. Three principles guide this explanation:

1. All the manifestations of the supernatural are the work of God and God alone. Prophecy is a grace, a gift which God has put into a human receptacle, who is then called a prophet. The prophet is mortal like other men. He cannot do without food or drink. He leads a normal married life. He cannot predict the future. Nor can he perform miracles, except under exceptional conditions otherwise it would be necessary to suppose that he had superhuman capacities. The prophet is merely an instrument of God's will, the receiver of supernatural visions.

2. God, who is unknowable and incorporeal, makes manifest his created Glory, the first of his creations, an air which is finer and more subtle than the visible air: the 'Second Air'. This Second Air is audible and visible, filled with light and colour, striking in its splendour. It is through the Second Air that the created word was produced which Moses heard, and the Ten Commandments heard in the visible air by the whole people of Israel on Mount Sinai.

It is the Second Air which the prophets saw and called

the Throne of Glory and Cherubim, Angels, Seraphim

3. God makes his glory visible in the manner of a teacher going from the easier to the more difficult. He created man in such a way that he was free to obey or disobey his commandments. His wish was that man should merit the highest reward, the world to come, and it is to this end that he made his orders and prohibitions. Among them are some which reason would have shown us were necessary, and others which revelation alone teaches us (though none of them is contrary to reason). These purely religious laws allow the faithful to prove their obedience and merit the reward which God wishes to give them: immortality and resurrection at the time of the Messiah.

Saadiah Gaon's thought remains very close to tradition, both in his conception of God and his exegesis of texts. His charm and optimism cannot fail to allure the modern reader. His simplicity ensures that he will remain for ever young.

Jewish Neoplatonists

Isaac Israeli was a slightly older contemporary of Saadiah's. He was a famous doctor, and he has the credit of having introduced into medieval Jewish thought texts and ideas taken directly from the Greeks. Like al-Kindî, he also used Greek texts which have not survived to modern times. His type of Neoplatonism is based on emanation. Between the perfection of God and the imperfection of the world below there are interposed more or less perfect essences which link the incorporeal deity to the world of matter. According to Isaac Israeli first matter and first form come from God. Intellect is engendered from these. From Intellect emanates the world of souls (that is, of the rational soul, the animal soul and the vegetative soul). There follows the world of the spheres, then the sublunary world with its four elements and what is made from them. Our earth is a mixture of the four elements: earth, water, air and fire. It is at the centre of the universe and without motion. The spheres, which are made of a more perfect matter, the quintessence, revolve around the earth and create by their movements the composite beings which are bodies.

Other Neoplatonists held that first form and matter emanated from God in a manner which was involuntary and outside time. But Isaac Israeli lays great stress on the creation. God creates first matter and first form. He makes them come to be from nothing, something which God alone can do. Isaac is, however, in agreement with other Neoplatonists in believing that first matter is intelligible, that is to say, absolutely incorporeal. First form contains all other forms which come into existence, but in a perfect way. Intellect, which is light and splendour, comes from the conjunction of first form and first matter. From Intellect emanates the rational soul, which is the human soul. The Intellect holds a high rank in the scale of being, since its source is a pure light, more elevated and brilliant than any body, even one as perfect as the sphere of the heavens. The so-called 'metaphysics of light' play an important role in this description of the higher world, and it is because the soul is part of this world that it is able to climb back up again towards its former habitation. The start of this return is knowledge of the higher world and certainty of the truth.

God, by his will and his power, has created and made manifest first matter and first form from nothingness. But it is by emanation a necessary action that Intellect, which is the source of souls and the universe, comes from these two created beings. Intellect and souls act in a different way from that found in the celestial sphere and the sublunary world. It can be said to create, in that nothing is lost of the essential light and lower beings are created from the shadow of this light. But in the world of the spheres and below, natural action is by generation and corruption, since the source of action is changed and diminished by the action itself which it carries out on bodies with qualities opposed to it. Below the celestial sphere all beings come into being from the four simple elements: fire, air, water and earth. Whereas in other bodies one or another of these elements predominates, in man they are in harmonious equilibrium. Every creature made of the elements is given a soul according to its capacity and each finds pleasure in bringing itself closer to the principal element in it.

The three degrees of the soul intellectual, animal and vegetative are not absolutely separate. For instance, certain animals have almost as much intelligence and prudence as man. All this is due to the inclination of one soul towards another. Sometimes, the rational soul tends towards the animal soul and its actions tend towards those of the animal soul which desires eating, drinking and pleasure. In the same way, the animal soul has a tendency to assimilate its actions to those of the rational soul when it is instructed and influenced by it. The rational soul tends to draw itself near to the Intellect and reach perfection, in which case it will be clear and pure, and it will seek good and true things such as knowledge and understanding, purity and saintliness, service of God and nearness to him. This all comes about from the influence of the higher substance.

Since man of his own accord raises himself towards the Intellect, and so towards God, what part does revelation play? Isaac Israeli divides mankind into types according to which of each of the three souls is dominant: the rational soul, the animal soul or the vegetative soul. Only a small proportion of the human race is, therefore, truly close to the light of the Intellect. These are the privileged individuals whom God will use as intermediaries in order to bring the divine word to humankind.

One of Isaac Israeli's pupils, Dunash ben Tamin, brings out his train of thought when he discusses Moses. Moses differs from the other prophets because he heard the word of God in the way described in Exodus 32:11: 'the eternal one spoke to Moses face to face.' Moses' soul was superior to that of other men: it was subtle, light and, even before it was separated from Moses' body, it was united with the world of the rational soul. For when souls are separated from their bodies, they remain alive and are united with the world above: the soul becomes intellect and, in an incorporeal, spiritual union, the intellect is united with light.

Prophetic visions are no longer conceived as real, external phenomena which are seen and heard, but as internal visions which reflect spiritual rather than sensory reality. So far from being inferior to sensory reality, spiritual reality is as much superior to it, as the soul is superior to the body.

One whose rational soul has withdrawn itself [i.e. from the lower souls] and upon whom intellect causes its light and splendour to emanate becomes spiritual, god-like, and longing exceedingly for the ways of the angels, as far as lies within human power. The Creator, exalted and blessed be He, therefore chose from among His creatures one qualified in this manner to be His messenger, caused him to prophesy, and showed through him His truthful signs and miracles. He made him the messenger and intermediary between Himself and His creatures, and caused His true Book to descend through him.

The Bible is not, however, a work of philosophy. It includes narratives which have a sense which is far from intellectual. The reason for this, Israeli explains, is that God speaks the language of men so that all will understand him. He bases his language on the capacities of his audience. Those among them able to discern the pure sense will find it; because they are distant from material things and their minds are detached and luminous, they will see God's words and his light. Those who are still incapable of seeing the light will ask the sages to expound the Bible to them and, little by little, thanks to their expositions, they will understand and will come nearer to the source of purity until they are so close to the Intellect that it will print its form in their soul. God himself provides the example which the Intellect follows. God puts himself within reach of human understanding: the Intellect imitates this divine way of teaching when it wishes men to know future events, and the philosophers in their turn take the same course when they explain *viva voce* what their pupils cannot understand in their written work. The superior beings are like a ray of light which penetrates through the entire breadth of a solid body. The Intellect, the prophets and the philosophers all follow God's own footsteps as they incline themselves towards lower beings and help each of them, so far as he is able, to climb the ladder of light.

It was not only philosophers who developed such themes: the quest for purity, freedom from bodily desires, and the desire for union with the Intellect. They were also taken up by scholars, rabbis, poets and courtiers during the tenth to twelfth centuries: for instance, Hai Gaon, president of the Talmudic academy; Bayâ ibn Paqudah, a judge on the rabbinical tribunal and author of the famous devotional work, *Guide to the Duties of the Heart;* the famous poet, Moses ibn Ezra; Abraham ibn Ezra, also a famous poet and biblical commentator; Joseph ben Jacob ibn addik (died 1149 at Cordoba), a judge on the rabbinical tribunal and a philosopher; Abraham bar iyyah (died after 1136 at Barcelona), an astronomer and mathematician who held an important post at the court of Alphonsus I of Aragon and of the counts of Barcelona; and Solomon ibn Gabirol and Judah Halevi.

Solomon ben Judah ibn Gabirol is well-known for his Hebrew poetry, both sacred and secular. His philosophy is expounded in a treatise which has not survived in its Arabic original but in the Latin translation, *Fons Vitae* made by John of Spain and Dominicus Gundissalinus in the mid-twelfth century. The *Fons Vitae* was widely read by thirteenth century Christian theologians, who knew its author as 'Avicebron' or 'Avencebrol' and took him to be an Arab or even a Christian thinker. In addition, there survive some extracts from the work, translated into Hebrew, made in the thirteenth century by Shem Tov ibn Falaqera. These do not preserve the dialogue form found in the *Fons Vitae*. Gabirol's treatise was known to Neoplatonic Jewish philsophers and was fiercely criticized by the first Jewish Aristotelian, Abraham ibn Daud. Then it was almost entirely forgotten until 1846, when Solomon Munk showed that the extracts made by Falaqera were from the work translated into Latin as the *Fons Vitae,* and so that 'Avicebron' was none other than the famous Hebrew poet, Solomon ibn Gabirol.

Gabirol's system is Neoplatonic. Through knowing his own soul, man can know nature, free himself from it and return to the spiritual world, his place of origin. Knowledge is knowledge of being. There are only three sorts of being: (1) primary substance, (2) primary matter and form, (3) God and the Will, which is an intermediary between God and matter-with-form. Man is able to grasp these types of being because he finds within himself equivalents of them: his understanding corresponds to primary substance, his soul to the Will and his matter and form to primary matter and form. Man can know God's actions but not his essence apart from his acts, since it is infinite and above all things. In the order of emanation, primary matter and form are the nearest to the divine Will. From them together is engendered Intellect, then Soul, and from Soul Nature, which is the last of the simple substances. It is from Nature that bodily substance derives.

The path which will take the soul back to Intellect goes by the knowledge of composite beings: spiritual beings which are called 'simple' although they are in fact composite. Indeed, 'simple' and 'composite' are relative terms: a being is simple with regard to that which is lower than it, and composite with regard to that which is above it. The entirety of things can thus be regarded as if it were arranged in a line, beginning with universal matter and form. The further it is from its source, the more composite a being is with regard to that which goes before it, although it remains simple in relation to that which follows it.

Matter, form and the Will are the true subject-matter of the *Fons Vitae*. Gabirol describes at length the various types of matter and form, universal and particular, which make up the universe. Beings are individuated in the first place by forms, material or spiritual, whereas matter is one and universal. But to the unity of form there corresponds a unity of matter and, in another passage, Gabirol makes it clear that the diversity of beings is not brought about because of form, since form is one and entirely spiritual, but by matter which can be perfect and subtle or thick and heavy.

The Will is the ultimate goal of man's quest. This Will is identical to the Wisdom of God and his *logos*. Conceived apart from its acts, the Will is indeed identical to the divine essence, but it is distinguished from it when its acts are considered.

In the former case, it is infinite, but finite in the second. It is an intermediary between the divine essence and form and matter. It penetrates all things and is their efficient cause; itself without motion, it is the cause of spiritual and bodily movement.

In Gabirol's philosophy, as in other Jewish Neoplatonic (and later Aristotelian) philosophies, God can be approached only through rational knowledge. Prophets and philosophers imitate God by their intellect, in thought, and prophetic visions are no longer considered to be dialogues with God or his angels but rather internal illuminations. Bodily acts have no value in themselves: they prepare the soul to separate from the body, since only then will it be able to fulfil its destiny.

It is this very approach to philosophy which Judah Halevi wishes to supersede in his *Kuzari*. Written in Arabic, the *Book of Refutation and Proof, in Defence of the Despised Faith* is a dialogue between the king of the Khazars and the defenders of philosophy, of Islam, Christianity and Judaism. From the beginning, Judah Halevi insists that good intentions are not sufficient to please God, who also cares about which rites and observances are used.

Above the natural manner of action, there is the supernatural way of acting of the *Amr Ilahi* (God's word and action): God has revealed himself in history, in his choice of a people, a land and a language. This choice is the only real proof of God's existence, and it is part of the order of the world. On to the mineral, vegetable, animal and rational kingdoms, there is added, in the hierarchical order, the prophetic order, that of Adam and his sons, of Noah and then of the whole people of Israel.

Man is able, by his own strength, to rise as far as the level of the Intellect. To do so, he must follow the discursive path, that of philosophy. But, in order to be marked out by the *Amr Ilahi,* he needs to follow the supernatural path, that of the Torah. God has reserved this path for his elect. In every generation since Adam there was one pure man, worthy of the *Amr Ilahi;* but then the whole people of Israel and it alone was chosen by God.

Along with the choice of the people of Israel goes the choice of the land of Israel and of its holy language, Hebrew. The land of Israel has a special place in Judah Halevi's work, and his Hebrew poems about Jerusalem are among the most beautiful of all Jewish literature. They are still recited today, and Judah Halevi's thought, with its particularist view of Judaism, remains as popular among modern Jewry as the thought of Maimonides.

The most original writing of the twelfth century, however, steps aside from debates between religion and philosophy. It is that of Abu'l-Barakât al-Baghdâdî, who lived in Iraq and died, at a very old age, after 1164. Towards the end of his life he converted to Islam. His *Kitâb al-Mu'tabar,* a sort of reply to Avicenna's philosophy, is based on his own personal reflections. He upholds the unity of the soul, denying that there is a distinction between it and the intellect. In his view, there is just one time, which measures *esse* and is similar for all beings, including God.

Maimonides

Moses ben Maimon was born in 1138 at Cordoba, where his father was a rabbinical judge. In 1148 Maimon and his family fled from the religious persecution which took place after the town fell to the Almohades. After wandering from town to town in Spain, and perhaps also in Provence, in 1160 they arrived at Fez in Morocco, In about 1165 the whole family fled from Fez and set off to Acre. For five months, Maimon and his children lived in the land of Israel, then they went to Cairo and settled at Fostat. Maimon's son Moses rose rapidly in Egyptian Jewish society, helped perhaps by family ties with some of the important people there. For about five years from 1171 he was 'Leader of the Jews'. He was subsequently deprived of this post, but twenty years later he regained it and kept it until his death.

Maimonides earned his living by practising and teaching medicine, which he had studied in north Africa. His fame reached its peak in 1185 when he was chosen as one of the official doctors of Al Fadil, Saladin's vizier. At the same time as he followed his profession and composed his medical treatises, Maimonides completed two great works, the *Mishneh Torah* in 1180 and the *Guide of the Perplexed* in 1190, as well as conducting a lengthy correspondence with the many Jewish communities of Egypt and in other countries. His death in 1204 was the occasion for public mourning among Jews everywhere.

With the exception of the *Mishneh Torah,* all Maimonides' works were written in Arabic. They were almost immediately translated into Hebrew. The *Guide of the Perplexed* was translated by Samuel ibn Tibbon in 1204, and a second, less precise, more literary translation was made a few years later by Judah al-Harizi. It formed the basis for the Latin translation used by Christian scholastics such as Thomas Aquinas.

Maimonides' reputation rests, in the first place, on his contribution to law. It was as a legal authority that he was first known to the Jews of the diaspora and still today many eastern Jewish communities follow his juridical and religious rulings.

The comparison between Maimonides and Averroes is inescapable, and one difference between the two thinkers is striking. By contrast with Averroes, who held that philosophy should be carefully hidden from the ignorant, Maimonides is a philosopher in all his works, legal as well as philosophical, in the texts intended for the general public as much as in those written for students of philosophy. After Aristotle, al-Fârâbî was Maimonides' real master. His influence is visible in a youthful work, the *Milot-ha-Higayon,* 'A Logical Vocabulary', written at the age of 16, and it remains in Maimonides' last work, the *Guide.* In a letter written to Samuel ibn Tibbon a year or two before he died, Maimonides told him:

Aristotle's intellect [represents] the extreme of human intellect, if we except those who have received divine inspiration. The works of Aristotle are the roots and foundations of all works on the sciences. But they cannot be understood except with the help of commentaries, those of

Alexander of Aphrodisias, those of Themistius, and those of Averroes, I tell you: as for works on logic, one should only study the writings of Abû Nar al-Fârâbî. All his writings are faultlessly excellent. One ought to study and understand them.

On Avicenna, his view is more qualified:

> *Though the work of Avicenna may give rise to objections and are not as [good] as those of Abu Nasr [al-Fârâbî], Abu Bakr al-Sâigh [Ibn Bâjjah] was also a great philosopher, and all his writings are of a high standard.*

And to read the other Jewish and Arab philosophers was, he thought, a waste of time.

The philosophical school to which Maimonides says he belongs, and which he recommends to Samuel ibn Tibbon, is that of the Andalusian philosophers, who strictly separated scientific knowledge from religion. Maimonides, however, did introduce philosophical principles into all his works, including those intended for the simple believer, such as Book I, part one of his *Mishneh Torah,* the *Book of Precepts* and the commentary on the *Mishnah.* These principles, thirteen in all, which are discussed afresh in the *Guide,* are presented by Maimonides as truths which everyone should accept by authority because they are the beliefs of the Jewish people, the necessary condition for belonging to it:

When a man has accepted these principles and truly believes in them, he forms part of the community of Israel; and it is incumbent upon us to love him, to care for him and behave towards him as God has ordered us to do: to love and comfort him; if he sins because of his corporeal desires or his bad instincts, he will receive the punishment proportioned to his crime, and he may [afterwards] have the part [that belongs to him in the world to come], he is a sinner within the community of Israel. But if someone casts doubt on one of these principles, he has foresworn his faith, he is a renegade, a heretic, an unbeliever, he has rebelled against God and it is a duty to hate him and to cause him to perish.

The 'Thirteen Principles' are divided into three groups.

The first five are concerned with God, who is one and incorporeal; the following four with prophecy and the Law; the last four with reward and punishment, the coming of the Messiah and the resurrection of the dead. The principles include certain articles of faith which were far from being unanimously accepted by the Jewish community, especially in these two respects:

(1) Divine incorporeality implies the rejection or allegorization of many biblical passages and of a certain number of texts which are an integral part of the oral Law. Maimonides was not the first to declare that God is not corporeal, but he was the first to exclude from the people of Israel those Jews who took the anthropomorphic comments in the Bible in their literal sense.

(2) By 'the world to come' Maimonides understands the immortality of the soul, and he does not make clear whether this is a matter of individual immortality. Traditional texts use two other expressions to talk about man after death: 'the days of the Messiah' and 'the resurrection of the dead'. For Maimonides, 'the days of the Messiah' means political independence of the Jews and their return to the land of Israel. The Messiah will easily be recognized, since his coming will coincide with a new period of history, totally different from the time of the diaspora. As for the corporeal resurrection of the dead, Maimonides holds that it is neither necessary from a scientific point of view, nor theoretically impossible. If one believes in divine omnipotence, it is a possibility. Clearly, this bodily resurrection is not of great importance to Maimonides, especially since it would be followed by a bodily death. Samuel ben Eli, Gaon of Baghdad, attacked Maimonides sharply for failing to insist on the resurrection of the dead and the survival of the individual human soul. In his final work, *The Letter on the Resurrection of the Dead,* Maimonides repeats his earlier view, unchanged, often with fierce irony.

A fourteenth-century versification of the Thirteen Principles became part of the daily prayers of almost every Jewish community, except for the Ashkenazim, thus impressing themselves on the great majority of Jews and definitively shaping the Jewish notion of God.

The Guide of the Perplexed is the Jewish philosophical work most known outside Judaism. By contrast with Maimonides' other works, which are models of clarity and order, the *Guide* is avowedly difficult to understand. Like the Torah, the prophetic books and the *Aggadot* of the Talmud, it is constructed in such a way as simultaneously to hide and reveal its inner sense. The difficulties of its plan and the ambiguities in its expressions can be traced back to the obscurities of the texts it discusses. He asks that it should not be read in the light of preconceptions, but that the reader should first have studied all that ought to be studied, and that he should not explain it to others. From the conceptual point of view, belief in the existence of God is inseparable from his absolute unity and his absolute unity is inseparable from his incorporeality. But it is quite otherwise when seen from the pedagogical or historical angle. The Law of Moses, a political law like every other religious law, was given to the Jewish people at a certain point in its history. For it to be accepted, it had to take into consideration the beliefs to which the people were accustomed. If it had not done this, the political and intellectual good it brought would have been lost. Before insisting on the existence of an incorporeal God it was necessary to bring about acceptance of the existence of God himself. When they fled from Egypt, the only type of existence which the Jews could conceive was that of a corporeal being: 'The minds of the multitude were accordingly guided to the belief that He exists by imagining that he is corporeal and to the belief that he is living by imagining that He is capable of motion'. 'God, may He be exalted above every deficiency, has had bodily organs figuratively ascribed to Him in order that His acts should be indicated by this means'. What was a gain in understanding at the time of Moses had become an inexcusable fault by the time of Maimonides: those who believe that God is corporeal were, as we have seen, to be excluded from the Jewish community. The Sages themselves had never committed this fault: 'the doctrine of the corporeality of God did not occur even for a single day to the Sages, may their memory be blessed and this was not according to them a matter lending itself to imagination or confusion'.

The problem which the *Guide* is intended to resolve is, therefore, that of the Law's double character. Sometimes its external sense, which results from the historical situation at the time when it was granted, serves to introduce and helps to discover the internal sense, which alone is true. Sometimes the external sense prevents the reader from reaching 'the knowledge of the Law in its reality' and is contrary to reason. The object of the *Guide* is to bring to light the two senses of the Bible: through this duality alone can knowledge from science and revelation be reconciled. In the *Guide* there can be found the elements of the method which allows the cloak of divine, scriptural allegory to be removed:

> Know that the key to the understanding of all that the prophets, peace be on them, have said, and to the knowledge of its truth, is an understanding of the parables, of their import, and of the meaning of the words occurring in them. You know what God, may He be exalted, has said: *And by the ministry of the prophets have I used similitudes*. And you know that He has said: *Put forth a riddle and speak a parable*.

The first half of Book I treats in general the expressions in the Bible and the Talmud which cannot be taken in their literal sense. In the second half, God's attributes are described and the *Mu'takalimun,* among them Saadiah, are attacked. Book II discusses philosophical doctrines, then prophecy. Book III begins with an allegorical explanation of the 'Account of the Chariot' and then considers providence and the fact that the world will end and not continue eternally. Maimonides gives a psychological explanation of the book of Job, a history of religions and types of worship, and he goes on to talk about religious commands. Clearly, it is beyond the scope of this survey to examine the great variety of interpretations of the *Guide*. Our discussion must be limited to mentioning a few of the especially important points in its doctrine.

(1) *God and his attributes*: According to Maimonides, only negative attributes can be applied to God. Any relation between two terms implies something they have in common. But there can be nothing in common between a being which is totally separate and another being which depends on every other being. Even existence is not common to them both, because 'existence' does not describe the same thing when one speaks of God and when one speaks of a created being, because God is a necessary existence and a created being a possible existence.

For Moses, the prince among the prophets, as for man in general, to know God means, not to know anything of his essence but to know his actions. Through the speculative method which God showed to Moses, it is possible to make progress in knowing the unknowability of God's essence. As we deny attributes of God, we understand better his supereminence and the lack of relation between his perfection and ours. To deny that God has emotions is already to be closer to the truth about him than just to deny that he has a body. To deny not only that he has emotions but that there is any relation between him and other beings is to take another step on the path of negative theology, a step which brings us closer to the idea that God is above all our categories of thought. We should, therefore, say nothing about God, and true prayer the only prayer which is befitting to God is silence, since every positive praise in fact consists of attributing to him what, to us, is perfection and, for him, a defect. Maimonides quotes with great praise a Talmudic story where a worshipper adds eulogistic adjective to eulogistic adjective in his prayers. Rabbi Haninah tells him that these praises are as unfitting as if one were to praise a king for all the silver coins he possessed, when his treasury was full of gold. Indeed, Maimonides says, were we left to follow reason alone, we would use none of these adjectives. We do so because men have need for images in order to understand and also just because the Torah used them. Since they were written in the Torah, we are allowed to read them as part of the biblical text. But we use them in our prayers only on the authority of the men of the Grand Synod, since they have taken the responsibility for this decision. Verbal prayer is, in fact, a concession to human weakness.

'Knowing God's actions' is the second aspect of knowledge of God. By knowing his creation, we learn what we should deny of God. Every branch of knowledge can teach us something about this. Arithmetic and geometry teach us that God's unity is not like the unity to which we add, or which can be multiplied. Physics and astronomy teach us how God puts the world into motion through the intermediary of separated intellects, in a perfect and absolute manner. It is only because we have a tendency to describe God in anthropomorphic terms that certain of God's, or nature's, actions seem beneficent and certain others seem destructive. In reality, God's action is intended to maintain the immutable order of nature, which includes the preservation of the human race as of other species of living things.

(2) *God's understanding*: In Part I, Chapter 68 of the *Guide,* Maimonides proposes a theory of understanding which seems to contradict his negative theology.

Now when it is demonstrated that God, may He be held precious and magnified, is an intellect *in actu*...It is accordingly also clear that the numerical unity of the intellect, the intellectually cognizing subject, and the intellectually cognized object, does not hold good with reference to the Creator only, but also with reference to every intellect. Thus in us too, the intellectually cognizing subject, the intellect and the intellectually cognized object, are one and the same thing wherever we have an intellect *in actu.*

Contrary, then, to the views of Aristotle and al-Fârâbî, Maimonides holds that God does not merely know his own essence but also every intelligible thing and the laws of nature: 'for through knowing the true reality of His own immutable essence, He also knows the totality of what necessarily derives from all His acts'. The commentators have not found a convincing explanation for this contradiction.

(3) *The origin of the world*: In the *Mishneh Torah,* the proof of God's incorporeal existence is based on the perpetual movement of the sphere and so on the eternity of the world. In the *Guide,* Maimonides shows the extent to which the philosophical point of view contradicts the religious one.

The belief in eternity the way Aristotle sees it that is, the belief according to which the world exists in virtue of necessity, that no nature changes at all, and that the customary course of events cannot be modified with regard to anything destroys the Law in its principle, necessarily gives the lie to every miracle, and reduces to inanity all the hopes and threats that the Law has held out.

If, however, one believed in eternity according to the second opinion we have explained which is the opinion of Plato—this opinion would not destroy the foundations of the Law and would be followed not by the lie being given to miracles, but by their becoming admissible. It would also be possible to interpret figuratively the texts in accordance with this opinion. And many obscure passages can be found in the texts of the *Torah* and others with which this opinion could be connected or rather by means of which it could be proved. However, no necessity could impel us to do this unless this opinion were demonstrated. In view of the fact that it has not been demonstrated, we shall not favor this opinion, nor shall we at all heed that other opinion.

Commentators have interpreted these passages in opposing fashions. Some take them to be a clear statement in favour of creation, whereas for others they seem rather to disguise Maimonides' view, which he proposes clearly elsewhere, in favour of the eternity of the world. Shlomo Pines, in the most recent discussion of the problem, suggests that problems of method came to occupy Maimonides increasingly as his thought matured, which can be summarized as follows:

1. Aristotle's physics are true so far as the sublunary world is concerned, but dubious with regard to the heavens and the order of intelligences.

2. Man cannot reach the level of intellectual

understanding except through the imagination, through the *phantasmata* of bodily things which, according to a quotation he makes from al-Fârâbî's Commentary on the *Nicomachean Ethics,* implies the denial of the immortality of the soul.

Maimonides' extreme intellectualism was not an easy doctrine to live with: his son, Abraham, who followed as head of the Jewish community in Egypt adopted a *sufi*-like mysticism and gathered around him a group of spiritually intense pietists. The descendants of Maimonides continued to practise this mystical approach to religion for two hundred years.

Ibn Kammûnah (thirteenth century) may be considered the last Jewish philosopher living in Islamic lands. In the fifteenth century, however, there was a sort of renaissance of Jewish philosophy, accompanied by mysticism, in the Yemen.

Jewish Philosophy in Christian Lands

From the twelfth century onwards, Christians and Jews discovered a whole body of Greek texts and their Arabic commentaries. They were translated into Hebrew for the use of Jews, just as they were put into Latin for Christian readers.

Jewish philosophy in Christian lands was based on Greek and Arabic sources, but also on the works of Jews who had written in Arabic. Maimonides had seen no need to use texts written by other Jews, since Greek and Islamic works provided what was essential in disciplined knowledge. But his successors, who lived among Christians, wanted to know this Jewish philosophy, and there were translators often dynasties of translators—who worked to make these texts available to them. The first of them was Judah ben Saul ibn Tibbon. He translated works by Bayâ ibn Paqudah, Judah Halevi and Saadiah. In 1204 Samuel ibn Tibbon put Maimonides' *Guide* into Hebrew. The work came as a revelation to educated Jews. All of a sudden, the passages of the Bible which offended reason became clear and rational. Maimonides, as the spiritual leader of Judaism, was already celebrated for his religious learning. Now, with the *Guide,* he showed that he was also a consummate philosopher, who accepted the true path of scientific knowledge that of Aristotle and showed that true Judaism was the religion which fostered this knowledge. The *Guide* became a manual of philosophy.

Aristotle could not be studied without a commentary, and Maimonides himself had recommended those of Averroes. From the beginning of the thirteenth century, Averroes' commentaries were translated into Hebrew but also, in the middle of the century, popularized through encyclopaedias: the *Midrash ha-Hokhma* of Judah ben Solomon ha-Cohen, the *Sha'ar ha Shamayim* of Gerson ben Solomon of Arles and the *De'ot ha-philosophim* of Shem Tov ibn Falaqera. Besides Averroes, there are frequent references to Aristotle, Plato, Alexander of Aphrodisias, Themistius, al-Fârâbî, Avicenna, Ibn Bâjjah, and Greek and Arabic mathematical, astronomical and medical texts. The Jewish philosophers were deeply affected by their reading of Averroes and this coloured their interpretation of Maimonides. Very often, Averroist ideas were preferred to those of Maimonides, thereby sharpening the opposition between philosophy and religion. Except in Italy, no Christian author is named and the influence of Christian scholasticism is not explicitly acknowledged. Indeed, the universities were Christian institutions to which the Jews had no access. Jews spoke the vernacular (French, Provençal, Italian or Catalan), but these spoken languages did not give them knowledge of Latin. Whereas Jewish philosophers in Islamic countries benefited from all the sources of inspiration open to their Muslim colleagues, those in Christian lands were limited to Hebrew texts. This gave a certain homogeneity to Jewish philosophy, but also limited it. In contrast with what had happened in Islamic lands, Jewish philosophy developed in parallel, but separately, from Christian thought, and the connections between the two are not easy to discern. Often they share common problems; their answers are usually different.

During the thirteenth century, many philosophical works

were written. Along with pursuing the sciences, authors engaged in the philosophical explanation of traditional texts, as Maimonides had shown, and of their anthropomorphic expressions. Philosophy was no longer the preserve of a learned or rich minority, but became available to a large section of society. An enlightened middle class had grown up in the south of France and Provence, in Catalonia, Spain and Italy. The existence of towns, material prosperity and the extensive links between the various Jewish communities encouraged the growth of a milieu where science and philosophy were keenly studied, and where scholars were numerous and influential within the community. Philosophy became the subject of public sermons. True, Jacob Anatolio was forced, by the opposition of some of his community, to abandon the set of philosophical sermons he had been giving on Saturdays in the synagogue. But the very fact that he had begun to give them, with the agreement of a certain number of the community, shows well how public philosophical teaching had become.

Both the upholders of traditional Judaism and the exponents of the kabbalah, which was developing in this period in Catalonia and Provence, were violently opposed to this surge of interest in philosophy. There was fierce anti-philosophical polemic in the Jewish communities during the whole of the thirteenth century, which reached its climax at several points: in 1202, about the resurrection of the dead (even before the *Guide of the Perplexed* had been translated), in 1240-2 and then at the very end of the century. This controversy about studying philosophy itself came to an end when the Jews were expelled from France in 1305, but the underlying differences of view continued until the end of the Middle Ages.

In the fourteenth century, Maimonides remained the fixed point of reference and provided the framework for Jewish thought. The central problems, however, and the way of tackling them began to be affected by the scholastic philosophy of the Christian universities: for instance, the question of individual forms in Yedaya ha-Penini, at the very beginning of the century; that of future contingents in the 1320s and 1330s; that of non-Aristotelian (Parisian) physics at the end of the century. In the second half of the fourteenth century, translations from Latin into Hebrew were more often of medical than philosophical texts, but they began to include works of logic. There was also a resurgence of interest in astrology, with a Neoplatonic emphasis.

Gersonides and Crescas

The dominant Jewish philosopher of the fourteenth century was Gersonides. Gersonides (Levi ben Gerson, Leo of Bagnols) (1288-1344) seems never to have left the south of France, where he lived at Bagnolsur-Cèze, in Languedoc, in Avignon and in Orange. He is often considered the greatest Jewish philosopher after Maimonides. Like Maimonides, he was a philosopher and a Talmudist, as well as being learned in the sciences.

Besides works on astronomy (where he attacks some of the fundamental principles used by Ptolemy and proposes his own solutions) and biblical commentaries, Gersonides wrote (still mostly unpublished) commentaries on the epitomes and *Middle Commentaries* of Averroes. They were composed between 1319 and 1324 and cover the greater part of Aristotle's oeuvre. These are purely philosophical works and do not deal with questions linked to religion. In the excursus, where Gersonides expresses his own ideas, he refers readers to his *Wars of the Lord.* This work, divided into six books, took ten years to write and was finished in January 1329. Its introduction shows how much it differs from Maimonides' writings both in method and in its thoughts:

I would like to examine in this book several important yet difficult questions on which many crucial doctrines relevant to man's intellectual happiness are based. First, is the rational soul immortal when it has achieved [only] some perfection? Second, when a man is informed by dreams or divination or prophecy of future events, is he informed of them essentially or accidentally?... Third, does God know existent things?... Fourth, is there divine providence over existent things?... Fifth, how do the movers of the heavenly bodies move these bodies, and how many movers are there, as far as we can know?... Sixth, is the universe eternal or created?...

Now it is without doubt essential that the reader of this book be familiar with the mathematical science, the natural sciences, and metaphysics. Of the questions mentioned so far, some belong to the sciences, others to metaphysics, and others require a knowledge of mathematics [including astronomy].

Gersonides has therefore written a work about science, and he deals with mathematical, physical and metaphysical that is to say, philosophical questions. His intended audience are those who are plunged into perplexity by scientific questions to which previous philosophers have found no solution. It is not the letter of the biblical text which causes problems:

The reader should not think it is the Torah that has stimulated us to verify what shall be verified in this book, [whereas in reality] the truth itself is something different. It is evident, as Maimonides (may his name be blessed) has said, that we must believe what reasoning has proved to be true. If the literal sense of the Torah differs from it, it is necessary to interpret those passages and accord them with reasoning. Accordingly, Maimonides (may his name be blessed) explains the words of the Torah that suggest that God is corporeal in such a way that reason is not violated. He, therefore, maintains that if the eternity of the universe is demonstrated, it would be necessary to believe in it and to interpret the passages of the Torah that seem to be incompatible with it in such a way that they agree with reason. It is, therefore, evident that if the course of speculation causes us to affirm doctrines that are different from what appears to be the literal sense of Scripture, we are not prohibited by the Torah to pronounce the truth on these matters, for this is not incompatible with the true understanding of the Torah. The Torah is not a political law that forces us to believe false ideas; rather it leads us to the truth to the extent that is possible.

In Gersonides' view, most of the prophets did not have revelations about things to do with the intelligible world. So Abraham did not know how many stars there are, because this number was not known in his day. Ezekiel thought that he had heard the voice of the celestial spheres, because this is how people thought of it in his times. Nor did the prophets have a political role (and here Gersonides rejected the whole Arab and Jewish political tradition); the purpose of dreams, divination and prophecy is to reveal the future, especially future contingents which will happen to individual human beings. These future events seem accidental. In fact, they can be known in advance, by dream, divination or prophecy, because they have been determined and arranged. The fact that accidental events are part of an order is proved by the existence of men who are said to have been born under a good star. They are granted every success whilst for other men misfortune is heaped on misfortune. But, if good or bad fortune were accidental, they would be distributed in fairly equal measure. Another argument is that, as the most eminent of creatures, man is taken care of by the celestial substances to such an extent that his actions and thoughts come from them. So astrologers know what people think and their predictions are often correct. When they predict wrongly, this is because of the distance of the stars from us and the limitations of the astrologers' knowledge. Since that which, for man, is an accident, is ordered and determined for the stars, these human events are in fact ordered and determined.

There are, however, acts which cannot be foreseen in the ordering of the stars: those which are freely chosen by men. But such acts are few. Indeed, almost all the thoughts of men and their movements are determined by the stars. Men are the most noble creatures and the order of the stars is intended for the good, and so men benefit more than other animals from the beneficent influence of the stars. It is rare that men set themselves against this order and, in fact, the great majority of events which we call accidental are determined and knowable. They are therefore the objects of scientific knowledge: of God's knowledge, eminently perfect; of the more partial knowledge of the Agent Intellect; and of the very limited and incomplete knowledge of man—a degree of knowledge which, none the less, gives him immortality.

God's thought is directed not merely toward himself but also to the law, order and organization of beings, which he considers in a single, unified concept. All the attributes which he has disseminated to the pure forms are perfect within him. To him then can be attributed those attributes which are the reflection of the perfection of the divine being in us: essence, existence, unity, substantiality, understanding, the joy which accompanies doing good and so on.

Gersonides discusses the creation of the world from an astronomer's point of view. God created the world by beginning with a first body lacking in form and therefore not being. This first body, entirely in potency, neutral and lifeless, has an existence which is known to the senses. It is the fluid body between the spheres and sometimes it is opposed to form. It can be seen in the spheres, where God has given it a geometrical form along with the ability to keep this form; whilst, in the sublunary world, it has the form of the elements and the ability to receive every form.

God created the world in time. Gersonides rejects the definition of the present instant as that which separates the past from the future. An instant can be the beginning or the end of an interval of time. In order to support the idea that the world was created in time, Gersonides also brings in the argument that history is still going on and is far from having reached its conclusion; consider the history of the branches of knowledge, or of the dissemination of God's law, or the history of languages.

Although he was deeply convinced of the truth of astrology, Gersonides upholds the existence of human free will, as all the other Jewish philosophers had done. The problems of determinism and future contingents which, in Christian scholastic philosophy, had taken a clear form in the work of Peter Aureoli, were raised in Jewish circles by Abner of Burgos. Abner's unqualified determinism was the justification for his conversion to Catholicism in the 1320s.

It is all the more astonishing to find an equally complete determinism in the thought of Hasdaï Crescas. Hasdaï Crescas was the leader of the Jewish community in Barcelona, already well known in 1367. His only son was killed in the anti-Jewish uprisings of 1391, though he himself survived. The wave of conversions to Catholicism which would go on through the whole of the fifteenth century had already begun, and Crescas dedicated himself to combating it and to reconstructing the Jewish communities which had been destroyed. His two polemical works were written in Catalan and his philosophical book in Hebrew.

Aristotelian philosophy was accused of having disturbed people's minds and of having driven the heads of communities rich men who were often interested in philosophy to convert and take with them other Jews. *The Light of God (Or Adonaï)* was planned by Crescas as just the first part of a more extensive project, intended to replace the whole of Maimonides' work, both in philosophy and rabbinical jurisprudence. But the second part of it was never written. According to Crescas, the very root of Maimonides' philosophy, like that of any thinker basing himself on Aristotle, was false. The route to God is not intellectual understanding, but fear and love.

The final purpose of human existence is the fulfilment of the divine commands given by God himself to the children of Israel, in order that they should love and fear him. Scientific knowledge, a preliminary to the knowledge and understanding of the commandments, must be based on a physics different from Aristotle's, because his physics is false. Book I of the *Light of God* is devoted to a critique of Aristotelian physics as it is expounded by Maimonides in the twenty-five propositions which precede Book II of his *Guide*.

Crescas argues that Aristotle gives to the infinite the

characteristics of finite bodies, and conceives the infinite only in relation to the finite. If it exists, the infinite is not contained within bounds. It has neither weight nor lightness, neither form nor shape. If it has a circular movement, it is not around a centre and, although it moves itself voluntarily, it has no need of any external object to bring about its movement. It can just as well be a simple being as a composite one. Similarly, place in the Aristotelian definition is the place of the elements, not the place of the world as a whole. Crescas holds that it is necessary to dissociate body and space. Space can be empty of bodies. In this case, the definition of the place of the world as being its external boundary no longer applies, and we can conceive an infinite space. Space is no longer the relation between bodies, but, as pure extension, it exists before bodies. The finite corporeal world is situated within an infinite void. Crescas does not deny the possibility of an infinite number of worlds and this hypothesis, although not explicitly adopted, is perhaps implied by his citation of a passage from the Talmud. In the same way, Crescas refuses to define time as the measure of movement: time is also a measure of rest.

If we can conceive an infinity of time and an infinite numerical series, we can no longer accept the proof of God's existence based on showing that he is the Prime Mover because this proof is based on the assertion that a series of causes cannot be infinite and so must end in a first cause.

Crescas' central intuition, then, is that, because God is infinite, space and time are infinite, and a numerical series can be extended infinitely. The human mind cannot reach the essence of an infinite God either through philosophy or through revelation. God is unknowable in his essence. But, like Gersonides, Crescas asserts the existence of positive divine attributes. Yet, for him, there is no possible relation or comparison between God and his creatures. We gain our idea of God's attributes in the way in which we gain our idea of the infinite from the finite. Equally, the number of divine attributes is itself infinite. Just as the final aim of human existence is not understanding, so our joy in God cannot be the contemplation or understanding of his essence: it is the joy of a gift, of the Good which gives of itself. God is the true agent of all creatures. He makes them act through will and intention, and maintains them always in being through the emanation of his goodness. God likes to spread goodness and perfection and his joy is that of always giving the being which he spreads over the whole of creation, in the most perfect way that can be.

The joy which God experiences in an infinite and essential way is a giving; it is also love and desire. God has loved and desired the patriarchs, and he loves and desires the love of Israel. God's power is infinite. If it has given rise to a finite world, that is a result of will and choice. It is not merely infinite in potentiality but also in act. God's omnipotence, which reason shows to be infinitely strong in act, is revealed in the biblical miracles, when substances are created or destroyed, as when Moses' rod was changed into a snake.

As a result of God's omnipotence, there is no place for free will. Only the feeling of freedom differentiates freedom from compulsion. All human acts are made necessary by their causes. The will of the agent who causes an act is itself determined by causes which might be external or internal or both. Divine commands and the rewards or punishments which follow obedience to them or their disregard are themselves links in the causal chain which leads to a human act. A man is said to act 'voluntarily' when a cause is internal and not perceived by him, and 'involuntarily' only when an external cause is perceived as forcing him, despite his internal dissent, to such and such an action. Joy accompanies the fulfilment of God's commandments as an effect accompanies a cause, but only when the soul has acted voluntarily, without any external obligation which it regards as contrary to it.

Beliefs, especially true beliefs, are obligations on the soul, not results of its will, since their reality constrains the soul to accept them. Beliefs, then, give rise neither to reward nor punishment, and they are unrelated to the knowledge of intelligible things. Nor are the intelligibles what one calls 'the survival of the soul'. Reward joy is brought by the effort towards knowledge, the desire to know, the wish to understand.

The goal of the Torah is to enable men to acquire perfection in behaviour and belief, material happiness and happiness of the soul. Most important is the happiness of the soul. This is the ultimate aim of God's law. The soul's eternal happiness is the love and fear of God. Love and fear of God are the final stage, not only of the Torah, but also of true philosophy.

Epilogue

In Crescas' thought, we can see the influence not only of Christian scholasticism, but also of the kabbalah, which became more and more important in Jewish thought, the worse became the political situation of Jews in Spain and the more eagerly they returned to the sources of their religion. It became necessary to define precisely what were the principles of Judaism. It is not correct to speak of 'dogma' in Judaism. Jewish tradition, the Bible and the Talmud, was considered as a whole, over a long period. It had to be accepted in its entirety, since belief was involved in each of the commandments. It was in confrontation with other religions that Judaism found itself obliged to clarify and systematize the principles of the faith. This problem was marginal up until the end of the fourteenth century, but it became a burning issue in the fifteenth century, culminating with Albo. Albo places his assertion of the superiority of the Torah within the context of a consideration of the different types of law: natural, conventional and divine. The Torah alone, he believes, is divine law, because it guides men towards the true good: the immortality of the soul.

Traditionally, the fifteenth century is taken to mark the end of medieval Jewish philosophy. Yet as many philosophical works were written as they had been during the previous two hundred years. Here as in the history of medieval Jewish philosophy in general history has been distorted in favour of the 'great philosophers', whose works were printed in the sixteenth century and so widely diffused. Here in this chapter an anachronistically disproportionate weight has been given to the better known philosophers, in order to avoid too thin a treatment of too many figures. More obscure philosophers, whose works are still unprinted, deserve to have a more important place. We would then see that the fifteenth century, far from being a barren period, witnessed a real renewal of all the types of philosophy which had previously flourished: the Aristotelian current with Joseph ben Shem Tov ibn Shemtob and his son Shem Tov, Abraham ben Yomtob Bibago, Isaac Abraham and, in the area of Padua, Elias del Medigo and his circle. In Italy, the Neoplatonic current was represented especially by Judah Abraham. In Provence, Africa and Turkey, as well as the Yemen, medieval philosophical texts were still read and taught to a wide audience. True, kabbalistic ideas came little by little to figure in the work of most philosophers. No longer did intellectual understanding play the only important part in the philosophers' systems too many political and religious events had shaken the philosophers' ivory tower. But philosophical ideas (the most important of which is that of God's incorporeality) had taken root in the Jewish community, and to this day they remain an integral part of Judaism.

Jewish philosophy includes all philosophical activity carried out by Jews, or, in relation to the religion of Judaism. Jewish philosophy, until modern Enlightenment and Emancipation, was pre-occupied with attempts to reconcile coherent new ideas into the tradition of Rabbinic Judaism; thus organizing emergent ideas, that are not necessarily Jewish, into a uniquely Jewish scholastic framework and world-view. With their acceptance into modern society, Jews with secular educations embraced, or developed, entirely new philosophies to meet the demands of a world in which they now found themselves.

Medieval re-discovery of Greek thought among Gaonim of 10th century Babylonian academies brought rationalist philosophy into Biblical-Talmudic Judaism, which later competed for the mainstream with emergent mysticism. Both schools would become part of classic Rabbinic literature, though the decline of scholastic rationalism coincided with historical events which drew Jews to mystical theology. For European Jews, emancipation and encounter with secular thought from the 18th century onwards altered how philosophy was viewed. Oriental and Eastern European communities had later and more ambivalent interaction with secular culture than in Western Europe. In the varied responses to modernity, Jewish philosophical ideas were developed across the range of emerging religious denominations. These developments could be seen as either continuations, or breaks, with the canon of Rabbinic philosophy of the Middle Ages, as well as the other historical dialectic aspects of Jewish thought, and resulted in diverse contemporary Jewish attitudes to philosophical methods.

7

Intellectual Context of Medieval Philosophy

Introduction

We limit ourselves to the consideration of theology, Paris led the way on the Continent. With the support of Popes Innocent III and Gregory IX, the University of Paris became the theological stronghold of the Christian world. The cathedral school of Notre Dame, the abbey of St Victor, the houses of the newly arrived Dominicans and Franciscans, formed an intellectual guild or corporation of masters and students, a *universitas magistorum et scholarium.* In the pursuit of their common interests they became a unified and autonomous community. This guild took the title 'University of Paris'. Across the Channel, Oxford outstripped the other English schools, owing mainly to the influence of Robert Grosseteste, student of scriptural wisdom, translator of Aristotle's *Nicomachean Ethics,* commentator on the Greek philosopher's *Posterior Analytics,* bishop of Lincoln, and chancellor of the young university.

Augustinian Model of Study

The programme of study for the cathedral, monastery and palace schools of the twelfth century, and for the early universities of the late twelfth and early thirteenth centuries, was inspired by St Augustine's *On Christian Doctrine*. Book II of Augustine's work viewed traditional pagan studies, if approached prudently, as helpful to those seeking understanding of the divine wisdom found in the sacred Scriptures. The seven liberal arts (the *trivium* of grammar, rhetoric and dialectic and the *quadrivium* of arithmetic, astronomy, geometry and music), along with geography, botany, geology and the mechanical arts all could assist those who read the Scriptures to attain a fuller grasp of the divine message. The twelfth-century schools of liberal arts became the faculties of arts in the universities of the thirteenth century. The arts faculty was a preparatory faculty, training students for further studies in law, medicine, and especially theology.

Richard Fishacre, in a sermon that he preached on the first day of class at Oxford in 1246, tells us that there is a threefold wisdom. The first kind of wisdom is that which is written in the book of life. This form of wisdom is the wisdom of God himself. To see God's meaning and plan for everything, to the degree that is possible for man, is the goal that all studies should strive to achieve. The way of attaining this goal is by carefully studying the two other books that manifest the divine wisdom found in the book of life: the book of the Scriptures and the book of nature. The Scriptures provide God's revelation to humankind of the riches of his own wisdom. The Bible is, thus, the principal help in coming to some understanding of divine wisdom. The Scriptures also give us a view of the book of nature that differs from the portraits of nature given by philosophers who are unaided by divine revelation. The Scriptures tell us that the natural world is a world created by and cared for by God. They likewise tell us that the created world provides vestiges and images of its Creator. The Bible uses natural things and the events of history to lead us to deeper understandings of God's wisdom.

We must therefore study the Scriptures to learn what they themselves say of God; but we must also, guided by the Bible, study the natural world to see how richly it tells us about the God who creates and cares for it, and whose imprint it bears. Both the Bible and creation thus help us to discover 'the depths of the riches both of the wisdom and knowledge of God'.

This sermon of Richard Fishacre at Oxford, following the Augustinian model of study, shows the way of investigation in the early medieval universities. The final goal of all study is to come to a greater understanding of God's view of reality, by taking as primary source the sacred Scriptures, which reveal the divine wisdom. The secondary instrument for discovering divine wisdom is found in the created world, which provides all the analogies for coming to a fuller understanding of God. They are the analogies used in the Scriptures: 'The kingdom of heaven is like a mustard seed'; 'You are the salt of the earth'; 'Behold the lamb of God, who takes away the sins of the world'; 'My kingdom is not of this world.' All other studies serve as helps in pursuing the divine wisdom that lies hidden in such scriptural declarations and that is manifested in some way in the created images of mustard seeds, salt, lamb, and earthly kingdoms that the Scriptures employ to speak of the hidden things of God. All the human disciplines, principally those of grammar, rhetoric, dialectic, arithmetic, geometry, astronomy, music and philosophy, in the more technical sense of the term are handmaids to be put at the service of the mistress, the wisdom of the Scriptures.

The Study of Aristotle

At the beginning of the universities, only in the area of dialectic (logic) did Aristotle fit into the traditional curriculum of studies that prepared students for the study of the sacred Scriptures. What became known as the *logica vetus,* or old logic, included Aristotle's *Categories* and *On Interpretation.* This old logic, available in Latin to the schools since the time of Boethius, also included the introduction to the *Categories* made by Porphyry and the commentaries on these two works of Aristotle done by Boethius himself. Before the middle of the twelfth century the *logica nova,* or new logic (the *Prior Analytics, Posterior Analytics, Topics* and *On Sophistical Refutations*) was also in use. Some of these works derived from the translation efforts of Boethius, but had been lost or neglected; others, by 1150, had been newly translated by James of Venice. Thus the whole of Aristotle's *Organon* or logic was available and had an ever deepening influence, transforming medieval Christian thinking from a sacramental or symbolic form of knowledge to a more scientific discipline through the study of various causal connections.

As the more properly philosophical works of Aristotle (e.g. *On the Soul, Physics, Metaphysics, Nicomachean Ethics* and *Politics*) were translated and began to be studied, more than the style or character of Christian knowledge was changed. The contents of Aristotle's works, his natural philosophy, slowly but surely also began to have their influence: his view of man, his teaching on the eternity of the world, his portrait of the unmoved Mover or supreme Being, his doctrine of virtues, his focus on the natural fulfilment or end of man. For the first time since the patristic era, Christian thinkers encountered a pagan philosopher directly. Many were struck by the brilliance of his intelligence and the strength of his argumentation; others were troubled by those of his teachings that seemed incompatible with those of the Christian faith.

Difficulties with Aristotle's Natural Philosophy

Attempts at moderating the disturbing influence that Aristotle's philosophy might have were made a number of times. The first intervention came in 1210 from the Provincial Council of Sens, presided over by Peter of Corbeil; it forbade the reading of Aristotle's 'natural philosophy' at Paris. Five years later, the papal legate Robert de Courçon also prohibited the reading of Aristotle's 'natural philosophy'. In 1231, Pope Gregory IX appointed a commission of William of Auxerre, Simon of Authie and Stephen of Provins to correct the prohibited books. Since William of Auxerre died shortly thereafter, the commission never met. Furthermore, this effort made by Gregory to correct Aristotle gradually became viewed as an admission that Aristotle was not necessarily wrong, but only wrong on certain issues. Little by little the prohibition against his natural philosophy was ignored. By 1255, all the known works of Aristotle, at least at an introductory level of understanding, were required in the arts faculty of the University of Paris.

Aristotle's works were read at many different levels. There was the introductory or beginner's level, where a first approach was made to one of his texts. In this beginning *lectio,* or reading, the Aristotelian text was read aloud and the basic direction and outline of the work was indicated. In a more advanced *lectio,* the text was explained in detail. In commentaries on the philosopher's works, the text was sometimes evaluated and on certain points questions were posed and answered. At the more advanced level of study, 'questions' concerning a text usually involved a deeper examination of the philosophical issues raised. In such a questioning approach, both sides of a debate were presented, and then a solution to the conflict was offered by the master. As teachers and students became more and more familiar with Aristotle's texts and philosophical positions, more specific conflicts between what he seemed to teach and what were matters of Christian belief became more evident.

Some points of Aristotelian teaching that caused problems for Christians had been passed down from the patristic era. St Augustine, for instance, had attributed to Aristotle the position that the world was eternal and therefore was not created in time. This was one of the grounds for the prohibitions at Paris against the public reading, before correction, of the natural philosophy of Aristotle in the early thirteenth century. Teachers who saw benefits for Christian theology that might come from the study of Aristotle, argued, however, that Aristotle never dealt with the question of creation. Aristotle, according to their reading of his texts, was simply giving a physical explanation, claiming that time did not exist before the world itself came to exist. Philip the

Chancellor and Alexander of Hales, for instance, claimed that metaphysics dealt with the issue of creation and that Aristotle did not pass metaphysical judgements on the nature of the world. According to their interpretation, Aristotle was only speaking as a physicist or natural philosopher; describing the world as it actually exists, not taking a position on whether it was created or not.

Other problems concerning Aristotle's teachings nonetheless gradually came to the fore as Christian thinkers became more familiar with his positions and with the commentaries made on them by earlier authors, especially the often conflicting commentaries of the Arabic philosophers, Avicenna and Averroes. St Bonaventure, in his Lenten sermons at Paris in the late 1260s and early 1270s, pointed out a number of problems in Aristotelian teaching at the university. The disturbing views at times might not clearly be positions of Aristotle himself, but rather positions of those in the arts faculty who show the strong influence of Averroes' interpretations of the Greek philosopher. The principal difficulties were: (1) the unicity of man's intellect, implying no personal immortality, and thus undermining individual moral responsibility; (2) the eternity of the world, entailing its independence from divine creation and a denial of divine concern or providence; and (3) the independent study of philosophy pretending to be a supreme and definitive wisdom separated from Christian wisdom.

The most detailed catalogue of the difficulties raised by the teaching of certain heterodox or radical Aristotelians in the arts faculty, however, is found in the list of 216 propositions condemned at Paris in 1277. They might be divided into two basic groups: (1) propositions concerned with the nature of philosophy and its relation to divinely revealed truths; (2) propositions of a specific kind that challenge particular truths of the faith. Among the first type of propositions we can find these condemned statements: (a) there is no more excellent state than to dedicate oneself to philosophy; (b) the only wise men of the world are the philosophers; (c) for a man to have any certitude about a conclusion, it is necessary for him to base his argument on self-evident principles; (d) nothing should be admitted as true unless it can be proved by a self-evident principle or by something based on self-evident principles; (e) man should not be content merely with authority if he is to achieve absolute certitude in regard to any question; (f) the Christian faith impedes learning; and (g) there are fables and false things in the Christian religion just as in other faiths. Among the specific positions condemned we find the propositions: (a) God does not know anything but himself; (b) the world, including all the species that are contained in it, is eternal; (c) it is impossible to refute the reasons of the philosopher concerning the eternity of the world without admitting that the will of God contains incompatibles; (d) the intellect is numerically one for all men; and (e) happiness is had in this life, not in another.

There were, then, in the late 1260s and throughout the 1270s-1280s signs of a real challenge to the Augustinian model of study, which stressed the unity of Christian wisdom. This challenge, of necessity, also affected studies in the faculty of theology as teachers and students moved there after learning or teaching in the arts faculty.

Theology as a Deductive Science

The 1253 university statutes at Oxford, confirming actually existing practice, indicate that a student could attain his degree in theology (which was considered a higher degree, as opposed to the degree taken earlier in the arts) by one of three routes: (1) he could study the Bible, a practice that usually entailed writing commentaries, using earlier exegetical efforts, on at least one book of the Old Testament and one book of the New Testament; (2) he could present a commentary on Peter Comestor's *Scholastic History* which presented a broader overview of all history, based primarily on the biblical account; and (3) he could comment on the *Sentences* of Peter Lombard, a collection of doctrinal questions organized in four books according to logical principles. The same options in practice were available even earlier in Paris, as is clear not only from the statutes of the Dominican Order listing these three options, but also from the practices that were in vogue after Alexander of Hales made the *Sentences* of Lombard a course textbook. Generally, we can say that the third option, the commentary on Peter Lombard's *Sentences*, was the one most frequently followed in the universities by the 1250s, if not earlier. Theology, through this instrument, thus became more and more a logically organized or scientific discipline.

The logical organization of doctrinal questions is evident in the many earlier authors, who followed Peter Lombard's *Sentences* by commenting in the margins of his text. His text was their text. It is also evident in the *Summae* of the late twelfth and early thirteenth centuries, which for the most part patterned themselves on his schema of questions. Explicit efforts to justify this procedure only come later. They can be found, for example, in the *Summa quaestionum* written by William of Auxerre in the 1220s, with its close structural correspondence to Lombard's *Sentences*. Lombard provides no discussion or justification of his method; nor do the people who gloss his *Sentences* or write *summae quaestionum* that slightly alter Lombard's organization. William of Auxerre, living in a university world more strongly touched by Aristotle's logical works, tries to give a methodological justification for writing such a work. For William, theology starts with certain principles or premisses and makes explicit, or deduces, the further knowledge implied in these premisses. The primary premisses in theology are the articles of the Christian faith. They are the starting points for theological reflection. They also set the boundaries for theological studies, in the sense that theology should not deviate from the articles of the faith nor pursue questions unrelated to basic Christian beliefs.

Other theologians immediately following William of Auxerre more deliberately attempted to set up parallel structures between Aristotle's model of science and their intellectual efforts in theology. Odo Rigaud, speaking of a 'science of the faith' maps out the correspondences and differences between the method he follows and the method sketched by Aristotle in the *Posterior Analytics.* Thomas Aquinas set up a parallel between Aristotle's description of a subalternated science, like optics, which used principles borrowed from a higher or subalternating science such as geometry, and the subalternated science of theology that uses principles borrowed from the higher science possessed by God and the blessed principles that God has revealed in the Scriptures. Just as geometry, which studies lines, helps the student of optics, which studies lines of vision, come to an understanding of the lines of vision, so God's knowledge of all that he has revealed provides the ultimate first principles which allow the student of theology to come to a knowledge or understanding of God and all things as they are related to him. Theology, then, is a science in the same way that optics is a science.

Critiques of Theology as a Deductive Science

The intellectual atmosphere in the late 1260s and throughout the 1270s–1280s had altered. Argument had become more precise and hard-nosed. Godfrey of Fontaines, who was a student at Paris during most of Thomas Aquinas' second teaching period there (1269-72) attacked, in question 10 of his *Quodlibet IV* (1287), Aquinas' claim that theology was like a subaltern science. Godfrey distinguishes two kinds of certitude: the certitude based on evidence and the certitude based on faith. Technically, he calls them certitude of evidence and certitude of adherence. He then argues that if we start with principles or premisses that we hold because of faith, then no matter how sure we are that the conclusions are true, still they will never be science, since science is based on evidence. Of course, a correctly argued conclusion can be a certain conclusion. Yet, since it still is based on faith, it is not an evident conclusion, and thus is not science. We might want to speak of the necessary way in which a faith conclusion flows from faith premisses and argue that there is a science of the consequence. Yet this in no way supplies evidence for the consequent or conclusion.

Godfrey also contested the example given by Aquinas. He argues that where a subaltern science must rely on principles received from an expert in a higher science which, within the subaltern science, are believed but cannot be *known,* then the subaltern science is not truly a science at all. Yet this is the case in theology as Aquinas presents it; the principles of theology, in so far as they are revealed by God, are believed. Just as human authority begets opinion which is a state of mind lacking both kinds of certitude, so divine authority produces faith which is a state of mind that only has the certitude of adherence. Of what advantage is it, asks Godfrey, for a theologian who is relying on such principles, which he cannot know but must accept as a matter of faith, that they are known evidently and with certitude to the blessed and that, in themselves, they are evident and certain? This does not bring the believing theologian evidence. He remains essentially a believer, without evidence. Theology is not a science, at least in the sense that it brings evidence for theological truths.

Henry of Ghent was also a critic of Thomas Aquinas. Whereas Godfrey of Fontaines criticized Aquinas from an Aristotelian viewpoint, Henry criticized him from an Augustinian one. One of Henry's main efforts in his approach to philosophy and theology was to show that Aristotle had a limited vision of reality, that he was deprived of the riches of Christian revelation, and that his philosophy was too pretentious in presenting itself as a complete human wisdom.

In his discussion of the nature of theology, Henry gave the strictest literal analysis of Aristotle's theory of subalternation, as found in the *Posterior Analytics.* Then he declared that none of the philosopher's types exactly fit what Thomas tried to make them fit. In effect, the philosopher never knew a case of subalternation of the kind that Thomas was speaking about.

Godfrey's and Henry's Alternatives to Deductive Theology

Godfrey's critique of Aquinas argued that any conclusion deduced from premisses held on faith could only be a conclusion of faith. In proceeding to such a conclusion or consequent we gain no evidence. The only way in which one might speak of any scientific progress is in the logical realm; we can by correct logical procedure guarantee science of the consequence. This critical side of Godfrey moved at least one later author to place Godfrey in the camp of those who held that theology is a science of consequences. For Godfrey, however, theology is, beyond a science of consequences, a science of Sacred Scripture. In a way that a layman does not, a theologian develops a habit whereby he can show in the texts of Sacred Scripture the justifications or warrants for the truths of the Christian faith. He knows, for instance, that the Trinity and the Incarnation are taught or anticipated in such and such texts of the Old and New Testament. He thus knows not only the truths of the faith as presented in the Creed; he knows the scriptural bases on which the Church supports herself in teaching them. And this knowledge is not just a habit based on memorization. A theologian comes to understand the Scriptures and sees that sense cannot be made of certain passages unless one admits a plurality of persons in God and a plurality of natures in Christ.

Godfrey's full position might even claim more of a role for a theologian than what we have stated so far, but most later portraits of his stance limit him to holding that theology is a science of Sacred Scripture. Theology as a science of Sacred Scripture was far too restrictive for Henry of Ghent, since it seemed to leave aside any knowledge of the realities of which Sacred Scripture speaks. It seemed to him that Godfrey's position abandoned the study of reality to philosophers and awarded simply the study of the sacred texts to the theologians. In question 2 of *Quodlibet XII*, Henry waged his attack on Godfrey:

It is very striking that teachers in every other faculty do their best to praise their science. It is only certain theologians, in an effort to promote philosophy, who put down theology, saying that it is not properly a science and that it cannot make the realities we believe in truly intelligible in the present life. Such theologians block any way of knowing or understanding the things we believe in. They lead others to the point of having no hope of understanding these realities. Surely, this is pernicious, dangerous to those who hear it, and harmful to the Church.

It is in reaction to Godfrey's main thesis, that theology is a science of Sacred Scripture, that Henry of Ghent was forced to pursue another route, which would admit a science of the realities spoken of in the Scriptures and presented by the Church for Christian belief. He claimed that theologians receive extra assistance from God to understand the realities of which the Scriptures speak.

It is important to realize that, for Henry, any certain knowledge that man might attain requires at least God's general assistance or illumination. A helpful analogy might be found by imagining a person inside a cathedral, looking at the colours and shapes of the stained glass windows. What that person immediately focuses on, of course, are the colours and shapes of the figures in the windows. When we reflect on the situation, however, we realize that this person could not see the colours or determine the shapes unless the sun, hidden from immediate perception, were present and active. Similarly, we would grasp nothing for certain, because of the darkness of the objects or the weakness of our sight, unless God, like the sun, were illuminating the objects and assisting our sight. For Henry, this is the general illumination required for any certain knowledge. In the case, however, when a theologian is dealing with the objects of faith, objects beyond man's natural perception even when aided with the general assistance of God's illumination, he needs a special assistance or illumination to grasp these supernatural objects of faith.

Henry presents this special light as a middle light between the light of faith, which elevates men with faith to know, by hearing the authority of Scripture, things that are above anything Aristotle ever grasped. It is also a light below that possessed by the blessed who behold the realities that at one time they may have only believed. This middle light is a special illumination given to theologians, as distinct from laymen and the blessed, to grasp the realities they believe in.

In regard to the divine world, by knowing the natures of the terms of faith, such as 'Father', 'Son', and 'Holy Spirit', he can, by the intellect's search, with the aid of supernatural light [faith] and with special divine illumination [the middle light], come to know that the Holy Spirit proceeds from the Father and the Son, and not from the Father alone. And the same holds for other realities that are proper to the science of theology and that pertain to faith.

The science of theology as developed by Henry thus appeals to a middle light between the light of faith and the light of glory. Theology thereby is very definitely aimed beyond the study of the Scriptures as such to a study of the higher realities of which the Scriptures speak.

Declarative Theology of Peter Aureoli

Criticisms of Henry of Ghent's position were strong. Godfrey thought that Henry was placing theologians beyond academic accountability. They could merely claim a superior light that others lacked. John Duns Scotus points to a predecessor who wondered why students and teachers spent so much time in the classroom sweating over theological arguments rather than in chapel praying for this theological light. In brief, to many theologians Henry seemed to be claiming more than he could warrant.

Peter Aureoli thought that the direction of theology had gone awry since the time of William of Auxerre, often acclaimed as the thirteenth-century apostle of deductive theology. Aureoli gives one of the most extensive discussions on the nature of theology that can be found among medieval authors. He presents in great detail the positions of Thomas, Godfrey, Henry and Duns Scotus, refutes each in terms of his own view of the character of theology, and then tells us what theology is really about.

When we say that he presents and criticizes the opinions of these theologians, he does not simply repeat the critiques others have given of these opinions. It is from his own perspective concerning the nature of theology that he produces his critique. What is that perspective? It is this:

theologians develop many cognitive habits when they study theology. Since they make many deductions, they develop strong logical skills. Since they use among their premisses, besides the premisses of faith, materials from physics and metaphysics, they become very able in Averroes' philosophy of nature and Avicenna's metaphysics. Since they trace revealed truths back to their biblical sources, they become very knowledgable in the texts of the Scriptures. Theologians thus develop cognitive abilities in many fields of learning. Yet none of the intellectual habits that we have mentioned are the proper habit of a theologian. Most recent theology, according to Aureoli, has been led astray from what it is really about. It has been led astray by the limping analogy that the articles of the faith are principles or quasi-principles in theology. Theology in the proper sense is surely about the articles of the faith, but not as principles from which we deduce new truths. It is rather about the articles themselves. Properly speaking, theology is declarative: it brings light to these very articles of the faith.

When Aureoli says that theology is declarative, he means first of all that the theologian, using analogies and probable reasons taken from other sciences, is able to gain and offer some understanding of the things he believes in, and is able to overcome doubts raised against them. He can, furthermore, make clear the meanings of terms that are used to express the truths of the Christian faith, and can appeal to and explain the scriptural bases that sustain these truths. In brief, he is 'ready to render an account of those things that are in him by faith'. Now, none of these abilities makes him believe. His faith is the ground for accepting these truths. Theology is declarative: it is a habit that makes the theologian more clearly grasp with his mind the things that the Church believes in. In the words of St Augustine in Book XIV of *On the Trinity*, theology is the kind of 'knowledge by which the most wholesome faith is begotten, nourished, defended, and strengthened'.

According to Peter Aureoli, Augustine, Thomas Aquinas and all doctors of theology in their practice formed questions concerning the very articles of the faith. They asked: Is there only one God? Is there in God a trinity of persons? Is the incarnation possible? They tried to answer such questions in their *summae* or commentaries on Lombard's *Sentences.* It is not that they doubted their truth. The *question* as a learning instrument was not developed to undermine the faith, nor to produce faith. It was a method designed to bring greater clarity to what they already believed. Instead of speaking of the articles of the faith as principles or premisses, as theologians have done since at least the time of William of Auxerre, Aureoli would have them speak of the articles of faith almost as conclusions. By responding to the *quaestio,* by clarifying the terms employed, by answering objections, by finding suitable analogies, and developing strong arguments, theologians not only make it clearer *that* there is one God, or *that* there are three persons in God, or *that* the incarnation is possible, but they make it clearer how these things are so.

Gregory of Rimini's Case for Deductive Theology

In the opening question of the prologue to his *Commentary on Book I of Lombard's Sentences* in 1342, Gregory of Rimini certainly had Peter Aureoli in mind when he tried to determine what is proper theological discourse. Proper theological discourse must focus, he contends, on the articles of the faith, not on the probable arguments that might be employed to bring some clarity to the articles of the faith. Probable arguments in themselves only beget opinion, and surely theology is not primarily a discipline aimed at producing opinion.

Gregory's own view of properly theological discourse is the type of argument made up of propositions contained in Sacred Scripture or propositions deduced from scriptural propositions. Everyone realizes, he argues, that something is proved theologically when it is proved from the words of Scripture. If a theologian proves that God is eternal and does so on the basis of the eternity of motion, as Aristotle does in Book XII of the *Metaphysics,* he is not involved in theological discourse. If he bases himself on John's Gospel, then this is proper theological discourse. This is the kind of discourse that marks Augustine's arguments in *On the Trinity:* he does not prove the Trinity by probable propositions, but rather by the authority of Scripture. Likewise, when the Church determined as a matter of Christian belief that the Holy Spirit proceeds from the Father and the Son, it did not declare this to be an article of faith because of analogies or probable arguments. It was because the Church saw that this truth followed necessarily from the statements of Sacred Scripture. The ultimate resolution of all theological discourse, according to Gregory, is the truth of the sacred canon of the Scriptures.

It is from the truths of Scripture that all other theological truths are ultimately deduced. Theology, then, according to Gregory, properly is deductive, not declarative.

Theology as Declarative and Deductive

Some theologians, such as Peter of Candia, who commented on Lombard's *Sentences* at Paris in 1378–80, evaluated the declarative theology of Peter Aureoli and the deductive theology of Gregory of Rimini, and judged that both approaches were necessary. He argued that the articles of the faith can, in fact, be appreciated in themselves and also as premisses for extending the domain of faith by deducing further legitimate conclusions. The method followed when the articles of the faith are considered in themselves is a direct or immediate approach to revealed truth; all the truths are seen as parts of a cohesive whole and are affirmed in an equal manner. When the articles of the faith are viewed as premisses, then the theological conclusions drawn from them are not affirmed directly. The believer adheres to them as derived, and as due to his adherence to the premisses from which they are derived and to which he directly assents.

8

Compass of Magical Philosophy

Introduction

The "compass" of philosophy he saw as being at the same time a pointer for directional orientation, the entire scope of a bounded field, and the geometer's tool for figure construction. We planned our book as an enterprise that would justify the title taken in all three senses. Descartes and Leibniz, among others, had talked about the differences in the same city seen from different directions. But they did not explicitly say from *opposite* directions. The reason probably was that they thought such extreme diversity of standpoint would not be appropriate to their intended comparison with philosophy. For as I suggested above in chapter two, it does not usually occur to philosophers that *anyone* could have an opposite concept of "being," "reality," and "actuality" from the one on which they base their own systems. These "orientation" coordinates seem intuitively evident. It is as though no navigator could believe that a compass would not point due north (for Western navigators) or due south (for Chinese explorers and sailors). But unlike actual, as opposed to imagined, navigators' compasses, which come both with *N* and *S* orientations, philosophers' compasses may be oriented to any of *four* metaphysical magnetic poles.

This fact, combined with the unshakable belief in directional invariance, plays hob with the comparison of comprehensive surveys in philosophy (whether we choose to call these metaphysics, or give them some other title). We might well gaze with incredulity at the coordinates taken from a Chinese map when compared to our own. But if there were only the two possibilities, we would sometimes notice the symmetry of their opposition. The practical results of these differences in mapping could be any of several. They might inspire a bloody holocaust by believers in "the true north" against their opponents; or there might be a tolerant skepticism that rejected questions of "direction" altogether; or there might be found a remarkable formula of transformation (at the expense of losing, for both parties, the common sense assurance that goes with having a unique and absolute coordinate location).

It is quite clear in Aristotle (though surprisingly often overlooked) that the Prime Mover acts by an *attraction* from its future that lures each specimen toward full maturity of its type. It is not quite so clear how the Form of the Good acts in Platonism. One reading, at least, would have that action always in the present, always from beyond the flow of time ("above" it in standard Platonic metaphor). These two relations of ultimate explanatory entities to time make it very tempting to equate the *x*-axis of our system scheme with a *time* line, a *t* coordinate, and Aristotelians schematizing the history of philosophy often make just that identification when they deal with Plato. But if we accept that identification, it seems that Aristotelian scientists, concerned with mature or excellent type specimens, must always be looking backward from completed final causes into the realm of change from which they have emerged. The completed final causes exist only in already perfected individual instances along the time line (hence always in a *t* direction from the observer of them) and in the mind of God (whose view of the universe is likewise as a *completed* natural order of perfect species). This way of writing history, then, raises problems for the Aristotelian, who always looks toward a *W* pole though his "natural histories" run toward *E*.

This diagram, with our metaphor of the compass, is so peculiarly able to make sense of Aristotle's criticisms of Plato (and later Aristotelian variations of them) that one is tempted to think Aristotle himself visualized some geometrical pattern of this kind. Reality for Aristotle runs *W* to *E*; and for what is "real," namely substances that are genuinely existent ("separate"), the *y* coordinate is equal to zero. Some formal entities are not equal to zero for the y coordinate, but these are not fully actual (they arise by abstraction, not intuition, and are not "separate"). Aristotle was concerned with the way in which Platonic forms could act causally in time and with the way they were located in a place. He hit upon the present model of divine attraction with a separate but unchanging being as agency, and he located the elusive forms in his Prime Mover's mind. However, all of Plato's formalist diagrams and metaphors of insight ran upward from the *x*-axis in increasing formal extension.

Now, every form with a location where *y* ? o is *separate from* Aristotle's *y* = o axis of actuality. We see here directly why Aristotle insists so constantly on Plato's error in "separating" forms from things. Only those Platonic forms that are also Aristotelian final causes have any temporal causal efficacy if this diagram is taken seriously.

The same way of schernatizing history, with *x* as *t* coordinate, will clear up another point that has puzzled historians of the Academy. At least, I find it very helpful. Aristotle, we recall, after Plato's death, was not elected his successor; and the reason seems ideological as well as personal. Speusippus and Eudoxus had developed a revised Platonism, just as Aristotle did. They saw themselves faced with the same problem, of the causal efficacy of Plato's form in time, that Aristotle had been troubled by. But (here following a line that Plato himself had put forward as a myth or likely story) they chose to have the forms relate to time via a divine creation. In other words, they chose another compass, oriented to the *E* rather than the *N* or *W* pole. (This idea is somewhat inferential; but I start with Eudoxus' claim that he was restoring the philosophy of Anaxagoras, and I note Speusippus' advocacy of emergence in his thesis that the good comes last, if at all. Also there is Aristotle's own account of his difference with Xenokrates about the *Timaeus*, Plato's "mythical" account of creation: Aristotle took this to be historical in its sequence, Xenokrates merely logical. I believe most other Academicians would have sided with Aristotle.) What we have, then, is a -90-degree rotation of the Divided Line, with the *x*-axis still a *t* coordinate, ideas in God's mind, and models used by him.

However we want to modify this figure to account for a possible difference in divine *planning* (from whole to part) and divine construction (sometimes, in Plato's account, this must be from part to whole), causality has become a *creative advance*, an impulse from the past, not a magnet in a posttemporal future. The metaphor of creation explained (I think better than Aristotle's metaphor of love or attraction) the limitations as well as the order of the world we live in. For God did not create the space-time medium he worked in; and so the best work still fell short of non-constructible idealizations. For example, in designing human beings, the creator had to choose between a nobility of life but fragile brevity and a durable but dull longevity. Being Platonic, he of course chose the nobler. Thus it is a consequence of God's work, but not of his will, that we die, and die young.

Aristotle, apparently conceding that this Academic plan would give a "location" (in creative mind) to the forms, argues that the Academicians translate philosophy into the language of mathematical construction plans. "These modern thinkers make mathematics the whole of philosophy." For their part, these members of the early Academy seem less concerned with criticizing Aristotle than with making incredible advances in mathematics and astronomy.

Aristotle groups together Anaxagoras and these later Academicians, both correctly, according to our compass scheme and to what Eudoxus is reported to have said he was doing to revise Plato's metaphysics. But then Aristotle could not understand the possibility of the result, a directed field of force without "forceful" separate individual substances. Academic Platonism, in its -90-degree rotation, retains the field concept of space and time, with time as flow. And the location of the forms in a creator's mind is not satisfactory to Aristotle, either. Plato had said "God always geometrizes," and the creative deity of the Academics seems to have had exactly the mind of a geometer. But that will not, Aristotle argues, give him ideas of concrete substances.

As earlier, these dotted lines are the *x*, *y* coordinates of method and direction. The slanted *t* line, however, is now the time line for a world in evolution, as evolution is treated in the systems of the type III quadrant. The time line changes, however (the underlined dotted line), in the systems of the type II quadrant to an Aristotelian time line, since in these systems evolution of more complex form is not possible.

With a certain justice, I treated the atomic theory as an atomic archive in our systems inventory. I dealt separately with physical, psychological, and semantic atoms, though keeping the claim that in principle the latter two were reducible to physical atomism. This kept us out of mischief. But if we had plotted the atomic theory on our coordinates with *x* as a time line, Plato and Democritus would both have emerged as systems in which $t = o$. Clearly, something is wrong with that, if we take modern philosophy to be a development of the Democritean model. For Democritean time must at least have extension, even if it has no preferred direction. And I had put "Atom" at the *S* pole, as the corresponding entity to the Good, the Prime Mover, and the Demiurge. That transformation seemed wrong somewhere, even if we took the atoms to be fragmented, shattered parts of an original Parmenidean being. But for the time, we let that ride and passed on to a more detailed account of process philosophy.

In our actual writing, Newton Stallknecht could not confine himself to neutral description, but gave such a brilliant presentation and defense of process philosophy that our earlier dispassionate accounts were shot down in flames.

He shifted focus from what we had proposed as a project of formal transformation to a material defense of process thought as philosophy's proper content. (I guess, looking back, that my own carefully neutral system accounts sound more like the work of a Platonic visionary than an Aristotelian taxonomist or a Democritean archivist.) The formalism of our introductory approach did not appeal at all to most contemporary process-oriented readers, who on the whole were Bergsonian in their lack of tolerance for complex abstraction; the material conclusions as to the actual truth coming out of the comparisons did not appeal to our contemporaries who were positivists or Aristotelians. There were no Platonists, so far as I ever learned, so I don't know (but can guess) what they would have thought. I still find very interesting ideas in our joint exploration.

However, as long as anyone myself, Aristotle, Speusippus, Whitehead -takes *x* to be a "time" line, there is no easy way to fit in both the atomic and Platonic theories. Since for both Platonic formalism and Democritean materialism *t* = o, the "actual" forms and "actual" atoms are alike indifferent to time. So are the "logical space" containing forms and the "physical nothingness" insulating atoms from one another. The transformation using the metaphor of compass poles has already been made somewhat irregular by evolution. But now we go from the atemporal *N* orientation +90 degrees to *E*, where *x* ? o, then to the +180 atomic *S*, where again *x* = o. From there, the scheme moves another 45 degrees to the *E* process pole, actually now *SE*. That word "Atom" at the end of the -*y*-axis seems an awkward match for the Good: There should be just the opposite order from elements to complexes as -*y* distance increases. The metaphor of "changing directions" has by now begun to require one Ptolemaic epicycle after another to sustain the figure. (The "Ptolemaic epicycles" are not quite literally descriptive of the inversions plus rotations we must make, but uncomfortably close.)

So the identification of the *x*-axis with a time line from -*t* to + *t*, illuminating as it is for some purposes, and likely to have matched Academic schematic thinking, does not lend itself well to a demonstration of system equivalence. The *E* pole differs by 135 degrees from the *W* pole of the Aristotelian, where the angle should be 180 degrees. (The *EW* distance is +225 and -135.) The Aristotelian *x*-axis must represent, simultaneously, opposed directions of physical history and final causality, one impelled from the past, the other attracted from the future. The identity of Platonism and atomism on the *t*-line (for both, $t = o$) picks out just the wrong property to compare for forms and atoms.

An intricate enough algebra could still compute some kind of equivalences in systems in logical space, but I know I would find it unconvincing. (After all, I recall Leibniz' claim that given *any* ordered set of points, he could find an equation of a curve that would pass through each of them in order.)

So my wife's and my work with systems and their relations had to move on to another stage. The crucial step was to separate the *x*-axis of method and the *t*-axis of temporality. The present chapter shows why the *identification* of these two was so tempting.

Ethics of Metaphysics in Philosophy

This idea is relevant, for after all the philosopher is human, and we would think an insight into reality would at least have to be consistent with this reality that includes a human life. Further, if there is a ground for preference in the lifestyles of applied metaphysics tested by developing each application in its pure, unmixed form we may be content to use something like William James' principle, that beliefs with desirable consequences are pragmatically true, to advocate one theory over the others. This possibility bypasses the metaphysical issue, but I, at least, would consider it seriously.

Unfortunately, as I think I can show, the experiment ends inconclusively. It begins, however, with an interesting promise. For it does seem possible to trace a correlation between even fine details of life-styles and the basic orientations toward reality that underlie them. I could predict, for example, that a Platonist would prefer a large living space that could be organized for different functions (foldaway beds, for example, would fit in here); where an Aristotelian would prefer less grandly expansive, separate functional, social spaces (a separate dining-room, for example, would be attractive). A thorough pragmatist would, as one whom I knew actually did, have house and grounds with *no* determinate spaces from furnace pipes to rose garden borders, there was constant disarray into ongoing projects of reconstruction. On the other hand, a consistent atomist like one I also know will concentrate on fine detail, and change incrementally, if at all. The compulsive concern with detailed neatness goes with complete insensitivity to total overall aesthetics.

So there is a traceable correlation. Let me, then, go on with my pragmatic project, and generalize this into whole life patterns, testing each for its consistency with reality.

Of course, to begin with systems of type IV, it is only by absentmindedness that strict atomists, that is, the group who accept strict metaphysical mechanistic determinism, have an "ethics" at all. But the penchant for analytic distinctions can apparently split objective and subjective domains for separate analysis, overlooking the contradiction. The least deviation from strict consistency in this mechanistic world a free agent observing its dichotomy is represented, not by an official atomist, but by some of the older Stoics. "Man is free," they wrote, "in the way that a dog chained behind a chariot going downhill is free." It can choose to run along or not. Earlier, Democritus had a physiological definition that would make very good sense if only his atoms had some sensitivity: "Happiness is nonperturbation." But then he advises his reader on the way to use a prudential calculus in *choosing* the physiologically most shockproof action. Epicurus and his school think that they must avoid the contradiction of physical determinism and ethical freedom and believe that a revision in physics will solve the problem. Epicurean atoms have a spontaneous, nonpredictable "swerve" that is supposed to leave room for human freedom. It leaves no room, though, as far as I can calculate, for any model of the mind that could exercise prudence and choice, but only explains a Dostoyevskian eccentricity.

Psychological and linguistic atomisms do not seem to me to fare any better. They are like the experiment designed to show that color, a secondary quality, is in fact a subjective contribution of the observer. A disk with a black and white pattern when at rest is set spinning, and the observer now sees it as blue, which is supposed to prove that motion of colorless waves, space, and brain cells can produce perception of apparent blue colors. But what, in the brain, corresponds to the observer who sees the blue in the laboratory experiment? Bertrand Russell once said, "We see a part of our brain." But wait! There is then an infinite regress of "seers" here, in each brain a smaller self who sees the blue appearance of part of its surrounding cortex. Variations on hedonic calculus are in much the same position as regards the hedonic calculator: *Who* is being pleased per moment or perturbed per hour? Not the atoms; not the void; then not any summation of them.

As a life-style, however, I am less concerned with the logical impossibility of this approach than with the tolerance the scheme holds for any sort of intangible coercive authority. Epicurus thought his physical atomism would "free men from fear of the gods." But its criteria of non-existence simply do not apply to imagined immaterial souls or malevolent deities. Atomic science cannot prove that they *are not* there, and if someone has pleasure or pain caused by following supposed supernatural directives, the moralist cannot change this by means of less exciting and self-admittedly inconclusive lectures on transfer of momentum. Sincere belief obviously has a positive hedonic value, regardless of what it is belief *in*. We still are waiting for biochemistry to explain this human anomaly; meanwhile, in the interest of democracy and utility we try to keep it in channels that are not destructive. The situation is awkward; the reader can study it in detail by comparing the text proper and the introduction of B. F. Skinner *Beyond Freedom and Dignity*.

So-called analytic philosophy is a style rather than a doctrine; it originates in the attempted transfer of a logic of natural science to questions of ethics. I think the essential point for my present inquiry was already made by Russell in his characterization of this movement in the *History of Western Philosophy* and in his application of it to education in his model school. We can be precise in finding out what terms mean if we take the trouble (this from Hume). But if that meaning is to have any objective status, it must be possible to connect it definitely with things we can verify or disprove in sense experience. These constitute a domain of knowledge, the remainder being a question of taste and opinion. By this criterion, Russell's own impassioned pacificism and concern with an education that avoids superstition are not any more rational than their contraries.

Hume and Confucius both had high hopes for the results of a clarification of language. It is certainly a sound objective, but in the end, we may find reality reduced to a second intention, if we take the project as the whole of metaphysics. Willard V. Quine's classic essay "What There Is" argues that "to be is to be the value of a bound variable." But the values of bound variables in Quine's article are the early letters of the alphabet, *a, b, c,* and so forth.

The problem of deriving consistent life-styles from metaphysical systems also runs into contradictions for systems of my type III. Again, the metaphysics needs to accommodate the possibility of a metaphysician; and this time, because the method is a dialectical one that admits self-reference, the problem comes to the foreground.

Ethics of the sort encountered in process theory are given a rousing historical send-off by Heraclitus. Death in battle is a noble thing; greater lives gain greater portions; the Ephesians should be hanged for preferring democracy to aristocracy. Unlike the jaded quest for *ataraxia*, freedom from perturbation, of the atomic theorists, we are back here with an ethics congenial to the heroic age of Homer. However much Heraclitus distrusts the old legends and their poets, he is the thinker who best carries on their way of thought. If reality is a one-way flow of time, each individual unique in its feeling, the world poised always for catastrophe and adventure, a romantic ethics is obviously also a "realistic" one.

One way of locating this view in its relation to two of the others is suggested by the psychology of a tripartite personality that still prevails in American criminal law. An "agent" has thought, will, and passion as three "faculties." The second of these, will, may ally itself with one of the other two against the third, or all three may agree on an act committed with "malice aforethought."

Reason

Will Passion (appetite)

Now if the notion of a self is changed by making the will dominant and directive of reason and appetite, what criterion can there be for better and worse action? It seems it will be the degree of commitment, the sheer force of will, that counts here.

The process theories have a self that is a center of creative novelty and one that has a drive toward intensity and originality in its adventures and expressions. We go forward with the flow of time itself, pausing briefly for visions of timeless beauty or a needed rest of peace.

Recall that, typical of this view (for example, in Henri Bergson's claim that metaphysics must exactly reverse the usual direction of reason), there is a rejection of "abstractions," which are deficient in reality. The last thing, then, that a process philosopher exploring ethics is looking for is a carefully balanced code of abstract validity. Whitehead says a number of times that he has little use for "ethics," obviously thinking of technical rule-books in the Greek Sophists' tradition. He goes on to say that ethics reduces to a special case of aesthetics, a kind of "aesthetic harmony," and that its language is not the imperative of law codes and commandments but that of persuasion. (He cites Plato *Timaeus*, where "reason [for the most part] persuades necessity," a passage that the scholar Francis M. Cornford effectively compares with the speech of Athena to the Furies at the end of Aeschylus' *House of Atreus* trilogy.) The problem one stumbles into here comes out clearly in Whitehead. Each "actual occasion" has an appetite for intensity: not conscious, but the driving force in its feeling. The sequence of these attained levels of intensity is what we recognize in physics as a transmission or transfer of electric charge, momentum, light. There are also levels of intensity of realization from simple organisms to higher living societies. The maximum aesthetic value, as we move up the scale, becomes a harmony of contrasts, which must be extended over progressively longer volumes of space and periods of time. The recognition of a musical theme, for example, requires an observer with a span of attention (a "specious present") equal to the time of the thematic statement.

Aesthetic interest accompanies contrast, but the contrast is more satisfying within an experience where it leads on to a resolution. The cumulative effect of multiple levels of contrasts and resolutions, dissonances and concords, is aesthetic harmony. It is because a principle of limitation is reflected in the multiplicity of plenitude that we find satisfaction. And the beauty is greater as the scope and intensity of the components is increased.

Beauty, however, requires novelty and energy ("zest") as well as limitation and harmony. Art must change style as one angle of vision becomes so familiar that it loses a feeling of creativity.

Ethics does not reduce to social expediency or authoritarian obligation. What is socially desirable is to maintain the impulse of adventure through the technical readjustments of art, fine and useful, without crystallizing in the harmony but frozen stability of peace.

The contrast between the goal of stability of the Democritean and the novel creativity emphasized as the goal by the process philosopher is, I believe, firmly grounded in their respective metaphysical determinism and indeterminacy. But a second contrast is that between the quantitative simple elements of concrete experience discovered by the atomic analyst and the infinite qualitative complexity of feeling found in the field-oriented concrete process realm. Something new under the sun is not only possible always but is actual, whether we look through the dark glasses of abstraction or see concretely.

What is good is sensitivity, engagement, competition, romantic love, and a contribution of one's own objectified immortality to cosmic history. The tightly connected occasions that are the history of a self in Whiteheadian process theory (or the successive crests of a continuous wave pattern in others) make it unnecessary to introduce an arbitrary postulate, that the ethicist must calculate future consequences in choosing present actions. For the self and choice are in reality already continuously extended into the future. The atomic theories need to specify an excess of positive over negative atoms of experience *integrated over a given period of time.* The units themselves, when present, have no tight forward connection. "For tomorrow we die" is sound atomistic admonition. "This enjoyment still will be with me tomorrow" is the process way of looking at the same thing.

The trouble is that the counsels of this type III class of ethical theories are couched in terms of what to avoid more than how far to vary course or which way to dodge in order to carry out the avoidance. By making feeling and intuition prior to thought and calculation, what we usually think of as "ethical criteria" are inverted. If we take Aristotle's counsel of "the mean" as selecting a 45-degree line from the go-degree arc of future options, process commends the whole +45 - +90 segment. But if to define the right way only can be done by a negation, the range of acceptable, since non Aristotelian, possibilities is a boundless one.

Now, if there were some law of progress in history, we might take that as a norm. But Hegel and Marx, for example, seem not to match the reversals of fact, while Oswald Spengler and Arnold Toynbee could probably find cycles in any sequence, by selection to match preconception, and by epicyclic additions.

Since we find no grand scale historical plans, there is a fallback to aesthetics. We would at the very least like to find an advance in human aesthetic sensitivity over history. Perhaps professional athletics can replace battles by mercenaries, and superiority in manners can substitute for superior adaptation by use of the stone axe. But the historic record is shot through with ambiguity. We praise the ecology of the South-Western American-Indians, but would never trade ours for their ghost-haunted, bleak subsistence culture. We praise, in schoolbooks, our progress toward liberty, equality, and fraternity; but our political policy may at the same time be accelerating economic inequity and devising ways to bypass democracy in elections.

There is, as a constant in history, however, a haunting wish for immortality through coming time. We want to be preserved personally–if not embalmed, as Egyptian pharaohs were, then sung in epic, like Beowulf and Hector, or, failing that, remembered for all time as part of a great collective deed, as the courageous Spartans at Thermopylae.

All thinkers of this type existentialist, Heraclitean, Whiteheadian, Bergsonian, Nietzschean, Schopenhauerian define the Good as something well outside the Aristotelian mean. Their theories are self-consistent in a way that atomism was not: All things have force admixed, and existence in time inspires pursuit of glory. The process philosopher would not care for tranquility, even if the atomist could offer it by microsurgery on some mechanical "soul organ" of small round atoms.

Turning now to systems of type II, we discover that perhaps the most consistent deduction of an ethics from a metaphysics is to be found in Aristotle. The central reality of independent substances, the presence of genuine contingency, the natural drive toward maturity, and the reflexive rationality of prudence–all these combine to form a world in which happiness can be defined and recognized. We have seen how Aristotelian practical science seems to take place by the substitution of one set of final causes by another, the pig turned into pork.

The problem for Aristotelian ethics is the considerable latitude in determining the final cause of man and the much more variable, but socially operative, *apparent* final causes of man. Reason, which enters nature with the human species, always has a "double potency." Thus a human character is a set of habits reflecting repeated choices that have become a "second nature." There is, though, a natural range and direction that limits human choices and a limiting final cause for man, though it is indeterminate in fine detail.

The Aristotelian project in ethics is to compose an inventory of the potentialities of a rational animal and to trace them to a portrait of full maturity in which earlier errors have not foreclosed later perfections, and good fortune has cooperated with good natural capacity.

The *Nicomachean Ethics* traces the stages of maturity, moving from the immature person-to-be pushed around by external praise and blame to the self-disciplined adult. The stages move from self-control through objectivity in social participation to a kind of self-enlargement in friendship and a final godlike contemplation of the order of nature, in which the self is at home.

The most important faculty for us, as self-creating, is prudence, practical wisdom, which is an ability to apply general rules, to anticipate consequences, and to redirect desires away from dangerous extremes. The Platonic problem of "participation" recurs here, reminding us that we are dealing with a formalism, though a compartmental one.

The metaphysics gives us, as foundation of our practical enterprise, an egocentric world with a general direction of orientation toward maturity and a predictable context that we should explore. The first main problem is *discipline*: We have a capacity for habit formation by nature, but no inherited habits. We have the power to decide between opposites and an inner compass of a sort of cosmic direction ("All things desire god"). But metaphysically considered, all stages of human life prior to full maturity at the age of 49, Aristotle indicates, are deprivations, needing *remedial* action. The teleology stresses future attainment, where the process philosopher would concentrate more on present engagement.

Aristotle, with the technique of an anatomist, undertakes a description of the moral habits and intellectual skills to be balanced in a self-respecting, socially well-adapted personality. Where Plato had talked about *metron*, "measure," as the intersecting point of ideal and instance, Aristotle talks about to *meson*, "the middle." For him, the two pretty much coincide; a type specimen is the measure appropriate to Plato's theory.

In the background of this anatomy of human character development is a theme that unites the ethics and metaphysics more tightly than most readers have noted: the desire for *autarchy*, self-rule. Nature is organized in a scale of entities that become progressively more self-sufficient and self-directed, and the attraction of final causality can also be described as the desire to be godlike in self-sufficiency. This motif rises to the surface in the argument-puzzling to commentators working from other philosophic points of view that contemplation is superior to action. The reason is that action depends on external instruments, opportunities, companions, while contemplating can be done independently. Aristotle, however, does not, as Plotinus did, characterize action simply as a "lower form of contemplation." In fact, he cannot, since although autarchy is the attractive aim, existence in Aristotle's world of nature is an *activity*.

The splendid objectivity of Aristotle's description takes place retrospectively, from the standpoint of an attained happiness. The picture from this vantage point is not a very optimistic one. Everyone can have *some* degree of balanced well-being, but true happiness is reserved only for a few persons of unusual excellence; in fact, one might conclude from the *Ethics* that the only fully human individual ever was Aristotle himself.

One special problem arises from the fact that intellectual insight is not the same as habit, though Aristotle thought Socrates had confused the two. So special attention must be paid to avoiding a split between a mature mind, which knows what is right, and a wayward character, which follows its own habits contrary to reason in pursuit of pleasure. (Modem psychoanalysis recurs to this theme, particularly in its concept of "fixation," a point of arrest in emotional maturity.)

Virtues must be learned by practice, not by lecture-so Aristotle tells his lecture audience.

Habits of action, not units of sensation, are the basis of Aristotle's analysis. To be human is to have and exercise natural functions. Level by level, Aristotle sees a personality develop. At the outset, we have a passive center of experience, guided by praise and blame of family and society. As the person becomes more adult, sharing in social responsibilities is learned; and intellectual skills are being developed along the same path. But intellectual maturity requires a longer time and more insight than social and emotional development. The overlapping levels of experience run from temperance through justice to wisdom.

And excellence is the result of fulfilling a normal drive toward human maturity. Where no rules can be given for the best process-oriented life. Aristotle's lectures were studded with techniques of self-evaluation and charts of specific virtues and vices, each virtue flanked by two off-course extremes.

If the trouble with atomist and process ethics was that neither was a specifically human life, the one devoted to the taking of pleasure and the avoidance of pain, the other to pure adventure and engagement, Aristotle's system seems to fail in a different way. His ideal case of full self-realization is not a life any more. The completely wise man is wholly self-sufficient; he may enjoy friends, but doesn't need even them. At home in a cosmic scale of contemplation, the excellence that has guided our aim throughout the *Ethics* is a completely isolated, self-enclosed life: upset by no passion, no conflict of what we want and what we know to be right, no motivation to engage in contests for prizes we deserve but do not compete for, a reconciliation with the order of nature. Short of that, the excellence that Aristotle recommends does run the risk of identifying the mean with the mediocre. The best society in general will be predominantly middle class. It cannot hope for happiness for slaves, children, women, or the working class; and for the adult males of the middle class, the requisite goods are not always available for the leisure that happiness requires. The ethics fits a metaphysical scene where species run true to type, though the human species admits an unusual range of varieties some of which Aristotle's most noteworthy student, Theophrastus, classified in a study, *Characters*.

The ethics of Platonism may be quite different from the ethics presented in Plato's dialogues. In fact, in my chapter on the next adventure of pure reason in history, I shall argue that it is different and can be revised to make it more satisfactory. But for the present comparison, I shall stay with those explicit texts that Platonists from the third century onward took as unqualified literal philosophical dogma and ethical prescription.

The ethics of Platonism is idealistic rather than romantic. There is a constant awareness of the forms refracted back through future time as the ideals that we want to realize as our own identities. This desire for full realization is our appetite for immortality, combining love of truth, rightness, and beauty. The metaphysics of field and form, with stable form limiting and attracting instances in flow, gives an ethics of pursuit of value, of wholeness, and at least of the immortality that comes from a realized identification of ourselves with an eternal good.

The quest for immortality is strenuous. Yet, if Odysseus' life was one he would not choose to live again (as is the case in one of Plato's myths that portrays him selecting a next incarnation). Socrates could not choose a life different in kind. Wherever his reincarnation lay, it would have a fixed star setting its course of inquiry and engagement and assurance that holding firm would bring ample adventure, not terror, exhaustion, or boredom.

Platonic idealism is a complex case in the study of the ethical projection of metaphysical systems. In spite of Socrates' example, the distance between ideal and actual may lend itself to a strategy of escape from the actual altogether, or an ironic skepticism that dismisses the relevance of the ideal. Plato's accounts of lower levels of knowing and existence can easily be misread and in fact, out of context, leading passages invite the misreading–as a program for rejection. And idealization can prove a dangerous strategy, as it does in the chivalrous idealization of women; they are *too* like a disembodied form to share in mundane prudential affairs, such as property ownership or public policy decisions.

The "Platonism" of the Hellenistic scene shared with the other schools of that era a materialist metaphysical direction until the sudden reversal of Neoplatonism transformed it into a dogmatic formalism. It is this revolutionary "new" Platonism that I will compare here, a much simplified and a more dogmatic version than its Hellenic original.

The two realms, those of form and creation, are maintained; but moral excellence becomes identified with an escape into the realm of forms, an escape that seems, metaphorically, a sudden ascent by instant supranatural illumination. Plato's mythology is now construed as the world's literal history. There is a divine creation (in Christianity, at least, from nothing, not from pre–existent matter) and a history of fall from a golden age to a last judgment. Piety now comes forward as a primary virtue. And piety means not being distracted by the created world, while admiring the eternal form and the Creator. Plotinus' succinct "action is a lower form of contemplation" is taken dead seriously.

Heaven and earth reflect a hierarchical order; so does, or should, human society. The idea of historical social progress does not fit into that picture. Still, some of us must compromise with the need for action, and for at least the necessary pleasures attendant on living. So a secondary this-worldly order of crusades, markets, and tenant farming goes along with the focus on otherworldly immortality.

It is this strongly polarized, religiously oriented, Neoplatonism that was the "Platonic tradition" whose restyling in the thirteenth century was brought about through the discovery and translation of Aristotle's texts.

The end of Aristotelian authority in the sixteenth century, though its eventual outcome proved to be modern science, also included a revolutionary recovery of a classical, humanistic "Platonism." The pagan Plato that the Renaissance recovered showed itself as far more this-worldly than the long Christian Augustinian tradition had taught. And its fondness for mathematics spilled over from the naturalism of fine art and the classicism of history of science to harmonies and observations of the new "scientific" scheme.

During the subsequent scientific age, Platonism was strategically relegated to theology. It was released, but exactly inverted, by the new energies of "process philosophies." Let the forms be transmuted from pure actualities to open future alternatives for evolutionary selection and the accommodation follows. But in this cabinet of varied options, values are now on the side of the concrete, not the abstract.

To sum up this moment of inquiry: We asked whether a metaphysics entailed a system of ethics, and if so whether, on William James' pragmatic principle, we could escape metaphysical argument because one of the systems so obviously excelled in this application. The answer to the first question, whether a metaphysics implies a class of ethical systems, dictating to them its direction and method, can be answered in the affirmative.

The following table shows the first explanatory principle of each metaphysical system and the deduced type of human life that is "most realistic" in a world where that principle is the criterion of reality. The causal connection is, I think, quite clear.

Form of the Good: love as desire for immortality	**Prime Mover:** happiness as full autarchy (love of self)
Demiurge: love of power, novelty, creativity positive increments of harmless pleasure	**Conservation Laws:** love of egocentric tranquility;

The answer to the second question is negative. No one of the pure ethical systems following consistently from a metaphysics is clearly superior as the prescription for or description of the good human life. Two of the cases seem not to be "lives." These are the atomistic theories, where sheer anesthesia would be calculated out as an ideal case of non-perturbation; and the Aristotelian, where full self-contemplative substantial independence, contemplating oneself as the same eternal order, would be a satisfaction hard to tell from catatonia. The other two cases seem not to be "human." A pure assimilation to violence and action does not distinguish a human life from the other venturesome and predatory branches of some "vital force" developing itself though evolution in various lines of natural selection. We could hardly tell the life of human beings from that of sharks. But the escapism of a Platonic formalism that discards time in favor of assimilation to contemplation of higher, non-temporal form, is an escape motivated by perpetual irony, in fact unattainable anyway, and explicitly non-human in its disgusted rejection of the natural order.

Although the systems we have described as basic philosophic families seem to be mutually exclusive, clearly the lives that fall within the class of "human life" at all must be "mixed" in some way, not consistent, pure applications.

It is clear, too, that the strategy of holding a sale of lives, hoping to bypass metaphysics by a pragmatic assessment that would single out one option as attracting the highest bidders, is not an open one. Either ethics cannot be realistic, or the systems of metaphysics cannot be exclusive, as our analysis has suggested that they must be.

The generalizations are then consistently extended to create a systematic explanatory scheme of concepts. The outcome, however, has been not just one such system but four. Now, so far as the abstract structures compared in chapter 5 are concerned, we have seen that even diagonally opposed schemes can be made conceptually intelligible to each other; that is, they are recognized as consistent formally. But at the same time, this is accompanied by a conviction that things that fit the alien frame, so different from those our common sense expects, are not actual. The other system may be logically consistent, but we would like to dismiss it as only hypothetical.

It proves, however, to be a fact that some things and events that exactly illustrate the opposed system and would have seemed, a priori, impossible in our own, force themselves on our attention. The result is a new relation between these systems; it is not a recognition of equal truth, but rather a feeling of magic that comes from encountering something we thought only fictional as actual. And this odd actuality is a thing that the philosophers whom we thought were unaccredited have predicted and are quite at home with.

So the relations along diagonals of my scheme not only represent an intellectual sense of mutual unintelligibility but also a feeling of fascination as we experience things that match the system alien to our own, things we would otherwise have entertained as only hypothetical. These things that match the other system, furthermore, usually appear in areas where we ourselves have not worked out much detail; and they sometimes prove to be very hard to explain. Of course, some odd appearances are only illusions; but something as evident as a talent for original musical creativity cannot be dismissed as one of them, nor can the simulated mathematical intelligence of an inanimate calculating machine. There is an excess of actuality over what the common sense based on any given metaphysics would expect, and this may explain why each of the four alternative systems renews its vitality, even after periods of suppression and latency.

For the moment, however, my concern is with the cross-system feeling, not with historical viability. I think, in fact, as I have said, that I was the occasion of my wife's discovery of the diagonal "magic" and its fascination. I am a Platonist by temperament, used to dealing with forms that take on space-time shape by way of minds and souls. But I have always been fascinated by calculating machines, digital or algorithmic. Mathematics obviously requires intelligence; in fact, digital sequences are the content of the messages we have designed to reach possible intelligences in other planetary systems. What am I to make, then, of a box of cogwheels that performs calculations faster and more exactly than I can? (I here will take the most elementary case an adding machine I recall from some years ago to make my point, because its operation is so obviously by mere transfer of momentum; electricity might suggest something less patently material.) Wheels with gear teeth do not have souls or intelligences. Yet the assemblage does, somehow, outdo me at addition. I cannot resist taking off the top of the machine, "just to see what's inside." Here is, indeed, a feeling of magic.

To generalize: Let us look at this cross-system feeling for each of the four pairs in turn. I will start with the Platonist (and the relation between systems I and IV). The Platonist is an archstructuralist who sees, for example, a symbolic and an efficient gesture as the same. This overlooking of non-formal differences in the light of similar symbolic structures can be quite disconcerting. For example, it can take such forms as "mopping the floor" that leaves twigs and puddles in the center; or "cleaning a rifle" that ends up with rust still in the barrel. It can work, too, as it does in my encounter with the adding machine, for where there is something that acts like an intelligent agent, the Platonist feels immediately that there must be some kind of soul present. Of course, after taking the machine apart, I see that my feeling was wrong. It imitates one special operation of intelligence, but while it can count, it can never write philosophy or fall in love. But it certainly is ingenious, and to me magical.

The I-IV magic works much more strongly, of course, for a modern computer, so far as the mental operations it can simulate are concerned; but the absence of mind or soul is not so tangibly, so inescapably obvious on the scale and speed of recent hardware as it is, invincibly, in the older cogand-axle machine. This experience, like an encounter with a Martian in its divergence from a built-in sense of normalcy, answers any question we may have had about the visibility of entities from other metaphysical systems. For the other three cases as for the I-IV diagonal there are things that we do in fact encounter, but feel to be intruders from beyond what we took to be normal and then absentmindedly generalized into what we took to be possible.

The IV-I effect of magic, for the atomist, lies in the whole domain of immaterial realities. The Platonic forms of mathematics unchangeable, public, wholly intangible are mysterious but demand recognition as objective. "Insight" is mysterious; so, of course, is any sort of "subjectivity." Since the primary criterion of reality for this philosophic family is some sort of *tangibility* (as *visibility* is for the Platonic systems), the whole domain of souls, persons, spirits, cosmologies, and non-computable constants is nonstandard. Enthusiasm often goes with a loss of any familiar criteria. Thus in physics today, there are some advocates of the thesis that since life is so improbable, only cosmic prevision can account for it. This is an elementary error in probability theory, but not a computable one. And for several generations, British analytic philosophers were enthusiastic patrons of spirit mediums and other experimenters with the occult. But we do not need to find anything occult to confront the atomist with something alien and a bother to explain. What about the mathematical expression .9999...= 1? The computer will run until doomsday without deciding the truth or falsity of that equation. Historically, we find this cross-system sense of magic admitted when Lucretius opens his toughminded account of the atomic universe with a hymn to love (which presupposes something just the opposite of his later statement that "poetry is an arrangement of letters").

What is magical to an Aristotelian, whose system family is type II, is the kind of novel creation that is found in fine art and paradigmatic in systems of type III. In a type II world, where things run true to form in fixed kinds, the creation of a unique new specimen is arresting. For example, Aristotle could not do much to explain artistic creativity. He said that the gift of metaphor cannot be taught and rests on a talent that (like that of dream interpretation) lies close to madness. "Imitation" is his characterization of fine art. But this is exactly what we do *not* find as the differentia of creative advance. An Aristotelian sense of the magic of creative artistry explains one side of the phenomenon of patronage. Ludwig II of Bavaria was fascinated by Richard Wagner, Frederick of Prussia by J. S. Bach, and Pericles, like statesmen ever since, admired and supported tragedians. To find something outside all previous taxonomy is like the surprise of Faust's student, Wagner, when in fact the small homunculus appeared in his laboratory flask. Besides, the artist may offer his patron immortality in sculpture, coin design, portraiture, or an onstage dramatic role.

The magic of patronage works the other way as well. This is the magic between systems of type III and those of type II. The creative artist can imagine plots, characters, and spectacles at leisure; but none of these imaginations creates a very real world of history. The criteria of aesthetic coherence make no distinction between the vivid fancy and the stubborn fact, yet the artist is the creator of one and only a spectator and participant, willing or not, of the other. To have mere plans and wishes become institutions and laws in historical space and time is the sort of thing the creative thinker finds magical. So the artist is attracted by his patron and does not compete with him. He is still puzzled, no doubt, over why this should be the actual history, rather than any of a thousand others. And the artist often wishes that his fantasies, too, could legislate for reality.

This cross-system attraction has now been found for each of the four diametrically opposed system pairs. The sense of magic arises when something makes us pay attention to extraordinary phenomena that at first seem outlandish intruders in the world of our ordinary inventory of normal things. Each intruder, though, in effect carries a letter of introduction: "If you are a metaphysician, and I am actual, I have a right to be recognized in your system." And that is right; we were so occupied with achieving precision somewhere else that we had neglected this particular area of the system until this strange thing forced us to notice it. But then it will probably prove to have a place, after all maybe an "unimportant" or "incurably vague" one. Consider the

IIV relation again. Plato and his students had not paid much attention to the operation of aesthetics on the level of simple particles until their attention was caught by the success of Democritean explanations of technology, using the postulate that atoms come in all shapes and sizes ("for why should they be one rather than another?"). The Academy must have worked for weeks, packing spaces with small blocks shaped like four of the five regular solids in different sizes. They needed to show that some conditions of value held as axioms in their atomic stereometry. This odd branch of formalism, packing and spacing of regular solids, would have stayed lost in a dusty corner forever if Democritus' work had not turned a spotlight on this group of phenomena needing explanation. In the end, Plato and his colleagues did explain the making of glass, tempering of iron, passage of light through air and water, even the underlying geometry of youth and age. In turn, their medical research turned up something Plato challenged the empirical doctors to explain: that ideas could cause physiological symptoms. This theory remains a problem for any physiology that recognizes only toxins and traumas; it does not surprise an Anaxagorean or Aristotelian.

In recent history, I did not dream, when I was teaching educational theory, that a cheap personal computer for every student could someday relieve fifthgrade drill in the tedious algorithm of long division with dozens of ill-mated pairs of numbers. Nor did the Aristotelians who opposed "symbolic logic" fifty years ago recognize the potentialities for information-handling in its elegance of simple truth-value operations. Their natural language "syllogism" (a word that also meant "calculation" in Aristotle's time) probably carried about 512 more bits of information than a 1 and 0 sequence in propositional calculus, but at a cost of considerable, slow inelegance.

So, even if I find it apractically unending job to give an exact abstract definition of what is a paradigmatic typical entity of another metaphysical system, because my own vocabulary has built in presuppositions that never wholly fit, I know that there is, in application, some mutual visibility.

What I am insisting on is that we can have a feeling for the non-hypothetical relevance of systems exactly other than our own, even when we have no rational proof that their formulations are consistent. The origin of systems in experience, and an experience in the domain of actuality, ensures that each has some existential application, and we must be able to grant this and at least be fascinated by the fact. My transformations show that there is no contradiction in form between system families; they say nothing about the respective ease, difficulty, or region of fit of that form to content. It seems that actuality will continue to make us reconsider any closed notion of what is a possibility, and so long as that holds, there can be profitable interaction between diverse systems of metaphysics, even if, formally, each would like to consider the other coherent but irrelevant. How the constructive interaction can be created will be the subject, in two stages, of the following two chapters. The project is both an interesting one and necessary if philosophy is to pursue its ideal of comprehensiveness in description and explanation.

Magic is a faculty of wonderful virtue, full of most high mysteries, containing the most profound contemplation of most secret things, together with the nature, power, quality, substance and virtues thereof, as also the knowledge of whole Nature, and it doth instruct us concerning the differing and agreement of things amongst themselves, whence it produce its wonderful effects, by uniting the virtues of things through the application of them one to the other, and to their inferior suitable subjects, joining and knitting them together thoroughly by the powers and virtues of the superior Bodies. This is the most perfect and chief Science, that sacred and sublimer kind of Philosophy, and lastly the most absolute perfection of all most excellent Philosophy. For seeing that all regulative Philosophy is divided into Natural, Mathematical and Theological: (Natural Philosophy teach the nature of those things which are in the world, searching and inquiring into their causes, effects, times, places, fashions, events, their whole and parts also.

Their track Abbaris the Hyperborean, Charmondas,

Danigeron, Eudoxus, Hermippus followed. There were also other eminent, choice men, as Mercurius Tresmegistus, Porphyrius, Iamblicus, Plotinus, Proclus, Dardanus, Orpheus the Thracian, Gog the Grecian, Germa the Babylonian, Apollonius of Tyana. Osthanes also wrote excellently of this Art, whose books being as it were lost, Democritus of Abdera recovered, and set them forth with his own Commentaries. Besides, Pythagoras, Empedocles, Democritus, Plato, and many other renowned Philosophers travelled far by sea to learn this Art; and being returned, published it with wonderful devoutness, esteeming of it as a great secret. Also it is well known that Pythagoras and Plato went to the Prophets of Memphis to learn it, and travelled through almost all Syria, Egypt, Judea, and the Schools of the Chaldeans that they might not be ignorant of the most sacred Memorials and Records of Magic, as also that they might be furnished with Divine things.

9

Henry of Ghent and Duns Scotus in Philosophy

Introduction

Reckoned to have been born in Ghent sometime before 1240, Henry undertook early studies at the cathedral school in Tournai, where he maintained lifelong and influential connections. He studied theology at Paris, where he became master in 1275 and actively taught and disputed for nearly twenty years. As a young master, Henry participated in Bishop Stephen Tempier's sweeping actions against Aristotelianism at Paris in March of 1277 involving the arts faculty, Giles of Rome, and certain doctrines of Aquinas. In fact, personal remarks by Henry about these closely connected events provide otherwise unknown details. Henry himself says that he sat on Tempier's episcopal commission *(assessores episcopi)* of sixteen masters that produced the syllabus of 219 propositions condemned by Tempier on 7 March 1277. The syllabus comprised in large measure the more extreme Aristotelian and Arabic philosophical positions taught in the arts faculty. Henry certainly represented a critical attitude to Aristotelianism on the commission, and indeed several articles on Tempier's syllabus appear traceable to him. Henry was also present at the immediately ensuing meetings of the theology faculty that resulted in the censure of the younger theologian, Giles of Rome, and in the masters' own condemnation of Aquinas's doctrine of unicity of substantial form. Henry's Augustinian orientation, so evident in Tempier's actions, continued throughout his career, encountering new Aristotelian foes within the faculty after 1285, when Giles of Rome was rehabilitated at the order of Honorius IV and Godfrey of Fontaines became master. A secular, Henry was also known as a strident critic of the mendicant privileges granted by Martin IV in 1281. His opposition was such that he was reprimanded and suspended in 1290 by the future Boniface VIII. Henry's death is usually given as 29 June, 1293.

Henry's two major works are the direct products of his long teaching career at Paris. The first is his *Summa of Ordinary Questions* and the second his fifteen series of *Quodlibetal Questions.* Cross-references establish that both works were disputed and written concurrently over the length of his career. His regular or 'ordinary' questions derived from his disputations held as master during the normal course of term. Revised for publication as a massive *Summa,* these ordinary questions represent Henry's systematic investigation of the nature of theology (articles 1-20), the divine nature and attributes (articles 21-52), and the Trinity (articles 53-75). Henry intended his *Summa* to include a part on creatures, but he never completed it. As such, Henry's *Summa* corresponds roughly in plan to the first forty-three questions of the first part of Aquinas's own *Summa theologiae,* yet approaches Aquinas's entire work in length. Unlike ordinary questions, which were disputed by the master at regular class hours throughout the academic year, quodlibetal questions were special university disputations only held before Christmas and Easter. Here the questions were not posed by the master himself on controlled topics, but by the audience, on any issue of interest. Hence they were designated *quodlibetales* or 'on anything whatever'.

Accordingly, while ordinary questions allowed for systematic investigation, quodlibetal questions forced the master to address the current controversies in the university community that at times involved the master himself. Henry's fifteen quodlibetal disputes represent one for nearly every academic year from 1276 to 1292. Each dispute itself contains up to forty separate questions, which were considerably expanded and revised by Henry for publication, including lengthy insertions, cancellations and digressions. Henry brought the quodlibetal question to its apex as a literary form of scholastic theology and was the first to make the quodlibet a principal vehicle for his thought.

Duns Scotus

It is perhaps no exaggeration to claim that less is known with certainty about the life, career and works of Duns Scotus than about any scholastic thinker of his rank. Aside from his own writings, only six slight documents provide what scattered facts are known of his life. Of Scottish origin, Scotus is thought to have been born about 1266, on the basis of the established date of his ordination to the priesthood on 17 March, 1291. The once widely accepted details of Scotus's place of birth, family, early education and entry into the Franciscan order are now considered unreliable owing their source to the discredited chronicle *Monasticon Scoticanum* of Marian Brockie. From about 1288, Scotus studied theology at Oxford, although it is disputed whether this was interrupted after his ordination in 1291 by several years of study at Paris. In either case, Scotus was certainly studying theology at the Oxford convent by 1300. On 6 July, 1300, he was one of twenty-two Franciscans from the Oxford diocese presented to John Dalderby, bishop of Lincoln, for permission to hear confessions. About this same time, he was beginning to revise his lectures on the *Sentences,* given as a bachelor at Oxford. This revised commentary on the *Sentences,* known as the *Ordinatio*, was under way in 1300, because in the prologue Scotus himself says that he is writing in that year. Further evidence of his activities as bachelor at Oxford during this same period is given by his participation in a disputation of the Franciscan master Philip Bridlington, who was also in the same group presented to Dalderby. Scotus, however, never incepted as master at Oxford. He was instead sent in the autumn of 1302 to study theology at Paris, where he began a new set of lectures on the *Sentences*. These were interrupted in June 1303 when, together with some eighty other Franciscans, he was expelled from France for declaring allegiance to Pope Boniface VIII against Philip the Fair in their escalating dispute over taxation of church property. Where Scotus went during his exile from Paris is unknown, but it is commonly assumed that he either returned to Oxford or went to Cambridge, where he is believed to have lectured at some point in his career. Scotus was back in Paris at the latest by the autumn of 1304 to finish lecturing on the *Sentences*. It is inferred that Scotus must have incepted as master at Paris by early 1305, because in a letter dated 18 November, 1304, Gonsalvus of Spain, the newly elected Minister General of the Franciscans and the Franciscan regent master when Scotus first arrived at Paris, recommended Scotus as next in line for promotion to master. In his letter, Gonsalvus testifies to Scotus's reputation, which he says had 'already spread everywhere'. During his regency at Paris, Scotus held one quodlibetal disputation and debated with the Dominican William Peter Godinus on the principle of individuation. For reasons unknown, Scotus was replaced as the Franciscan regent at Paris by Alexander of Alexandria in the autumn of 1307 and abruptly transferred to the Franciscan convent in Cologne, where he is listed as a lector in early 1308. Nothing is known of his activities during his Cologne period. Before his career could reach full maturity and with his major work the *Ordinatio* still in a state of revision, Scotus died in Cologne later that year, where he remains buried today. The date of his death is traditionally given as 8 November, 1308.

As with the details of his life and career, uncertainty about Scotus's writings is unparalleled for a medieval thinker of his stature. While much progress has been made in establishing Scotus's genuine corpus, important questions of chronology and canon still remain. Scotus's genuine works can be divided into philosophical and theological writings, and roughly speaking the former are regarded as earlier. Scotus's logical works are generally considered to be his earliest. These include sets of questions on Porphyry and the *Categories,* two works on *De interpretatione,* and questions on the *Sophistical Refutations*. The important *Questions on the Metaphysics* have traditionally been considered an earlier work as well, though somewhat later than the logical treatises, but this has been disputed by commentators since the sixteenth century. Current evidence suggests that the latter books, VII-IX (only the first nine books are authentic), show revision from later in Scotus's career, perhaps even very late. Finally, there are two philosophical works that fall outside this main group owing to uncertainty over their dating and degree of authenticity: questions on *On the Soul* and the *Theoremata*. While *On the Soul* is surely Scotistic, manuscripts attest that it has been edited by a follower of Scotus *(scotellus),* perhaps Antonius Andreas (d. *c.* 1320). Both manuscripts and contemporaries assign the *Theoremata* to Scotus, but their authenticity has been debated owing to a section entitled *Treatise on Articles of Faith (Tractatus de creditis),* which denies the philosophical demonstrability of the existence of God.

The bulk of Scotus's reputation rests, however, on his more mature and longer theological writings. These are essentially four: various versions of his commentaries on the *Sentences,* two sets of disputes known as *Collationes,* a set of twenty *Quodlibetal Questions,* and the *Treatise on God as First Principle (De primo principio)*. The textual situation of Scotus's commentaries on the *Sentences* is one of the most complicated in medieval scholarship. First of all, Scotus lectured on the text at Oxford, again at Paris and, at an undetermined time, at Cambridge. Second, his secretaries and students conflated these different versions in an effort to fill in places apparently left incomplete at his death. Finally, Scotus revised by means of numerous additions and annotations to the primitive text, so that these had to be distinguished from the intrusions inserted by his students and secretaries. The better part of modern textual criticism on Scotus has been devoted to teasing apart these various versions and layers of his

Sentences. This research has established that there are two versions of his Oxford *Sentences,* an earlier *Lectura,* which was then considerably expanded to form the *Ordinatio,* previously termed the *Opus oxoniense*. As indicated, Scotus read the *Sentences* again when he went to Paris in the autumn of 1302, which commentary survives as neither a *lectura* nor an *ordinatio* but as what students' reports called *reportationes*. A major point of dispute is the chronological relation of these *Parisian Reports (Reportationes parisienses)* to the Oxford *Ordinatio*. The long-held view was that Scotus constructed the *Ordinatio* from both the early Oxford *Lectura* and the Parisian *Sentences,* rendering the *Ordinatio* later than the Parisian commentary and according it a status as the most definitive of Scotus's works. Recent studies have tended to revise this view, placing at least the first book of the *Ordinatio* before rather than after the corresponding part of the Parisian *Sentences*. This revised chronology seems required not only by Scotus's own statement dating the prologue of the *Ordinatio* to 1300, two years prior to his theological studies in Paris, but also by the Parisian commentary's noticeable independence in organization, topic and treatment relative to both of its Oxford counterparts. Scotus's two series of *Collationes,* one held at Oxford and the other at Paris, are known from the eye-witness testimony of his secretary, William of Alnwick, to represent the proceedings of oral disputation. It has been suggested that these *Collationes* were exercises carried out by Scotus within the Franciscan houses while still a bachelor, but this is not certain. His *Quodlibetal Questions* are assigned to his regency at Paris, perhaps in the academic year 1306/7. As the product of a formal university disputation by a regent master in theology, they must certainly be regarded as Scotus's mature thought. Finally, the *De primo principio* is a systematic treatise on the transcendentals, containing Scotus's proof for the existence and infinity of God. While the authenticity of the *De primo* is uncontested, it none the less betrays the influence of an editor. More than half of the *De primo* has been supplied verbatim from the *Ordinatio,* indicating that it is to some extent a compilation of material. Despite this, it has received more contemporary attention by way of translation and commentary than any other single work in Scotus's corpus.

Relation of Henry of Ghent to Duns Scotus

Henry's significance, both historically and philosophically, stems from his position in the thirteenth century of having an important and immediate relationship to both Aquinas and Scotus. On the one side, Henry mounted the most sustained and sophisticated Augustinian response in the later thirteenth century to the Aristotelianism of Aquinas. Adopting a critical attitude towards Aristotle on fundamental points, Henry returned to more Augustinian principles, which he infused with certain elements of Avicenna. In comparison with Aquinas, Henry can fairly be said to exhibit a doctrinal tendency called Avicennizing Augustinianism', a label coined by Etienne Gilson to describe the exploitation by certain scholastic thinkers of similarities between Augustine and Avicenna, such as their mutual denial of knowledge by abstraction. Thus, where Aquinas argues 'according to Aristotle and the truth' *(secundum Aristotelem et veritatem rei),* Henry will instead argue 'according to Augustine, Avicenna, and the truth'. In particular, Henry reverted to certain positions considered Augustinian by thirteenth-century standards, such as the compatibility of faith and demonstration, a need for a special divine illumination in natural knowledge, a heavy emphasis on the reality of the divine ideas and their role in both knowledge and creation, and above all a strong voluntarism against the intellectualism of Aristotle. Henry specifically criticized Aquinas on numerous points, including the concept of theology as a sub-alternated science, the exclusivity of faith and demonstrative reasoning, the definition of self-evidence and related criticism of Anselm's ontological argument, the pre-eminence given to Aristotle's argument for the unmoved mover, the denial of any positive knowledge of God's essence *(quid est)* in the present life, the limitation of each Aristotelian separate form or angel to a species in itself, the real distinction of essence and existence (at least as defended by Giles of Rome), the indemonstrability of the temporal beginning of the world, and a variety of theses connected to the relationship of the intellect to the will. In the words of one of Henry's editors, 'No theologian immediately after the death of Aquinas so sharply criticized the philosophical basis of his theology as Henry of Ghent.'

On the other side, Henry's own revised Augustinian outlook was itself subjected to an extensive, critical evaluation by Duns Scotus. What led Scotus to focus on Henry is not known. Perhaps in view of the restrictions placed by the Franciscans in 1282 on reading Aquinas's *Summa,* the Order turned to Henry's *Summa* to supply the systematic training in current theology during Scotus's formation. A high regard for Henry is evident in Oxford Franciscans just prior to Scotus, such as Roger Marston, who in 1283 described Henry as 'a recent, solemn doctor, renowned and studious in philosophy from infancy'. Whatever the explanation, Henry constitutes not just a source, but the source, for Scotus's thought. This is in fact so true that Scotus appears to be the first major scholastic thinker to base his principal work explicitly on the systematic examination of a contemporary. On many important questions, Scotus develops his own position as a critical reaction to that of Henry, often after extensive reporting, analysis and refutation of Henry's reasoning. This is the case, for example, on such fundamental issues as the relation of faith and reason, natural knowledge of God, the nature of transcendental concepts, the primary object of the intellect, necessity and contingency, the divine ideas, creation, illumination, causality of the will, connection of the virtues and on numerous points of Trinitarian theology. All the same, however, it would be a distortion to see Scotus as simply rejecting Henry's positions. Even when clearly repudiating a view of Henry, Scotus will none the less presuppose much of Henry's underlying philosophical framework and formulate his own position in terms of Henry's basic concepts, distinctions and technical vocabulary. This is not to say that Scotus was unoriginal and derivative but only that his originality cannot be fully understood apart from his relationship to Henry. Nowhere is the relationship between Scotus and Henry better illustrated than in their dispute over the nature of the transcendental concepts.

Univocity and Analogy

One of the most striking results of the metaphysics of Duns Scotus was that the concepts of being and the other transcendentals applied univocally to God and creatures, substance and accidents. Scotus broke with the unanimous and traditional view that being, conceived in its utmost generality, could only be predicated analogously and not univocally of substance and accident, much less of God and creatures. Scotus made his innovative move to univocity in specific and explicit response to the peculiar version of analogy advanced by Henry of Ghent. Indeed, it would be more accurate to say that Scotus's path to univocity was paved by Henry's prior and equally innovative interpretation of the traditional view of analogy itself. Here, perhaps more than in any other area of disagreement between them, it would be a distortion to portray Scotus as simply rejecting, rather than building upon, an antecedent position of Henry. None the less, in advancing beyond Henry's own version of analogy to univocity, Scotus had to solve fundamental difficulties connected with univocity that had always been compelling motivations for the traditional view of analogy, difficulties which Henry evidently saw but could not resolve.

Scotus advances his theory of univocity as part of a critical and exhaustive revision of Henry's account of our natural knowledge of God. At issue was an abiding concern of the period: how to reconcile the possibility of attaining some knowledge of the divine nature from creatures with God's total transcendence of creatures. The difficulty involved was long recognized, having a formulation as far back as Gaunilo's reply to Anselm that the argument of the *Proslogion* appeared to put God in a genus or species. In order for God to be totally transcendent, the divine nature can have no reality in common with creatures. But if God and creatures agree in nothing real, then a creature can never yield a positive notion of the divine nature that conveys any of its reality. One standard solution was to stress the negative character of natural knowledge of God. For instance, Aquinas attempted to reconcile divine transcendence with our natural knowledge of God by way of the Aristotelian distinction between knowing that something is *(quia est; si est)* versus knowing its essence or nature *(quid est)*. According to Aquinas, our intellect in its present, natural state can only know through sensible creatures that God is or exists *(si est)*. As for the divine essence, we cannot know what it is *(quid est)* but only what it is not. This solution was attacked in the condemnations issued by Stephen Tempier on 7 March, 1277. Article 215 on Tempier's syllabus repudiated such attempts to protect the transcendence of God at the expense of restricting natural knowledge of the divine nature to the bare fact of its existence. As censured the article read, 'That it can only be known that God is, or that God exists.' *(Quod de Deo non potest cognosci nisi quia ipse est, sive ipsum esse.)* Both Henry and Scotus agreed that some positive knowledge of the divine nature and attributes was naturally attainable from creatures, thereby fully reinstating the tension between the transcendence and knowledge of God. Henry, for his part, attempted to account for this positive knowledge while maintaining the traditional view that being and the other transcendentals were only analogously common to God and creatures. Henry none the less saw that he had to revise the traditional doctrine of analogy, and in so doing extended that traditional view as far as it could go without actually becoming a doctrine of univocity. Scotus rejected Henry's revised theory as unworkable and argued that only univocity could ensure a naturally attainable concept of the divine essence.

Henry of Ghent on Analogy

Henry of Ghent followed the common opinion in holding that being is predicated of God and creatures neither univocally, nor purely equivocally, but analogously. The traditional understanding of the terms was based on Aristotle. The definitions of univocity and equivocity derived from the opening chapter of the *Categories,* while the notion of analogy was taken chiefly from the treatment of being as an equivocal by reference in the *Metaphysics*. Thus, a term is univocal if it has a single meaning or concept *(ratio, intentio, intellectus, conceptus)* when applied, such as 'animal' when predicated of a horse and a human being. It is a pure or chance equivocal *(aequivocum in casu)* if it is applied according to completely discrete and unrelated meanings, such as the 'bark' of a dog and a tree. Analogy, however, is intermediate between these two extremes of univocity and equivocity. An analogous term has different but connected meanings, so that one is primary and the other is related to it, usually either as a cause or an effect. Aristotle's own example of 'healthy' served as the standard illustration. The primary meaning of 'healthy' is the state of a well-functioning, living organism, yet clearly things are said to be healthy which do not possess health in this sense. Both medicine and urine, for example, are called 'healthy' not because they possess health in the primary sense, for they are not living at all, but because they bear some relationship to it. Medicine is a cause of health and urine a sign or effect of it. The scholastics adapted Aristotle's conception of analogy as a middle way between the extreme positions of univocity and equivocity, to account for some knowledge of God based on creatures while ensuring divine transcendence. Being was not univocal to God and creatures, but rather analogous, so that it applied to God primarily and to creatures in a secondary but related sense, although appropriate distinctions had to be made to avoid equating the relation of divine and created being with that of substance and accident. In this regard, Henry was in conformity with the common view.

Being therefore does not belong to God univocally nor purely equivocally but in a middle way, namely, by analogy, because it signifies one thing primarily and principally and the other as in some way ordered, related, or proportional to what is primary. And in this way, being in the most common sense primarily signifies God, secondarily creature, just as created being primarily signifies substance and secondarily accidents, although the relation in each case is different.

Aristotle, however, was not the only authority on the transcendentals. Even more important for the scholastics was Avicenna, who had not only made being, in explicit contradistinction to God, the subject of metaphysics, but also one of the primary conceptions of the mind. These claims of

Avicenna for the primacy of being had to be addressed, for together they implied that there was a concept of being antecedent to either God or creatures. Henry's formulation of the Avicennian objection is important, not only because it states sharply the impediment to univocity, but also because in Henry's reply Scotus clearly saw that the denial of univocity involved highly unacceptable consequences.

What is predicated of several things, but has an essential concept different from the concepts of those things [of which it is predicated], is something really common to them, for every concept is based upon some thing. Being is this sort, because according to Avicenna, 'Being is imprinted on the mind by a first impression,' even before the concept of God or creature are impressed on it.

The argument is that being must have a concept different from those of God or creature, because it is known prior to either one. Since being is predicated of both God and creature, that concept must also be common. Thus, the noetic primacy of being entails that it have a concept distinct from and common to those proper to God and creatures. Because any such common concept must be based on some common reality, being must be something really common to God and creature.

It is the major premiss which constitutes the underlying impediment to making any concept univocally common to God and creatures: every concept must be based on some reality *(omnis conceptus fundatur in re aliqua)*. Accordingly, a common concept must be of some common reality. But, obviously, no reality can be admitted as common to God and creatures. This will prove to be the most formidable difficulty for Scotus's doctrine of univocity: how to sustain a real concept univocally common to God and creatures without positing any reality common to them. The minor premiss, based on Avicenna's famous text on the primary intelligibles, is meant to establish that being has a concept outside of those of God and creatures owing to its position as a primary notion. The burden of Henry's reply will be to deny that there is any concept of being apart from those of God and creatures.

It is in this reply that Scotus will find his argument that, on the contrary, being must be a distinct concept, and hence univocal.

In reply to Avicenna's text, Henry is emphatic that there can be no concept of being absolutely taken apart from the concepts of God and creature, as if there were some single, simple concept of being common to them *(aliquis unicus intellects simplex communes),* for there can be no such concept. Rather, any real concept of being is either of the being proper to God or of the being proper to creatures, but not of anything common to them. Henry's position is governed by the requirement in the major premiss that a real community must underwrite a real, common concept. Since there can be no such real community between God and creatures, there can be no real common concept. Demanding therefore a strict correspondence in unity between a real concept and its foundation in reality, Henry concludes that at the transcendental level being forms two proper and distinct concepts corresponding to the two separate and diverse realities of divine and created being. These concepts, while proper and diverse, none the less have a community of analogy, the real foundation for which is the causal dependence of the creature on God. This agreement in being by virtue of the connection cause and effect, while real, is not sufficient to support a single, common notion of being but only two proper concepts related as primary and secondary.

Had Henry gone no further than this in his reply to Avicenna, his account would have conformed to what Peter Aureoli later identified as the common opinion. Being conceived at its most general level does not form a single, simple *ratio* common to God and creatures, but two proper *rationes* related in attribution as primary and secondary. Henry, however, did go further in his reply, motivated by a need not only to explain Avicenna's text on the primary intelligibles, upon which he would depend heavily in his proof for the existence of God, but also to account for how the mind could move from a concept proper to creatures to one proper to God.

Henry explains that if there appears to be some common concept of being, this is only because the divine being or created beings have been conceived in an indistinct or indeterminate way. But to conceive of either the being proper to God or proper to creatures in an indistinct way is not to have some third, distinct concept of being as absolutely undetermined and common to both. That is, there is no separate concept of being as absolutely undetermined that can be abstracted from the proper concepts of God and creature, as if each proper concept comprised a common notion of being as undetermined and a determining concept, such as finite and infinite or created and uncreated. Rather, the proper concepts of God and creatures are in each case already concepts of being as undetermined. Any concept of being as absolutely undetermined, which appears to be single, simple, and prior to the proper concepts of God and creature, is merely the result of confusing the two different ways in which the being proper to God and creatures is in each instance undetermined.

Divine being is undetermined in the sense that it cannot be determined by any advening perfection or entity. This is what it means to say that the divine being is infinite, for it cannot be determined or limited. Created being, however, when taken in its utmost generality as common to all creatures, is undetermined in the sense that it has been abstracted from all determinations with which it is found in reality, such as 'existing in itself' and 'existing in another', which determine or limit created being to substance and accident. Henry's technical terminology for this distinction is that divine being is undetermined negatively, for it is to be denied all determination, and created being privatively, for it can be conceived without the determinations with which it is found. As Henry explains in slightly different terms elsewhere, to conceive of being absolutely, that is, without any determination or qualification, can mean two different things. It can mean either being in its singular, most perfect instance *(in quadam singularitate)* or in its widest generality *(in quadam universalitate)*. Being taken absolutely in the first way is God, in the second way is the notion of being common to the categories. There is no sense in which being can be conceived as undetermined apart from these two.

Having made this distinction, Henry replies to the objection that what appears to be an absolutely undetermined concept of being univocally common to God and creatures is in fact a confusion of the two different ways in which being is undetermined. The divine being is undetermined by negation, because it lacks all determination in both act and potency; created being is undetermined by privation, because it is conceived as lacking determination in act but not in potency. The confusion between the two arises because both are concepts of being without determination, and to this extent they are similar. The mistake is to think that from this similarity one can extract a single notion of being as absolutely undetermined common to both God and creatures. Rather, what appears to be a simple, common notion of undetermined being is in fact a conflation of two proper notions of being, which resemble each other in their removal of determination.

Against the challenge presented by Avicenna's text that there is a concept of being common to God and creatures because, as a primary notion of the mind, the concept of being is prior to both, Henry upholds the traditional position of analogy. Being, conceived in its utmost generality, cannot be reduced to a single notion but only to two distinct concepts, one proper to God and the other to creatures, which are none the less related through attribution or analogy. Yet, in his answer to Avicenna Henry went considerably beyond this traditional view by explaining that being could be conceived with sufficient indeterminacy so as to *appear* univocal. While insisting that there was in truth no univocal notion of being, Henry none the less allowed that the being of either God or creatures could be conceived so indistinctly that the concept proper to the one actually was known in a confused way along with the concept of the other, because both were concepts of being without determination. This was a critical move past the traditional view of analogy and was clearly but a step away from Scotus's univocity, where a simple common concept would replace a confusion of two proper but similar concepts. After Henry went so far as to admit an apparently univocal concept of being, Scotus would conclude that such a concept must in fact be univocal.

Thus Henry revised the common opinion on analogy, according to which the concepts of being proper to God and creatures were united through attribution, by adding that they were also united by confusion in an indistinct notion that appeared univocal. Henry's underlying motivation for this extension of the traditional view was to provide some cognitive bridge between the two proper notions of being which allowed the human mind to pass from its knowledge of creatures to one of the divine nature. This bridge could not be provided by any concept common to both, so Henry supplied it by allowing the two concepts to be conceived together as though they were one. That is, Henry permitted the being of a creature to be conceived in such an indeterminate fashion that it in fact comprised, in an indistinct and confused fashion, the concept of being proper to God. In this way, Henry was attempting to explain, where the traditional view of analogy had not, how one could arrive at a proper concept of the divine nature from creatures. This is clear from Henry's account of the mind's ascent from creatures to God.

In the context of Tempier's condemnation of the position that we can only know that God exists *(si est),* but not what God's nature is *(quid est),* Henry undertook an extensive examination in nine questions of the categories of *si est* and *quid est* as they applied to our knowledge of God, paying particular attention to the extent to which knowledge of the divine nature had to be negative *(quid est non).* In express opposition to the assertion of Aquinas, Henry denied that in the present life we cannot know what God is but only what God is not. If our knowledge of the divine nature were limited only to negations about creatures, then we would know no more about the nature of God from creatures than we would about Socrates by saying that he is not a rock. That is, to have purely negative knowledge of the divine essence is to have no knowledge of it at all. The reason is that negation is always negation of something, so that all meaningful knowledge of what something is not presupposes, to some degree, knowledge of what it is. Furthermore, a purely negative knowledge of the divine nature could not account for our love and desire of God in the present life, for, as Augustine says, we can love what is unseen but not what is unknown. Accordingly, against the assertion of Aquinas, Henry concludes that there must be some positive knowledge of the divine *quid est* naturally available in the present life from creatures.

In effect, Henry sees a complete reduction of our knowledge of the divine nature to negations about creatures as inconsistent with analogy, because it is tantamount to making all predication about God purely equivocal. On the other hand, the positive knowledge of the divine nature provided by analogy does not compromise the transcendence of God to the human mind, because it is not of God's essence in its own particularity and individuality. Analogy can only yield a knowledge of God's *quid est* which is general, indistinct and, as it were, incidental to the substance of the divine nature itself. Yet, even this imperfect knowledge of the divine nature provided by analogy requires a sophisticated manoeuvre by Henry, utilizing his special understanding of the doctrine of analogy itself.

Henry's account of the mind's ascent to the divine *quid est* from creatures involves three main stages, designed to conform broadly to the traditional understanding of the pseudo-Dionysian ways of causality, eminence and negation. At each stage the divine essence is known in a progressively less general fashion, so that ascent is made by degrees to an increasingly distinct knowledge of God, which none the less always remains in some way general and universal. In these three stages Henry says that God is known most generally *(generalissime),* less generally *(generalius),* and least generally *(generaliter),* which involve, respectively, abstraction, eminence and negation. The first or *generalissime* stage is both the most elaborate and important, for it is here that the initial move is made from creatures to God. This first stage itself comprises three degrees of knowledge based on two types of 'abstraction' *(abstractio).*

According to Henry, a formal perfection can be abstracted from its instances in two ways: either as a universal or as something separate. In the first type of abstraction, for example, goodness can be abstracted from this or that particular good as a common and universal form in which they share. Here, while the form is abstracted from its instances, it is none the less still seen in relation to them as that in which they all participate, for the universal is 'one in many'. In the second type, the form is considered in absolute separation from any material instance, for it is seen not as something common divided among many particulars but as transcendent and subsistent in itself *(in se subsistens)*. Quite clearly, these two types of 'abstraction' are for Henry the noetic procedures that result in the concepts of being, goodness or any other perfection as indeterminate by privation and negation. These two kinds of abstraction produce the three steps of the *generalissime* way of knowing the divine nature.

In the first step of most general knowledge of God, any perfection in a creature already reveals, at least in a very confused and indistinct fashion, something of the divine nature. For instance, in knowing this or that particular, created good, Henry says that we know two things: the 'this' and 'that', which are proper to creatures, and 'good' which is something common to God and creatures. Thus, even in 'this created good' we know something of the divine good, even if it is not known as distinct from the creature. If, however, by the first type of abstraction we remove the 'this' proper to the creature, we attain a notion of the good that is less determined to the creature than before, and this is the second step of the *generalissime* stage. Here the good is not seen as proper to creatures or God but as something analogously common to both *(commune analogum ad Deum et creaturam)*. Although in fact the good of God and of the creature form two diverse and distinct concepts *(diversos intellectus distinctos faciunt)*, just as is the case with being, nevertheless these notions are so similar that our intellect at this point conceives both together in a confused way as one *(quia tamen proximi sunt, intellectus noster concipit modo confuso utrumque ut unum)*. By performing a second abstraction, we can distinguish within this confused, analogous notion those two proper concepts, so that we differentiate between what is abstract in the sense of universal and in the sense of separate. This is the third and final step of most general knowledge of the divine nature, where some perfection, such as goodness or being, is viewed as subsistent in itself. Such a concept is proper to God alone.

Once Henry has reached this point, he can easily apply the Dionysian techniques of eminence *(prae-eminentia)* and negation *(remotio)* to this proper concept to ascend to respectively the *generalius* and *generaliter* levels of knowing the divine essence. In eminence, the note of excellence is added to that of subsistence to result in the notion of God as a most perfect nature. In negation, all composition and diversity are removed from this most perfect nature, so that its goodness, wisdom and so forth are taken to be identical with its being. In this way, Henry concludes, we can know what God is, not just what God is not, from creatures in the present life, although 'by comparison to the beatific vision of God's nature, this knowledge is almost nothing'.

Henry's claim for a natural knowledge of the divine *quid est* from creatures would appear to face an insuperable obstacle in his denial of any conceptual community between God and creatures. By restricting our knowledge of God and creatures solely to two wholly proper, simple, and diverse notions, Henry seems to have completely undermined any epistemological basis for claiming that we can derive any concept of the one from the other. Henry clearly saw this obstacle and used considerable ingenuity to overcome it. He conceded that God and creature could be brought together in a common concept, yet found a way to deny that such a notion was univocal.

Henry's strategy, naturally enough, is to explain the derivation of knowledge of God from creatures by means of abstraction. Thus, as outlined above, we begin with some perfection of a creature, such as being or goodness, and detach the particularizing and determining elements with which that perfection is found in its material existence to reach a universal and general notion of it. In Henry's above scheme this abstraction marks the transition from the first level of most general knowledge, in which being and goodness are conceived as most proper to creatures, to the second. Henry is clear that in this step he has in mind the familiar and broadly Aristotelian kind of abstraction that yields common and universal concepts. When taken to its end, however, this process of abstraction does not result merely in a universal concept of being or goodness applicable to creatures alone, which is to say one proper to them, but in one that is *common* to both creator and creature. To be sure, this notion is not univocally common, for it is not a distinct concept *included in both* those of God and creature. It is rather 'analogously common', for it *includes both* the concepts of God and creature in a confused way as one. Thus, for Henry, a perfection can be abstracted from a creature and conceived with such indeterminacy that it is not just the universal knowledge of a creature but a confused knowledge of *both* God and creature. This exceedingly abstract notion, which Henry calls 'analogously common', provides the necessary epistemological bridge from creature to God by constituting a concept of both at once.

Henry attempts to span the cognitive gulf between God and creatures, the knowledge of which he has otherwise limited to proper, simple and diverse notions, by means of his 'analogously common' concept. He has constructed it to perform the required epistemological functions of a truly common concept, for it is universal and applicable to both of its instances, but in such a way that it cannot be called univocal. None the less, Henry's solution is remarkable for how close it comes to an admission of univocity. Indeed, his analogous common concept so nearly functions as a univocal one that even Henry himself at times slips into seeing it as such. In describing how we abstract the general notions of being and the other transcendentals from creatures, so that we do not distinguish in such a notion what is proper to God from what is proper to creatures, Henry adds, 'just as also in univocal things we abstract a common nature'. Elsewhere, Henry describes the universal concept of being abstracted from creatures as 'indifferently common to what belongs to

God and creature'. It is little wonder that Scotus will argue that Henry cannot consistently deny univocity, if for no other reason than he appears to have all but admitted it.

As will be clear, the distance between Henry's revised analogous concept and Scotus's univocal one is accordingly not as great as the opposition in their positions might suggest. They both agree that being and the other transcendental perfections can be thought of without determination to either God or creature and that this is the result of abstraction from creatures. They diverge sharply, however, on the exact nature of this indeterminate conception. Henry denies that it is in fact a separate and distinct concept but holds rather that it is a confusion of two proper notions of being which are themselves simple, ultimate and irreducible. Scotus argues against Henry that to admit such an indeterminate apprehension of being and then to deny that it forms a bona fide, distinct, simple and univocal concept is a contradiction. However, in seeking to avoid the inconsistencies that he sees lurking within Henry's analogously common concept, Scotus must show that a truly univocal notion does not violate the real transcendence of God, which Henry's revised doctrine of analogy, whatever its faults, tried to preserve.

Duns Scotus on Univocity

In his commentaries on the *Sentences,* Scotus addresses the issue of the univocal concept of being in three separate but related contexts: the natural knowledge of God, the primary object of the human intellect and divine simplicity. All three discussions are closely connected, as Scotus's own numerous cross-references indicate. The first, on natural knowledge of God, is a lengthy, critical examination of Henry's position and contains Scotus's most sustained arguments for univocity. After a detailed and systematic summary of Henry's account of our knowledge of God, Scotus replies that, while agreeing with Henry that such knowledge is possible, he departs from his position on five points. In the second of these five points, Scotus maintains against Henry that God is known not only in a concept analogous with, but also in one univocal to, creatures. It is an important but at times overlooked point that Scotus is not here rejecting the traditional view, upheld by Henry, that we have proper notions of God and creatures united by analogy or attribution. Rather, he is rejecting Henry's view that there can be *only* such proper concepts united only in that way. Scotus's point against Henry is that when perfections such as being and goodness are conceived in their utmost generality, they must be univocal not analogous notions. The precise target of Scotus's attack, then, is not Henry's commitment to a traditional doctrine of analogy, a version of which they both concede, but his conclusion that such excludes any univocal conception of being.

In an annotation to his criticism of Henry, Scotus at one point itemizes as many as ten arguments in favour of univocity, but gives five main proofs in the body of his discussion. Three of these are generally singled out as most important. The first of the five, the so-called arguments from 'certain and doubtful concepts', Scotus's own contemporaries labelled the 'Achilles' of his position. It runs as follows:

Major: An intellect certain about one concept, but doubtful about others, has a concept about which it is certain that is different from the concepts about which it is doubtful.

Minor: We can be certain that God is a being, but doubt whether God is infinite or finite being.

The concept of being is different from the concept of infinite or finite being, and hence univocal, since asserted of both.

Scotus takes the major premiss to be evident, for one cannot be both certain and doubtful of the same concept. That is, one and the same concept predicated of the same subject cannot result in a proposition whose truth is both certain and doubtful. The minor premiss is *de facto* true, because past thinkers, such as the pre-Socratics, never doubted that the first principle was a being, but disagreed as to whether it was even material or immaterial, much less finite or infinite. Since the concept of being is different from those of infinite and finite being, but obviously predicated of both, it must be univocal.

Scotus's point, which he establishes more explicitly in

the ensuing arguments, is that some univocal notion of being is presupposed in any natural knowledge of God. Ultimately, however much one doubts whether the concepts of infinite being or uncaused cause apply truly to God, such concepts are doubtful with respect to something that is certain. To be doubtful in all respects of some notion of God is simply to concede that one has no meaningful concept at all.

While Scotus has formulated his argument in sufficiently general terms to give it a universal force and appeal, he has none the less engineered it to expose what he sees as a fundamental absurdity lurking in Henry's analogously common concept of being. In effect, Scotus has crafted the minor premiss around Henry's analogous concept, substituting his own terminology of infinite and finite being for Henry's corresponding notions of negatively and privatively undetermined being. According to Henry, this analogously common notion of being is so abstract that we are in doubt as to whether it is a concept of negatively or privatively undetermined being. At the same time, Henry denies that there is any concept of being apart from these two proper concepts about which we are in doubt. Scotus's argument points out the inconsistency of these two claims: Henry must either concede that we have no certain knowledge of being at all in this analogous concept, for he allows only the two proper concepts of which we are admittedly doubtful, or that we are both certain and doubtful of the same concept. Thus, Henry's abstract, indeterminate notion of being is either vacuous or else it must be distinct from, and hence common to, either of the concepts proper to God and creature.

Recall that Henry's explanation was that there is no concept of being distinct from these two proper ones, but only a confused notion of both which *appears* univocal owing to their similarity. Accordingly, Henry would reply to Scotus that we are not certain of some distinct, common concept, as Scotus concludes, but only of a confused notion that seemed common. Scotus perceives Henry's manoeuvre as introducing scepticism at the most fundamental level of human knowledge. According to Scotus, it would destroy all univocity, for any allegedly univocal concept could always be denied on the grounds it was not one but two very similar notions which merely seemed to be one. Scotus's evident point is that if univocity cannot be ascertained with certainty at the level of our most abstract concepts, which are therefore primary, simple and irreducible, then it can never be determined. Furthermore, according to Henry, these two proper concepts of being must be ultimate and hence wholly simple otherwise they would be resolvable into more primitive notions and are therefore known in their totality and distinctly or not at all. Therefore, either they will always be seen as one or never will be, for, being wholly simple, no distinguishing element can be discovered in them which was not evident in the first place. Finally, either they were initially seen as wholly different concepts of being proper to God and creatures, and then it seems impossible in view of their disparity that they could have ever been confused as one, or they were seen in a relation of similarity owing to analogy. In the latter case they could not be initially known as one, for any two things seen as united in some relation must first be known as distinct. Therefore, these two notions would never appear to be one, simple concept, but only as distinct under a relation of similarity.

Scotus's first argument, then, attempts to draw out the apparent inconsistency in Henry's open admission, on the one side, that the intellect can conceive of being without determining it to God or creature, and his emphatic denial, on the other, that there is any concept of being distinct from those proper to God and creature. Scotus argues that Henry cannot claim that this indeterminate conception contains any certain knowledge of being at all unless he admits that it is a concept distinct from the concepts of being proper to God and creature. The reason is that, by Henry's own admission, the intellect is not certain at this point that it has either proper concept, for it has not yet distinguished between the two. It thus is either certain of no concept of being or is certain and doubtful of the same concept. Henry's device of making this analogous concept an *apparently* common and univocal concept, which is then later discerned to be two proper notions, collapses under scrutiny. Even if the simplicity of these two proper concepts of being did not make it impossible for them to be confused at one time and distinguished at another, they can only be seen as similar, and hence one, after first having been known as distinct and proper. As an epistemological explanation for the natural origin of our proper concept of God, Henry's analogously common notion simply begs the question. It presupposes the very proper concept of God that it is supposed to explain.

In his second argument, Scotus is explicit that denial of a univocal concept renders natural knowledge of God impossible. Specifically, Scotus attacks Henry's position on the grounds that no creature can be the immediate cause of a concept which is both simple and wholly proper to God. Yet this is Henry's only available account for the natural origins of our knowledge of God, given that he admits only two proper and simple concepts of being and excludes any which is common. Scotus maintains that it is patently absurd to hold that a creature can directly cause a simple and wholly proper concept of God, simply because such cannot be the concept of anything contained within the creature. Scotus argues that an object can only cause a concept of that which it contains either as an essential part (e.g. its *differentia* or genus) or virtually (e.g. an essential property). Obviously, the creature contains nothing proper to God as an essential part. Similarly, a creature cannot virtually contain anything proper to God, for one thing virtually contains another as the naturally prior contains the posterior or the cause its effect. For instance, premisses virtually contain their conclusions in the sense that their greater truth and certitude has the 'power' *(virtus)* to produce or cause certitude of the conclusion. The creature, however, is naturally posterior and inferior to divine nature as its effect and therefore cannot virtually contain anything proper to God. Rather, just the reverse is true; God virtually contains the creature. Thus, if a creature can produce any concept of God at all, it must be one that is common to both, which Henry denies.

Scotus pursues a similar line of reasoning in his fourth

proof, which examines the commonly admitted basis for natural knowledge of God, the so-called 'pure perfections' *(perfectiones simpliciter),* such as intellect, will or wisdom. Scotus argues that either these perfections have some meaning common to God and creature or not. If not, this is either because they are wholly proper to creatures, which no one admits, or they are wholly proper to God. If they are wholly proper to God, then they are not attributed to God because they are pure perfections, but are rather pure perfections because they are attributed to God. This, however, would violate the traditional and universally accepted procedure given by Anselm for determining what can be assigned to the divine nature. According to Anselm, we attribute to God those perfections which are pure in the sense that they contain of themselves no imperfection. As defined by Anselm, such a perfection is 'what absolutely taken is better to be than not'. But on Anselm's definition, one can determine what is a pure perfection without any reference to God. That is, on the received and accepted account of natural knowledge of God, something is first determined to constitute a pure perfection and then on that basis attributed to God, not the reverse. Consequently, something is not a pure perfection precisely because it is attributed to God but is such prior to that attribution. Pure perfections must therefore have some meaning that is common apart from the meaning it has as attributed and proper to God alone.

Once again Scotus argues that some common and hence univocal notion is presupposed by our analogous, proper concepts of God. In this case, the traditional doctrine of 'pure perfections' is seen to entail just such a common notion. If there were no common but only proper concepts of these perfections, then they could not be known apart from their attribution to God. Yet, exactly the opposite is prescribed by the traditional concept of pure perfections, for they are known independently of and prior to any relation to God.

Scotus makes the same point in a confirmation of this argument, this time using the equally traditional Dionysian procedures of removal and eminence. According to Scotus, all metaphysical enquiry about God proceeds by taking some formal notion *(ratio formalis)* and removing from it all imperfections with which it is found in a creature. For example, we take the formal notion of the will a power for opposites and remove any limitations connected with its existence in a creature, such as variability in its act of willing over time. We then attribute will to God by conceiving of it not just as lacking imperfection, but as possessing the greatest degree of perfection, such that it is infinitely powerful. This process presumes that the formal notion of the will which has been stripped of creaturely limitations is the same notion of will as is assigned the highest degree of perfection. If this is not the case, so that nothing of the notion of will abstracted from creatures remains when we attribute will to God, then perfections found in creatures tell us nothing about the perfection of God. As Scotus puts it, we could then no more say that the divine nature was an intellect, a will or wise than it was a rock. That is, the distinction traditionally made within creatures between pure perfections, which can be applied to God, and their other formal features, which cannot, would be meaningless on denial of any common notion of such perfections. If to be a 'perfection' has absolutely no common meaning as applied to God and creature, then perfection in creatures becomes tantamount to imperfection. Thus, 'wisdom' would be no more applicable to God than 'rock'.

The point of Scotus's fourth proof and its confirmation is that the traditional concepts and methods that are the accepted basis for natural knowledge of God presuppose a common notion of being and other such perfections. Elsewhere Scotus is more pointed: 'All masters and theologians seem to use a concept common to God and creature, although they deny this verbally when they apply it'. There can be little doubt, however, that Scotus has Henry specifically in view. This is particularly evident in Scotus's corroborative argument based on the Dionysian procedure, from which, as shown, Henry constructed his own three-stage ascent to God. Scotus has pared this procedure to the two minimal steps of removal and eminence, which correspond respectively to what Henry calls knowing God *generalissime* and *generalius*. (In his third point of disagreement with Henry, Scotus discards Henry's final stage of conceiving God as wholly simple through negation and limits our highest simple concept of God to that of a pre-eminent or infinite being.) Scotus's point is that the Dionysian procedure requires that the notion or meaning *(ratio)* yielded by removal be the same notion to which eminence is applied, otherwise the first step would simply have no relevance to the second. Removal and eminence would not, as all theologians assume, form two stages of a continuous process of reasoning leading from a knowledge of creatures to God. As Scotus says, 'There would be no such process, but inquiry of this kind would have to be avoided' *(nullus esset talis processus, sed vitanda esset talis inquisitio)*. But this is exactly the situation in Henry's interpretation of the Dionysian process, for he holds that the *ratio* of a perfection arrived at by the abstraction and removal of created limitations is wholly other than that to which eminence is applied *(illud est alterius et alterius rationis)*. Distinguishing between the epistemological functions of the ways of causality and eminence, Scotus denies that these two diverse *rationes* can be sufficiently connected by means of causal dependence, as Henry maintains. Something is not formally or essentially predicated of God, in the manner of a pure perfection, simply because it is an effect. A rock is an effect of God as exemplary cause in so far as it has an idea in the divine mind, yet the formal notion of 'rock' cannot be predicated of God in the same way as that of goodness, justice, truth or any other such perfection. Rather, perfections found in creatures must have some univocally common concept if they are to be predicated essentially of God as divine attributes, whereas things predicated of God as their cause need not have such a common notion. Henry cannot therefore use the way of causality to underwrite the way of eminence, for the epistemological requirements for the latter are greater than for the former. Thus, he must admit that his first stage issues in some notion common to God and creature.

The force of all this argumentation is that Henry cannot consistently uphold natural knowledge of the divine nature and then deny that being has some concept common to creatures and God. If being and the other perfections have only two simple and wholly diverse *rationes* or notions, one proper to creatures and the other to God, then creatures simply cannot yield any concepts relevant to the divine nature. The causal dependence of the creature on God is irrelevant here, because being, goodness and such are seen as divine *attributes* revelatory of God's nature, not because they are effects, but because they are perfections of a certain sort. Henry himself seems to have appreciated the limitations of the way of causality and attempted to supply the required conceptual unity by means of an 'analogously common notion', in which the two proper and diverse *rationes* were conceived in a confused way so as to appear univocal. Scotus saw this as an unworkable contrivance vulnerable to the most obvious of absurdities, such as that the intellect could lack certitude about its most fundamental concepts. In the face of Henry's strained and artificial attempts to sustain natural knowledge of God while denying any bona fide common concept, Scotus replaced Henry's 'analogous', confused notion of two proper *rationes* that appeared univocal with a distinct concept of a single, simple *ratio* that in fact was univocal. Accordingly, where for Henry being conceived in its utmost generality and community was a complex and confused concept, and the concepts proper to God and creatures were simple and distinct, for Scotus just the reverse became the case. The most general and indeterminate concept of being was irreducibly simple and common, and thus known in a distinct rather than a confused way, while the concepts of being proper to God and creature were complex, or at least not irreducibly simple. By admitting a simple and univocal concept of being, Scotus provided a true conceptual community between God and creature and placed the project of natural knowledge of the divine nature on a firm epistemological footing.

Scotus's univocal concept of being clearly had great epistemological advantages over Henry's revised version of analogy. It eliminated Henry's unsatisfactory attempt to make an unstable conflation of equivocal notions do the epistemological work of a genuinely univocal concept merely because such a conflation appeared univocal. Univocity not only provided a true conceptual community between God and creature, but made being suitable as a primary object of the mind by rendering its conception certain, simple and prior. In granting univocity, Scotus replaced Henry's two concepts of being with a single one, his doubtful concepts with a certain one, his relational concepts with an absolute one, and his confused concepts with a distinct one. Yet these epistemological advantages of univocity came at a very high metaphysical cost, which is precisely why Henry went to such extreme lengths to deny that there was in truth any such concept. The cost of Scotus's univocal concept of being, as one objector put it, was nothing less than 'to destroy the whole of philosophy'.

While Scotus portrayed univocity as contained with the tradition of natural theology, so that it could be found in 'arguments frequently made or implied by doctors and the saints', he had to reconcile it with a daunting array of philosophical authorities to the contrary. Scotus himself did not fail to raise and confront the various conflicts that a univocal concept of being appeared to present to the philosophical tradition, particularly that of Aristotle. Thus, for instance, univocity would remove a pillar of Aristotle's metaphysics, namely, that 'being is said in many ways', which meant that being was not univocal but a type of equivocal. It would destroy the categories as ultimate classifications or genera, for they would become species under the higher class of being. Similarly, it would render the five predicables of Porphyry inadequate, for being would form a sixth universal. Worst of all, God would enter a community of being with creatures. The divine nature would not be a wholly simple and pure act, but a composite of being and difference.

All of these impossible conclusions really expressed one and the same difficulty in different ways. Scotus's univocal concept of being appeared to his contemporaries to destroy all of philosophy Aristotle's conception of metaphysics, the categories, the predicables, and even the distinction between God and creatures because it appeared to destroy being itself as a transcendental. On the common view, a 'univocal transcendental' was a contradiction in terms, precisely because the categories or supreme genera were regarded as the highest classes of univocal predicates. Since a transcendental was by definition beyond the categories, it could not be univocal. This conviction was clearly stated by Peter Olivi, a theologian writing in the generation before Scotus: 'The nature of being, one, and true is so common to all things that it transcends the nature of a genus and everything univocal.' In other words, on the common view, univocity destroyed being as a transcendental because it reduced being to a genus. Indicative of this common view was the use of Aristotle's claim that being and one could not fall under a genus as a standard authority against univocity.

This conventional identification of univocal and generic concepts resulted from the requirement, explicitly invoked by Henry in this connection, that there must be a strict correspondence between real and conceptual community. Any real, univocal concept, as opposed to a purely logical or mind-dependent notion, had to be based on some type of corresponding real community or agreement. Since the categories by definition constituted the highest classes of reality, they formed the outer boundaries of real agreement. Accordingly, there could be no univocal concept of anything more universal than these categories or genera, for to such a notion would correspond no real community. If this was true of the categories, so much more of God and creatures, whose real diversity was immeasurably greater than that between any two genera. The challenge facing Scotus was thus clear if his doctrine of univocity was not to destroy all of philosophy by reducing being to a genus. He had to explain how there could be a truly univocal notion of being to which there corresponded no real agreement. Scotus himself was completely aware that this was the universally perceived impasse to making being and the other transcendentals univocal. The central difficulty to be overcome was that 'God and creatures are wholly diverse in reality, agreeing in no reality and nevertheless agree in one concept'.

This is the problem Henry saw but could not solve. He could not see how to unite God and creatures under some common concept of being without also uniting them in some common reality, that is, without bringing them under being as a genus. For Henry the one required the other, as exemplified by Plato, who held being was univocal because it was a genus. Because Henry could not resolve this difficulty, he tried to construct a type of conceptual community by conflating proper concepts rather than admit a single, common one. Scotus was the first to find a way around this impasse, and his solution involved some of the most innovative aspects of his metaphysics.

Scotus's solution is found in his question on divine simplicity, which he specifically formulated to draw out just his difficulty: 'Is it compatible with divine simplicity that God, or anything formally predicated of God, be in a genus?' As the lead objection to the question makes clear, the issue is whether Scotus's position of univocity, previously established in distinction 3, entails that God is in a genus.

It seems that [God is in a genus], because God is formally a being. Being, however, signifies a concept predicated of God quidditatively *(in quid).* This concept of being is not proper to God, but common to God and creature, as was said in distinction 3. Therefore, in order for this common concept to become proper [to God] it must be determined by some determining concept.

The above line of argument is precisely why Henry so adamantly refused to admit both a common and proper concept of divine being and allowed only a proper one. It is impossible to admit both concepts of God without conceding that the proper one itself is a composite of common and distinguishing notions which must be related in effect as potency and act, or as the objection puts it, as determined and determining. This is simply to admit that the common notion is a genus and the distinguishing one a *differentia.* This conclusion follows especially from Scotus's position, because he admits that the common concept of being applies to God quidditatively, which means that it is the concept of a 'what' *(quid).* The distinguishing concept will accordingly specify or qualify being as a kind *(quale),* so that the two will conform exactly to the classical relation of genus to *differentia* as *quid* to *quale.*

In his lengthy reply to the objection, Scotus concedes that there is a common concept of being and that it is 'contracted' or determined by the notions of infinite and finite to result in concepts proper to God and creatures. He even concedes that the common and contracting or determining concepts are related as *quid* and *quale*. He denies, however, that they are respectively concepts of a genus and its *differentiae*. As for the first point, Scotus argues that the univocal concept of being cannot be that of a genus. The reason is that being so conceived is common to both the finite (creatures) and the infinite (God), and this community exceeds that of any genus. No generic concept can be so common, for by definition the concept of a genus is that of a reality potential to some further, perfecting reality added by the *differentia*. What is infinite in being, however, cannot be potential to any further reality. Accordingly, since a genus by definition involves potentiality, the concept of being common to God and creatures cannot be that of a genus, for the infinite being of God can never be conceived, however commonly or indeterminately, as some reality potential to further perfection. The second part of Scotus's response is that the determining concepts of infinite and finite do not correspond to those of specific *differentiae*. Here the reason is that infinity and finitude do not indicate the addition of some reality outside that given in the common concept of being, but only degrees or grades of perfection intrinsic to the reality of being. The concept of a *differentia*, however, is always of some reality outside of and added to that of the genus.

Scotus's response relies on his technical conception of a formal, extramental distinction of two realities, on the one hand, and his so-called 'modal' distinction between a reality and its intrinsic grades or modes of perfection, on the other. As for the first, Scotus recognizes within one and the same thing *(res)* a distinction of realities, formalities or entities *(realitates, formalitates, entitates)*, as he variously calls them, corresponding to our different concepts of that thing. Such realities are said to be 'formally distinct', but really identical or united within one and the same thing. Such a 'formal distinction' is for Scotus not merely conceptual but real in the sense that it obtains prior to any consideration of the intellect. Scotus holds that at minimum this formal distinction between two realities is required to provide a real basis for the concepts of genus and *differentia.* According to Scotus, this degree of distinction is minimally needed to sustain any real relationship of potency to act required for genus and difference. The concept of a genus is taken from the one reality, which is perfected by and potential to, the formally distinct reality from which the difference is taken. Scotus argues that unless genus and *differentia* are at least formally distinct realities, the concept of the genus would coincide with the entire reality of the species, rendering the addition of specific *differentia* in a definition redundant.

In addition to this formal distinction of realities in one and the same thing, Scotus recognizes a lesser distinction between a reality and its degree of perfection, or in Scotus's terminology, its intrinsic mode. This is the distinction, for instance, between an accidental form, such as white, and the degrees of intensity with which it is actually found. For example, white can be differentiated into degrees or shades, yet these degrees do not form different species of colour. Or again, a species of precious stone, such as diamond, can be distinguished according to the various degrees of perfection that make up the gemmologist's scale, from imperfect to flawless, yet these gradations do not each one constitute a different species of gem. Such grades or modes are said to be 'intrinsic' because they do not add, as a specific *differentia* does to a genus, a new reality extrinsic to the form of which they are the grades. They rather indicate different quantitative degrees, as it were, of one and the same reality or form. Scotus's model here is the medieval theory of intension and remission of accidental forms. According to this theory, accidental forms, such as colours, heat, and cognitive and moral habits, are said to have a certain extension or 'latitude' *(latitudo)* within which they can be increased *(intensio)* or decreased *(remissio)* without a change in the essence or species of the form itself.

In light of these technical refinements, Scotus's answer to the above objection is that the relationship of the common concept of being to its contracting or determining notions of infinity and finitude does not correspond to that of genus and *differentia,* for this requires two formally distinct realities related as potency and act. The common concept of being cannot involve the element of potentiality found in a genus, for this would render it inapplicable in any way to the divine being, and hence not common to God and creatures. Rather, being and its qualifying concepts of infinity and finitude correspond to the relation of a reality and its intrinsic modes of perfection. The categorical analogue for the common concept of transcendental being is not therefore a genus and its specific differences, but rather a specific form and its grades of intension and remission. Clearly, Scotus thinks he has found in this categorical analogue of intension and remission a model for common and differentiating concepts which escapes the real relation of potency and act required in genus and *differentia.* The various degrees of intensity are *real* but not *specific differentiae* of a form. As it actually exists, white is found in different degrees of brilliance or intensity, and these are *real differentiae* of that form. Yet this diversity within the form of whiteness is not one produced by specific *differentiae,* otherwise every shade of white would constitute a different species of colour. Rather, the intensive grades of a form result from *differentiae* less than specific, albeit real, because they are intrinsic to the nature of the form itself. Specific *differentiae* by contrast always add a new reality in kind. By appealing to a recognized distinction within the categories between a form and its degrees, which is less than that of genus and *differentia,* Scotus thinks he can explain how the common concept of being can be 'contracted' by the finite and infinite without reducing being to a genus.

Yet Scotus realizes that this reply does not fully resolve the difficulty of the real basis for this common concept of being, so that univocity still poses a threat to divine simplicity. The problem is that Scotus holds that the concept of being univocally common to God and creatures is both *real* and distinct from the concept of infinite being proper to God. Since this common concept is *real,* it must be taken from some corresponding reality in God that is common. The original objection now reappears, because Scotus still has to admit that there will be two realities in God, one which is common to account for the real, common concept of being and another to account for the proper concept of God. These realities will be related as potency to act and hence as genus and *differentia*. The problem thus seems inescapable. If the common concept of being is real, it must be of something real in God. But to admit a common reality in God is nothing less than to place God under a genus. Scotus himself sharply focuses the difficulty: 'Here is doubted how a real concept common to God and creature is possible unless it is taken from some reality of the same genus.'

Scotus replies that both the common concept of being univocal to God and creatures and the concept proper to God are taken from one and the same reality of infinite being. The implicit assumption of the objection denied by Scotus is that in order for a common concept to be real, it must always be an adequate or perfect concept of the reality conceived. Rather, the common and proper concepts of God are related as imperfect and perfect conceptions of one and the same reality, not as perfect or adequate concepts of two distinct realities. Scotus's response exploits his distinction between a reality and its intrinsic mode or grade of perfection to account for how one and the same reality can cause both a perfect concept, which is proper, and an imperfect concept, which is common. For example, some particular instance of white existing at the tenth grade of intensity can be conceived perfectly, and then it is known according to the degree of perfection with which it is actually found. That same instance of white can be conceived imperfectly, and then only the nature of 'whiteness' as such, apart from the real condition of its grade of intensity, is known. The former is a proper concept of whiteness in some determinate grade, the latter a concept common to the various instances of white differing in degrees. No concept common as a genus, however, can ever result simply from conceiving a reality in an imperfect way. Rather, as just seen, to the concepts of genus and *differentia* there must correspond two different realities, and, in each case, there can be a perfect and adequate concept of the corresponding reality.

As applied to the renewed form of the initial objection, Scotus's distinction means that our univocally common concept of being does not entail a corresponding common reality in God, because that common concept is not a perfect or adequate concept of any reality. Rather, it is an imperfect concept of the reality of infinite being proper to God or of finite being proper to creatures. To put it another way, that concept of being is common to God and creatures because in it the two wholly diverse realities of infinite and finite being are conceived in an imperfect way. In an annotation to this reply, Scotus expresses in technical language his answer to the difficulty of the real basis for the univocal concept of being:

> Note [in this answer] how there can be a primary intention [i.e. a real as opposed to a secondary or merely logical concept] of 'a' and 'b' that is common and nothing of a single nature corresponds in reality, but two wholly diverse formal objects [i.e. God and creature] are understood in one first intention, although *either imperfectly*.

This constitutes Scotus's ultimate resolution of the metaphysical impasse to a univocal concept of being. It consists of recognizing a distinction that is real but less than that of two different realities. Only given such a lesser distinction is it possible to provide an ontological foundation for common and proper concepts that not are related as genus and *differentia*. Scotus himself is clear that the solution to the objective basis for a univocal concept of being requires such a lesser distinction, namely, that of a reality and its intrinsic mode: 'Therefore, a distinction is required between that from which the common concept [of being] is taken and that from which the proper concept is taken, not a distinction of reality and reality, but of reality and the proper and intrinsic mode of the same reality'. In Scotus's view, Henry and his contemporaries were led to deny univocity because they demanded that every distinction in real concepts be based upon a corresponding distinction of realities. They failed to see that the boundaries between our concepts can be more refined, so that they do not always answer to a distinction of realities but can be based on one between a reality and its degree of perfection. Such is sufficient for perfect and imperfect conceptions of the same reality, which are related as proper and common concepts of it. A concept of being which is common by virtue of its imperfection is all that is required for it to be univocal to God and creature.

Having solved this problem, however, Scotus faced a final hurdle to univocity in the authority of Aristotle, who repeatedly states that being is a type of equivocal. From this it is concluded that being cannot be univocal. Scotus replies that this reasoning assumes that analogy and univocity are incompatible, which he denies. First, according to Aristotle himself, there is a first in every genus, which is the measure of all in that class, such as is the case with human being in the genus of animal. Despite this relationship of attribution, in which human being constitutes the primary instance of animal to which all others are referred, Scotus argues that all still admit a single notion of animal univocal to all in the genus. Similarly, the order and attribution existing between the proper and analogous concepts of being is consistent with some univocal notion common to both. Second, the real or natural philosopher (i.e. the physicist, who deals with material beings) takes as equivocal the diverse genera which the logician sees as univocal, for in reality only the form of the ultimate species is truly univocal. So, Scotus concludes, all of the citations of Aristotle where being is claimed to be analogous should be read as referring to a real diversity of beings among which there is attribution, which is none the less consistent with some univocally common concept abstracted from them. Scotus's second response will form the basis for ensuing attempts by Scotists to reconcile his doctrine of univocity with Aquinas's position on analogy. In reconciling the two views, Aquinas is portrayed as maintaining real analogy among beings, while Scotus is seen as holding a purely conceptual unity.

Summary

There can be no question that in maintaining a concept of being univocally common to God and creatures, Scotus moved beyond the common view of the transcendentals in a dramatic and important way. The doctrine of univocity counts as one of the genuinely original results of Latin medieval philosophy, and its impact was felt well into the modern period. At the same time, Scotus's achievement depended in an intimate way on prior developments by Henry of Ghent. As has been repeatedly stressed, this is in fact so true that Scotus's doctrine of univocity should properly be seen not as a complete rejection but as a revision of Henry's own unique understanding of analogy. Specifically, Scotus's simple, univocal concept was a modification of Henry's revised 'analogously common' notion of being. Henry's extended sense of an 'analogous concept' had many features in common with Scotus's univocal one: it was a conception of being as completely undetermined, the result of abstraction from creatures, and the epistemological foundation for natural knowledge of the divine nature. Scotus accepted these aspects of Henry's indeterminate conception of being, and then argued that Henry could not consistently deny that such a conception formed a truly unified, distinct, and common notion unto itself. Scotus accordingly abandoned Henry's analogous notion of being, but did so by making it into the very univocal concept Henry claimed it appeared to be, but in truth was not. In other words, the univocal concept of being for which Scotus argues is, in many important respects, the very one that Henry described but rejected as merely apparent: a single, simple concept common to God and creature and different from concepts of both. These words of Henry answer quite closely to the concept demonstrated by Scotus, particularly in his first argument for univocity. To be sure, in upholding the univocal notion which Henry had rejected Scotus had to move beyond Henry's understanding of univocity in an important and creative way, most notably by detaching univocal community from the ontological limitations of a genus. On the other hand, it is not true that Scotus advanced a univocal concept of being which Henry had simply failed to see altogether; Henry saw a good part of it, but could not see how to sustain it.

The close connection between Scotus and Henry examined here in their disagreement over the nature of transcendental concepts is found to various degrees in many other areas of their thought. For example, Scotus rejects more and appropriates less in his attacks on Henry's version of Augustinian illumination and his theory of exemplar causality, according to which creatures have a necessary and eternal 'essential being' *(esse essentiae)* as divine ideas. In other areas, Scotus appropriates more and rejects less, such as in his proofs for the existence of God. In nearly all cases, however, a proper understanding of Scotus will depend on appreciating his relationship to Henry.

10

Medieval Logic in Philosophy

Introduction

Medieval logic encompassed more than what we call logic today. It included semantics, philosophy of language, parts of physics, of philosophy of mind and of epistemology.

The logical writings of Aristotle were all available in Latin by the mid-twelfth century. In addition, except for the theory of 'proofs of propositions', the characteristic new ingredients of medieval logic were already in place or at least in progress by the end of the twelfth century or the beginning of the thirteenth century.

The theory of inference or 'consequence', for example, was studied as early as Peter Abelard (1079–1142). Again, after about 1120 the circulation of Aristotle's *Sophistical Refutations* in Latin stimulated a study of fallacies and the many features of language that produce them. Out of this investigation there arose twelfth and thirteenth century writings on semantic 'properties of terms', like 'supposition' and 'ampliation'. At the same time, treatises on *sophismata* or puzzle-sentences in logic, theology or philosophy of nature began to be produced. (A good analogy for this literature may be found in modern discussions of Frege's 'The morning star is the evening star'.) Likewise, studies were written about the logical effects of words like 'only', 'except', 'begins' and 'ceases' that offer many opportunities for fallacies and involve complications going far beyond syllogistic or the theory of topical inferences. Treatises on 'insolubles' or semantic paradoxes began to appear late in the twelfth century. Simultaneously, a literature developed on a new kind of disputation called 'obligations'. Collectively, these new logical genres are known as 'terminist' logic because of the important role played in them by the 'properties of terms'.

These developments continued into the thirteenth century. By mid-century, authors such as Peter of Spain, Lambert of Auxerre and William of Sherwood were writing summary treatises *(summulae)* covering the whole of logic, including the material in Aristotle's writings as well as new terminist developments.

Then, after about 1270, something odd happened, both in England and on the Continent. In France, terminism was eclipsed by an entirely different theory called 'speculative grammar', which appealed to the notion of 'modes of signifying' and is therefore sometimes called 'modism'. This theory prevailed in France until the 1320s, when John Buridan suddenly restored the theory of supposition and associated terminist doctrines. After Buridan, supposition theory was the leading vehicle for semantic (as distinct from grammatical) analysis until the end of the Middle Ages.

Modism never dominated England as it did elsewhere; terminism survived there during its period of neglect on the Continent. Still, few innovations in supposition theory or its satellite doctrines were made in England during the last quarter of the thirteenth century. But then, in the very early fourteenth century, Walter Burley began to do new work in the terminist tradition.

This temporary decline of terminism on both sides of the Channel at the end of the thirteenth century, and its sudden revival shortly after 1300, are mysterious events. But, whatever the underlying causes, when supposition theory and related doctrines re-emerged in the early fourteenth century, they were importantly different from how they had been earlier.

In England, logic after 1300 may be divided into three stages: first, 1300-50, when the best work was done. Burley and William of Ockham (*c.* 1285-1347) were the paramount figures during this period. Both made important contributions to supposition theory, and Ockham in particular developed sophisticated theories of 'mental language' and 'connotation'.

In the next generation, several men associated with Merton College, Oxford, were influential in specific areas. Richard Kilvington and William Heytesbury, among others, applied the techniques of *sophismata* to questions in natural philosophy, epistemic logic and other fields. Thomas Bradwardine wrote an *Insolubles* that was perhaps the most influential treatise on semantic paradoxes throughout the Middle Ages. Around 1330-2, Adam Wodeham devised an important theory of 'complexly significables' *(complexe significabilia),* the closest medieval equivalent to the modern notion of 'proposition'. Richard Billingham (fl. 1340s or 1350s) seems to have originated the important theory of 'proofs of propositions'. His treatise *Speculum puerorum* or *Youths' Mirror* will be discussed in section VIII below.

The second stage of English logic after 1300 lasted from 1350 to 1400. This was a time of consolidation, of sophisticated but no longer especially original work. The period has not yet been well researched, but at least three trends can be distinguished. First, there was a remarkable number of school-manuals written in logic, compilations of standard doctrine with little innovation. Works of Richard Lavenham (d. 1399 or after) provide a good example. Gradually, certain of these school-texts congealed into two collections called the *Libelli sophistarum (Little Books for Arguers),* one for Oxford and one for Cambridge. These were printed in several editions around 1500.

Second, English logic from 1350 to 1400 had a special interest in the doctrine of 'proofs of propositions' associated with Billingham. As time passed, the labour devoted to this topic grew enormously. John Wyclif dedicated a large part of his *Logic* (before 1368) and especially of his *Continuation of the Logic* (1371-4) to this theory. So did Ralph Strode, a contemporary of Wyclif, in his own *Logic.* John Huntman wrote a *Logic* sometime near the end of the century, showing the continued expansion of the Billingham tradition.

A third concern of English logic in this period was the signification of propositions. The most influential work here was probably *On the Truth and Falsehood of Propositions* by Henry Hopton (fl. 1357). There Hopton discussed and rejected several previous views before setting out his own theory.

Several other English authors during this period should be mentioned, although their works are not yet fully understood. They include Richard Feribrigge (fl. probably 1360s), author of an important *Consequences* and a *Logic or Treatise on the Truth of Propositions.* Of lesser importance are: Robert Fland (fl. 1335–60); Richard Brinkley, the author of a *Summa* of logic probably between 1360 and 1373; Thomas Manlevelt (or Mauvelt), who wrote several treatises around mid-century that were influential on the Continent; and near the end of the century, Robert Alington, William Ware, Robert Stonham, and others.

One of the most significant events in English logic late in the century was the arrival at Oxford in 1390 of the Italian Paul of Venice (*c.* 1369–1429). Paul studied there for some three years. On his return to Italy, he taught at Padua and elsewhere, and was an important conduit through which English logic became known in Italy in the fifteenth century. His writings include a widely circulated *Little Logic (Logica parva)* and the enormous *Big Logic (Logica magna).*

The third stage of late medieval English logic includes the whole fifteenth century. This was a period of shocking decline. Except for a few insignificant figures around 1400, not even second-rate authors are known. The manuscripts from this period and by 1500, early printed books offer little hope that further research will change this assessment. The Oxford and Cambridge *Little Books for Arguers,* already mentioned, testify to the deterioration of logic during this period. Medieval logic was effectively dead in England after 1400.

Logic on the Continent during these same two centuries cannot be so neatly divided into stages. Still, there as in England, the most important work was done before about 1350. The pre-eminent figure was doubtless Buridan. His writings include a *Consequences,* a *Sophismata* and a *Summulae of Dialectic.* Buridan's students included many influential logicians of the next generation, among them: Albert of Saxony (d. 1390), the author of a *Sophismata* and *A Very Useful Logic,* and the first rector of the University of Vienna; and Marsilius of Inghen (*c.* 13300–96), the first rector of the University of Heidelberg and the author of an *Insolubles* and of treatises on 'properties of terms'.

On many points, Buridan's logical views were like Burley's or especially Ockham's in England. There are differences, but the similarities are more striking, especially when contrasted with logic on either side of the Channel before 1300. The extent of Ockham's own influence on Buridan is doubtful, but Ockham's confrère Adam Wodeham was instrumental in transmitting much English learning to Paris.

The Parisian Peter of Ailly (1350–1420/1) wrote several interesting logical works, including: *Concepts and Insolubles,* a pair of treatises on 'mental language' and the Liar Paradox; *Destructions of the Modes of Signifying,* against 'modism'; *Treatise on Exponibles*; and *Treatise on the Art of 'Obligating'* (perhaps by Marsilius of Inghen instead).

Before 1400, the Italian Peter of Mantua (fl. 1387–1400) wrote a *Logic* that already shows knowledge of earlier English work, particularly that stemming from Billingham. Around 1400 Angelo of Fossombrone, who taught at Bologna (1395–1400) and Padua (1400-2), wrote an *Insolubles* maintaining an elaborated version of Heytesbury's theory. About the same time, the newly returned Paul of Venice spread the gospel of Oxford logic further in Italy. Among his students, Paul of Pergula (d. 1451/5) wrote a *Logic* and a treatise *On the Composite and the Divided Sense* (on the scope of certain logical operators) based on Heytesbury's own work of that name, and Gaetano of Thiene (1387–1465) wrote detailed commentaries on works by Heytesbury and Strode. Other authors in Italy and elsewhere continued to write on logic to the end of the Middle Ages and beyond.

Even these few names will suffice to show that the logical landscape after about 1400 was by no means so desolate on the Continent as in England. Still, on either side of the Channel logical work after 1350 was largely derivative and, while sometimes very sophisticated, not very innovative. There was certainly no one, for example, with the stature of Burley, Ockham or Buridan.

This and the following sections will concentrate on five important topics in late medieval logic: (a) the theory of 'mental language', (b) the signification of propositions, (c) developments in supposition-theory, (d) semantic paradoxes, and (e) connotation-theory and the 'proofs of propositions'.

In *On Interpretation,* 16a3-4, Aristotle stated that 'spoken sounds are symbols of affections in the soul, and written marks symbols of spoken sounds'. These words were translated by Boethius and interpreted as implying three levels of language: spoken, written and mental. Through Boethius this three-level hierarchy of language became a commonplace in medieval logical literature.

Of the three, mental language was regarded as the most basic. Its semantic properties are natural ones; they do not originate from any convention or custom, and cannot be changed at will. Unlike spoken and written languages, mental language is the same for everyone.

Careful authors sometimes distinguished 'proper' from 'improper' mental language. The latter occurs when we think 'in English' or 'in French'. Thus a public speaker might rehearse a speech by running through silently the words he will later utter aloud. What goes on there is a kind of 'let's pretend' speaking that takes place in imagination and is in that sense 'mental'. But it is not what most authors meant by 'mental language'. Since silent recitation varies with the spoken language one is rehearsing, it is not the same for everyone. Proper mental language is different. It includes, for example, what happens when one suddenly 'sees' the force of a mathematical proof; in that case there is a 'flash of insight', an understanding or judgement that need not yet be put into words, even silently. This kind of mental language, the theory goes, is the same for everyone.

Spoken language, by contrast, has its semantic function parasitically, through a conventional correlation between its expressions and mental ones. The arbitrariness of this convention is what allows the multitude of spoken languages. Written language plays an even more derivative role, through a conventional correlation between its inscriptions and the sounds of spoken language. The arbitrariness of this convention too allows for different scripts among written languages. Only through the mediation of spoken language, the theory went, are inscriptions correlated with thoughts in mental language. This view implies that one cannot read a language one does not know how to speak. Most medieval authors accepted this consequence.

Following Boethius, the correlations between written and spoken language and between spoken and mental language were often regarded as relations of 'signification'. This claim had theoretical consequences, since signification was a well-defined notion in the Middle Ages. A term 'signifies' what it makes one think of ('establishes an understanding of'=*constituit intellectum*+genitive). While there was dispute about what occupies the object-pole of this relation, there was agreement over the criterion. Signification is thus a special case of causality, and so transitive. (Certain authors added to signification in general the particular notions of immediate and ultimate signification. The general relation of signification thus became what modern logicians call the 'ancestral' of the relation of immediate signification; a term *t* then ultimately signifies *x* if and only if *t* signifies *x* and *x* does not signify anything else.) Terms in mental language signify (make one think of) external objects only in the degenerate sense that they *are* the thoughts of those external objects.

According to this view, to say that expressions of spoken language immediately signify expressions of mental language is to say that the function of speech is to convey thoughts. Certain authors, e.g. Duns Scotus, Burley and Ockham, regarded this as too restrictive. For them, spoken (and written) terms may be made to signify anything, not only the speaker's thoughts. In fact spoken words do not always make us think of thoughts; sometimes we are made to think directly of external objects. For these authors, the relations between written and spoken language and between either of these and mental language are not relations of signification. Ockham described them neutrally as relations of 'subordination'.

Although authors since Boethius had recognized mental language, it was not until the fourteenth century that it began to be investigated in detail. Ockham was the first to develop a full theory of mental language and put it to philosophical use. Shortly thereafter, Buridan began to work out his own view. His theory agrees with Ockham's on the whole, although Ockham's is the more detailed. In the early 1340s, Gregory of Rimini refined certain parts of the theory, and applied it to a solution to the Liar Paradox. In 1372, Peter of Ailly's *Concepts and Insolubles* incorporated the work of both Ockham and Gregory. Other authors made contributions to the theory, but these were the major ones. The presentation below will follow Ockham's account except as indicated.

Terms in mental language are concepts; its propositions are judgements. The fact that mental language is the same for everyone explains how it is possible to translate one spoken (or written) language into another. A sentence in Spanish is a correct translation of a sentence in English if and only if the two are subordinated to the same mental sentence. More generally, any two spoken or written expressions from the same or different languages are synonymous if and only if they are subordinated to the same mental expression. Again, any spoken or written expression is equivocal if and only if it is subordinated to more than one mental expression.

If mental language accounts for synonymy and

equivocation in spoken and written languages, can there be synonymy or equivocation in mental language itself? The textual evidence is mixed. There are passages in Ockham supporting a negative answer in both cases. Nevertheless other texts, where Ockham is discussing the semantics of certain connotative terms, perhaps imply the existence of mental synonymy. As for equivocation, Ockham's theory of tense and modality, as well as his theory of supposition, commits him outright to certain kinds of equivocation in mental language. But apart from textual considerations, there are philosophical reasons for saying that, given other features of Ockham's theory, mental synonymy or equivocation makes no sense.

What is included in mental language? In two passages (*Summa logicae,* I, 3=[17.7] *OP* 1:11.1-26; *Quodlibet* 5, q. 8=[17.7] *OT* 9:508-13), Ockham remarks that, just as for spoken and written language, the vocabulary of mental language is divided into 'parts of speech'. Thus there are mental nouns, verbs, prepositions, conjunctions, etc. But not all features of spoken and written language are found in mental language. Ockham acknowledges doubts about mental participles (their job could be performed by verbs) and pronouns (presumably 'pronouns of laziness', as for example in 'Socrates is a man and *he* is an animal'). Moreover, not all characteristics of spoken and written syntax are found in mental language. While mental nouns and adjectives have case and number, and mental adjectives admit of positive, comparative and superlative degrees, they do not have gender and are not divided into grammatical declensions (like Latin's five declensions). Mental verbs have person, number, tense, voice and mood, but are not divided into grammatical conjugations.

Ockham's mental language looks remarkably like Latin. This fact led some modern writers to reject the theory as a foolish attempt to 'explain' features of Latin by merely duplicating them in mental language, which is then regarded as somehow more 'basic'. But more is involved than that. Ockham's strategy is to admit into mental language exactly those features of spoken or written language that affect the truth-values of propositions. All other features of spoken and written language, Ockham says, are only for the sake of decorative style, or in the interest of brevity. They are not present in mental language.

Mental language is thus a logically perspicuous language for describing the world. It has whatever is needed to distinguish truth from falsehood, nothing more. In this respect, mental language is reminiscent of the 'ideal languages' proposed by early twentieth-century philosophers.

How are mental words combined in mental propositions? What is the difference, for example, between the true mental proposition 'Every man is an animal' and the false 'Every animal is a man'? In written language, the difference is the spatial configuration of the words. But the mind does not take up space, so that there can be no such difference there. In speech the difference lies in the temporal sequence of the words. But since proper mental language at least sometimes involves a 'flash of insight' that happens all at once, neither can temporal word order account for the difference between the two mental propositions.

Because of such difficulties, authors such as Gregory of Rimini and Peter of Ailly held that mental propositions (although not all of them for Peter) are simple mental acts not really composed of distinct mental words at all. Ockham too had considered such a theory (*In Sententias* II, qq. 12-13=[17.7] *OT* 5:279; *Exposition of 'On Interpretation'*, proem=[17.7] *OP* 2:356). It is hard to reconcile this view with the claim that mental vocabulary is divided into 'parts of speech'; distinct mental words would appear to have no job to do if they do not enter into the structure of mental propositions.

There was a dispute over ultimate signification. Metaphysical realists, such as Burley, maintained the traditional view that general terms ultimately signify universal entities, while nominalists (e.g. Ockham and Buridan) held that they ultimately signify only individuals.

Some authors extended the notion of signification to ask not only about the signification of terms but also about the signification of whole propositions. Do they signify anything besides what their component terms signify separately? Do they signify, for example, states of affairs or facts?

Ockham did not explicitly address this question. But Buridan did, and his answer was no. For him, a proposition and in general any complex expression—signifies whatever its categorematic terms signify, nothing more. ('Categorematic' terms are those that can serve as subject or predicate in a proposition; they were regarded as having their own signification. Other words were called 'syncategorematic' and were regarded as not having any signification of their own; they are 'logical particles' used for combining categorematic terms into propositions and other complex expressions.) Thus in the spoken proposition 'The cat is on the mat', when I hear the word 'cat' I am, on Buridan's account, made to think of all cats and when I hear 'mat' I am made to think of all mats. That is all the proposition makes me think of, and so all it signifies.

Elsewhere Buridan maintained a different and incompatible theory. The proposition 'Socrates is sitting', for example, signifies *Socrates to be sitting*. And what is that? Buridan held that if Socrates really is sitting, then *Socrates to be sitting* is just Socrates himself. But if he is not sitting, then *Socrates to be sitting* is nothing at all. This view bears some similarity to a theory held earlier at Oxford by Walter Chatton and discussed as the first previous view in Henry Hopton's *On the Truth and Falsehood of Propositions*. Similar views were defended by Richard Feribrigge and John Huntman. The details of their texts have not been thoroughly investigated, and there is much that is still obscure; it is not certain that all these authors maintained variants of the same doctrine. Still, the motivation is the same in each case: to find something to serve as the significate of a proposition in an ontology that does not allow anything like facts, states of affairs or 'propositions' in the modern sense.

But there were other opinions. As early as Abelard, some authors held that what propositions signify falls outside the Aristotelian categories, and is something like the modern notion of 'proposition'.

Sometimes this new entity was called a 'mode', sometimes a *dictum.* In the fourteenth century, such theories continued to find their defenders. Perhaps a version of it may be seen in the early 1330s in William of Crathorn. Perhaps too Henry Hopton intended such a theory as the second previous view he considered, according to which a proposition signifies a 'mode' of a thing, where a 'mode' is not a *something* but a *being-somehow (esse aliqualiter).* But an unequivocal statement can be found in the theory of 'complexly significables'. According to this theory, complexly significables are the bearers of truth-value. They are not propositions in the medieval sense, not even mental propositions, but are what is expressed by propositions. They are the significates of propositions, and the objects of knowledge, belief and prepositional attitudes generally. Complexly significables do not exist in the way substances and accidents do. Before creation, for example, only God existed. But even then God knew *that the world was going to exist.* This complexly significable cannot be identified with God himself, since God is a necessary being but it was contingent that the world was going to exist. Yet as distinct from God, it cannot have existed before creation. Such extralogical considerations were an important motivation for the theory of complexly significables. Authors such as Buridan and Peter of Ailly rejected the theory; Peter, for example, claimed that the argument about God's knowledge before creation is based on an illegitimate substitution of identicals in an opaque context involving necessity.

All these theories offered a real entity (even if an odd one, like a 'complexly significable') as the correlate of a true proposition, and so as the ontological basis for a 'correspondence' theory of truth. Other authors took a different approach. They too maintained a correspondence theory, often expressed as: a proposition is true if and only if it 'precisely signifies as is the case', or if and only if 'howsoever [the proposition] signifies, so it is the case'. For them, the proper question is not *what* but *how* a proposition signifies. This 'adverbial' notion of signification allowed a correspondence theory without being obliged to find any ontological correlate for a true proposition to correspond to. After rejecting earlier views, Henry Hopton's own theory was like this. Heytesbury had earlier held a similar view, as did Peter of Ailly later.

The theory of 'supposition' is a mystery. Although it is central to the theories of 'properties of terms' that developed from the twelfth century on, it is not clear what the theory was intended to accomplish, or indeed what the theory as a whole was about.

Throughout its history, there were two main parts to supposition theory. One was a theory of the reference of terms in propositions, and how that reference is affected by syntactic and semantic features of propositions. The question this part of the theory was intended to answer is, 'What does a term refer to (supposit for, stand for) in a proposition?' That much is clear. But from the beginning, there was another part of supposition theory, an account of how one might validly 'descend to singulars' under a given occurrence of a term in a proposition, sometimes combined with a correlative account of 'ascent from singulars'. The mystery surrounds this second part.

Before the decline of terminism after 1270, there is some evidence that the second part of supposition theory, like the first, was intended to answer the question of what a term refers to in a proposition. The first part of the theory says what kind of thing a given term-occurrence refers to, while the second specifies how many such things it refers to (in much the way one finds even today accounts purporting to say whether the terms of a syllogism are about 'all' or 'some' of a class). The evidence for this is mixed, but even if this was the original intent of the second part of supposition theory, some authors quite early realized its theoretical difficulties.

When supposition theory re-emerged with Burley in England and later with Buridan in France, the two parts of the theory had been separated once and for all. By that time the theory of descent and ascent clearly was not about what a term refers to in a proposition. What it was about instead is uncertain.

The account below will mainly follow Ockham, although other authors will be mentioned. Their theories differed from his in detail, sometimes in important detail, but Ockham's is fairly typical.

The first part of supposition theory divided supposition or reference first into proper (literal) and improper (metaphorical). The latter is illustrated by 'England fights', where 'England' refers by metonymy to England's inhabitants. Medieval logic, like modern logic, did not have an adequate theory of metaphor. Ockham, Burley and a few others list some haphazard sub-divisions of improper supposition, but really mention it only to set it aside. Their emphasis is on proper supposition.

Proper supposition was divided into three kinds: personal, simple and material. The origin of these names is unclear, although the term 'personal' suggests a connection with the theology of the Trinity and the Incarnation. But it should not be thought that personal supposition has anything especially to do with persons.

Personal supposition occurs when a term refers to everything of which it is truly predicable. Thus in 'Every man is running', 'man' refers to all men and so is in personal supposition. But so too 'running' refers there to all things now running, and hence is likewise in personal supposition. It does not refer there only to some running things, for example, only to the running men. Again, in 'Some man is running', 'man' refers to all men, not just to running ones.

A term has material supposition when it refers to a spoken or written word or expression and is not in personal supposition. Thus, 'man' in 'Man has three letters' has material supposition. Although there are obvious similarities, material supposition is not merely a medieval version of modern quotation marks. For in 'It is possible for Socrates to run', the phrase 'for Socrates to run' has material supposition. But it refers to the proposition 'Socrates is running', of which the phrase 'for Socrates to run' is not a quotation.

The definition of simple supposition was a matter of dispute, depending in part on an author's metaphysical views and in part on his theory about the role of language in general. As a paradigm, 'man' in 'Man is a species' has simple supposition. In general, terms in simple supposition refer to universals. But for nominalists like Ockham, there are no metaphysical universals; the only universals are universal terms in language, most properly universal concepts in mental language. Thus for Ockham terms in simple supposition refer to concepts. It is they that are properly said to be species or genera. To prevent the term 'concept' in 'Every concept is a being' from having simple supposition (it has personal supposition, since it refers to everything it signifies to all concepts), Ockham added that a term in simple supposition must not be 'taken significatively', i.e. that it not be in personal supposition.

But for a realist like Burley, terms in simple supposition refer to real universals outside the mind. It is they that are species and genera. Furthermore, for Burley and certain others, general terms in language signify those extramental universals. Thus the term 'man' signifies universal human nature, not any one individual man or group of men, and not all men collectively. For Burley, therefore, it is in simple supposition that a term refers to what it signifies. For Ockham, general terms do not signify universals, not even universal concepts; they signify individuals. Even a term like 'universal' signifies individuals, since it signifies concepts, which are metaphysically individuals and are 'universal' only in the sense of being predicable of many things. Hence for Ockham, it is in personal supposition, not simple, that a term refers to what it signifies.

Personal supposition is the default case. Any term in any proposition can be taken in personal supposition. It may alternatively be taken in simple or material supposition only if the other terms in the proposition provide a suitable context. In such cases, the proposition is strictly ambiguous and may be read in either sense.

From this first part of supposition theory alone, certain authors, e.g. Ockham and Buridan, although not Burley, developed a theory of truth-conditions for categorical propositions on the square of opposition. Thus, a universal affirmative 'Every *A* is *B*' is true if and only if everything the subject term refers to the predicate term also refers to (although it may refer to other things as well). Truth-conditions for other propositions on the square of opposition can be derived from this.

Subordinated to this first part of supposition theory was a theory of 'ampliation', accounting for the effects of modality and tense on personal supposition. A term in personal supposition may always be taken to refer to the things of which it is presently predicable. But in the context of past or future tenses, the term may also be taken to refer to the things of which it was or will be predicable. Likewise, in a modal context (possibility, necessity), the term may also be taken to refer to the things of which it *can* be truly predicable. This expansion of the range of referents was called 'ampliation'.

Ockham and Burley regarded the new referents provided by ampliation as alternatives to the normal ones. Thus in the proposition 'Every man was running', 'man' may be taken as referring either to all presently existing men or to all men existing in the past. The proposition is thus equivocal. But on the Continent, Buridan and others regarded the new referents as additions to the normal ones. For them, in the proposition 'Every man was running' 'man' refers to all presently existing men and all past men as well.

The second main part of supposition theory, the theory of descent and ascent, was a theory sub dividing personal supposition only, into several kinds. First, there is discrete supposition, possessed by proper names, demonstrative pronouns or demonstrative phrases (e.g. 'this man'). All other personal supposition is *common,* and was typically subdivided into: determinate (e.g. 'man' in 'Some man is running'), confused and distributive (e.g. 'man' in 'Every man is an animal'), and merely confused (e.g. 'animal' in 'Every man is an animal'). The details varied with the author.

Sometimes these sub-divisions were described via the positions of terms in categorical propositions. Subjects and predicates of particular affirmatives, and subjects of particular negatives, have determinate supposition. Subjects of universal affirmatives and negatives, and predicates of universal and particular negatives, have confused and distributive supposition. Only predicates of universal affirmatives have merely confused supposition.

More helpful is the description in terms of descent and ascent. For Ockham (Burley's and Buridan's theories are equivalent), a term has determinate supposition in a proposition if and only if it is possible to 'descend' under that term to a disjunction of singulars, and to 'ascend' to the original proposition from any singular. The exact specification of the notions of 'descent', 'ascent' and 'singular' is subtle, but an example should suffice. In 'Some man is running' one can 'descend' under 'man' to a disjunction: 'Some man is running; therefore, this man is running or that man is running', etc., for all men. Likewise one can 'ascend' to the original proposition from any singular: 'This man is running; therefore, some man is running.' Hence 'man' in the original proposition has determinate supposition.

A term has confused and distributive supposition in a proposition if and only if it is possible to 'descend' under that term to a conjunction of singulars but *not* possible to 'ascend' to the original proposition from any singular. Thus in 'Every man is running' it is possible to descend under 'man': 'Every man is running; therefore, this man is running and that man is running', etc., for all men. But the ascent from any singular 'This man is running; therefore, every man is running' is invalid. Hence the term 'man' in the original proposition has confused and distributive supposition.

A term has merely confused supposition in a proposition if and only if (a) it is not possible to descend under that term either to a disjunction or to a conjunction, but it is possible to descend to a *disjoint term,* and (b) it is possible to ascend to the original proposition from any singular. Thus in 'Every man is an animal' it is not possible to descend under 'animal' to either a disjunction or a conjunction, since if every man is an animal, it does not follow that every man is this animal or every man is that animal, etc. Much less does it follow that every man is this animal *and* every man is that animal, etc.

But it does follow that every man is *this animal or that animal or,* etc. Again, if it happens that every man is this animal (i.e. there is only one man and he is an animal), then every man is an animal. Hence the term 'animal' in that proposition has merely confused supposition.

It is hard to see what this doctrine was intended to accomplish, particularly with its appeal to odd 'disjoint terms' in merely confused supposition. At first, modern scholars thought it was an attempt to provide truth-conditions for quantified propositions in terms of (infinite) disjunctions or conjunctions. But if that was its purpose, the doctrine is a failure. The predicate of the particular negative 'Some man is not a Greek' has confused and distributive supposition according to the above definitions, but the conjunction to which one can descend under 'Greek' does not give the truth-conditions for the original proposition. Suppose Socrates and Plato are the only men.

Then the conjunction 'Some man is not this Greek [Socrates] and some man is not that Greek Plato' is true, but the original proposition is false.

The problem is that rules for ascent always concern ascent from any one singular, never from a conjunction. Certain later authors, e.g. Ralph Strode, Richard Brinkley and Paul of Venice, do explicitly discuss ascent from conjunctions. But earlier writers such as Burley, Ockham and Buridan conspicuously did not.

Another attempt to explain this second part of supposition theory suggests that the rules for ascent and descent were used in detecting and diagnosing fallacies. This is doubtless correct as far as it goes, but does not account for the details in the theory as we actually find it. In the end, the exact function of this part of the theory in the early fourteenth century remains a mystery.

Medieval discussions of 'insolubles' (semantic paradoxes like the Liar Paradox, 'The sentence I am now saying is false') began in the late twelfth century. By around 1200, theories on how to solve them can be distinguished. Thereafter, three periods in the medieval insolubles literature can be distinguished: (1) *c.* 1200-*c.* 1320, (2) *c.* 1320-*c.* 1350 and (3) everything after that.

The earliest known medieval theory of insolubles (*cassatio* or cancelling) maintained that one who utters an insoluble is simply 'not saying anything', in the sense that his words do not succeed in making a claim. This view, although it has its supporters today, quickly disappeared in the Middle Ages. Other early theories rejected some or all self-reference; these too have their modern counterparts. Still other early theories sound less familiar to modern ears. A few authors argued that, despite the surface grammar, the reference in insolubles is always to some *previous* proposition. For example, 'What I am saying is false' really amounts to 'What I said a moment ago is false'. The insoluble is true or false depending on whether I did in fact say something false a moment ago. Others, e.g. Duns Scotus, appealed to a distinction between signified acts and exercised acts. This is the distinction between what the speaker of an insoluble proposition says he is doing (the signified act) and what he is really doing (the exercised act). Although the distinction is suggestive, it is far from clear how it solves the paradoxes.

Many of these early views are cast in the framework of Aristotle's fallacy of what is said 'absolutely' and what is said 'in a certain respect'. Discussing that fallacy in his *Sophistical Refutations,* Aristotle made some enigmatic remarks that suggested the Liar Paradox. Consequently, many medieval authors tried to treat insolubles as instances of that fallacy, although there was little agreement on the details. Some held that insoluble propositions are true 'absolutely' but false 'in a certain respect'. Some had it the other way around. Others said they were both true and false, each 'in a certain respect'. Still others applied the Aristotelian distinction not to truth but to supposition, so that they distinguished between supposition absolutely and supposition in a certain respect. Long after the early period in the medieval literature, the fallacy *absolutely/in a certain respect* was retained as an authoritative framework for many authors' discussions, even when the real point of their theories was elsewhere.

These early theories predominated until about 1320; some

of them survived much longer. Burley and Ockham offered nothing new here. Both maintained a theory that merely rejected problematic cases of self-reference without being able to identify which those problematic cases were.

The first to break new ground was Thomas Bradwardine, in the early 1320s. Bradwardine's theory was based on a view linking signification with consequence. He appears to have been the first to hold that a proposition signifies exactly what follows from it. Since he was also committed to saying that *every* proposition implies its own truth (e.g. Socrates is running, therefore 'Socrates is running' is true), this means that the insoluble 'This proposition is false' signifies that it itself is true. Since it also signifies that it is false, it signifies a contradiction, and so is simply false. The paradox is broken.

Bradwardine's view was enormously influential. Buridan later maintained a broadly similar theory, and others held variants of it to the end of the Middle Ages; it was one of the predominant theories.

Shortly after Bradwardine, Roger Swyneshed, an Englishman associated with Merton College, proposed a theory in which truth is distinguished from correspondence with reality. For a proposition to be true, it must not only correspond with reality ('signify principally as is the case'), it must also not 'falsify itself, i.e. not be 'relevant to inferring that it is false'. (This notion of 'relevance' is not well understood.) Swyneshed drew three famous conclusions from his theory: (1) There are false propositions (namely, insolubles) that nevertheless correspond with reality. (2) Valid inference sometimes lead from truth to falsehood. Validity does not necessarily preserve truth, although it does preserve correspondence with reality. (3) Sometimes, two contradictory propositions are both false. The insoluble 'This proposition is false' is false because it 'falsifies' itself. But its contradictory 'That proposition is true' (referring to the previous proposition) is also false, since it fails to correspond with reality the previous proposition is *not* true. These conclusions generated much discussion in the later literature. Swyneshed's theory did not have many followers, but it had at least one important one: Paul of Venice maintained a version of Swyneshed's theory in his *Big Logic*.

In 1335, William Heytesbury proposed a theory that rivalled and may have surpassed Bradwardine's in influence. He maintained that in circumstances that would make a proposition insoluble if it signified just as it normally does ('precisely as its terms pretend'), it *cannot* signify that way only, but must signify some other way too. Thus 'Socrates is uttering a falsehood', if Socrates himself utters it and nothing else, cannot on pain of contradiction signify only that Socrates is uttering a falsehood, but must signify that and more. Depending on what else it signifies, and how it is related to the ordinary signification of the proposition, different verdicts about the insoluble are appropriate. Heytesbury himself refused to say what else an insoluble might signify besides its ordinary signification; that could not be predicted. But some late authors went on to fill in Heytesbury's silence. They stipulated that insolubles in addition signify that *they are true,* thus linking Heytesbury's theory with Bradwardine's.

Heytesbury's view has an important consequence. Since signification in mental language is fixed by nature, not by voluntary convention, mental propositions can never signify otherwise than they ordinarily do. Given Heytesbury's account of insolubility, this means that *there can be no insolubles in mental language.* Heytesbury himself did not draw this conclusion, but it is there none the less.

All important developments concerning insolubles between 1320 and 1350 originated with Englishmen and are associated in one way or another with Merton College. Later writers, in the third and last stage of the medieval insolubles literature, sometimes developed this English material in interesting new ways. Thus Gregory of Rimini and Peter of Ailly took the above consequence of Heytesbury's theory to heart. They maintained that there are no insolubles in mental language, and that insolubles arise in spoken and written language only because they correspond (are subordinated) to *two* propositions in the mind, one true and the other false. Apart from these developments of earlier views, there seem to be no radically original theories of insolubles in the Middle Ages after about 1350.

Ockham's theory of connotation has antecedents in Aristotle's remarks on paronymy (*Categories,* 1a12-15). It is the most highly developed such theory in the Middle Ages.

For Ockham, some categorematic terms are absolute; others are connotative. 'Bravery' is absolute since it signifies only bravery, a quality in the soul. But 'brave' is connotative since it signifies certain persons (brave ones), but only by making an oblique reference to ('connoting') their bravery. Connotative terms have nominal definitions; absolute terms do not. The notion of a nominal definition is difficult to state exactly, but all nominal definitions of a connotative term are 'equivalent' for Ockham in a sense that is perhaps as strong as synonymy. Furthermore, it appears that the connotative term itself is synonymous with each of its nominal definitions, and may be viewed in fact as a kind of shorthand abbreviation for them. Thus the adjective 'white' is a connotative term having the nominal definition 'something having a whiteness' or 'something informed by a whiteness'. All three expressions are synonymous for Ockham.

Since Ockham's 'better doctrine' is that there is no mental synonymy, the elementary vocabulary of mental language (simple concepts) includes no connotative terms. Mental language contains the absolute term 'whiteness' and syntactical devices to form nominal definitions like those above. But it does not, on pain of synonymy, contain a distinct mental adjective 'white'.

All primitive categorematic mental terms are thus absolute. This has important consequences for Ockham's philosophy. For (barring miracles) the mind has simple concepts only for things of which it has had direct experience ('intuitive cognition'). The supply of absolute concepts is therefore a guide to ontology.

There is a related theory in Ockham, the theory of 'exposition' or analysis. The outlines of this theory were established by the mid-thirteenth century. In brief, an exponible proposition is one containing a word (the 'exponible term') that obscures the sense of the whole proposition. It is to be analysed or 'expounded' into a plurality of simpler propositions, called 'exponents', that together capture the sense of the original. Thus 'Socrates is beginning to run' might be expounded by 'Socrates is not running' and 'Immediately hereafter Socrates will be running'.

Ockham's own theory of exposition is not especially innovative, except that he explicitly links it with the theory of connotation. This is an attractive move, since whereas the theory of connotation provides explicit nominal definitions for connotative terms, it is plausible to view exposition theory as providing contextual definitions of exponible terms treated as incomplete symbols. Hence, just as the absence of synonymy in mental language means that it contains no simple connotative terms, so too it would mean that mental language contains no exponible propositions, but only their exponents. Since contextual definitions provide the more general approach, it is not surprising that connotation theory quickly declined after Ockham, and is treated only perfunctorily in Strode and Wyclif. Its place is taken there by much more elaborate treatments of exponibles. Buridan does retain a fairly full theory of connotation, but it is not so detailed as Ockham's.

Although the theory of exposition continued to have a life of its own, by mid-century it had also been incorporated into the theory of 'proofs of propositions'. Billingham's *Youth's Mirror* was a seminal work here.

The notion of 'proof' involved in this literature was broader than the Aristotelian demonstration of the *Posterior Analytics*. It meant any argument showing that a certain proposition is true. Not all propositions can be 'proved'. Some of them serve as ultimate premisses of all proofs; they must be learned another way. Such elementary propositions Billingham calls 'immediate' propositions, containing only 'immediate' terms that cannot be 'resolved' into more elementary terms. Immediate terms include indexicals such as 'I', 'he', 'this', 'here' and 'now', and very general verbs such as 'is' and 'can' and their tenses. Hence a proposition like 'This is now here' is immediate.

Other propositions can ultimately be 'proved' from immediate propositions. Billingham recognized three methods for such proofs: exposition, 'resolution' and proof using an 'auxiliary' *(officialis)* term.

Exposition has already been explained. Resolution amounts to proof by expository syllogism. Thus 'A man runs' is 'proved' by the inference 'This runs and this is a man; therefore, a man runs'. But there is a problem. The premisses of this inference are not immediate, since their predicates are not immediate terms. And there appears to be no way to reduce them to yet more basic propositions by any of the three ways Billingham recognizes.

'Auxiliary' terms govern indirect discourse. They include epistemic verbs such as 'knows', 'believes', etc., and modal terms such as 'it is contingent'. To 'prove' a proposition containing an auxiliary term is to provide an argument spelling out the role of the auxiliary term. One of the premisses of this argument states how the proposition referred to in indirect discourse 'precisely signifies'. Thus 'It is contingent for him to run' is proved by: '"He runs" is contingent; and "He runs" precisely signifies for him to run; therefore, it is contingent for him to run.' There are still many obscurities in the theory of 'proofs of propositions'. But it was very widespread.

Our knowledge of late medieval logic has advanced enormously since the 1960s. The availability of previously unpublished texts has shed great light on this fertile period. Yet, as this chapter shows, there is still much that is unknown.

11

Silver Age of Scholasticism and Philosophy

Introduction

There are, however, remarkable similarities between the golden and silver ages. Both ages were guided by the scholastic aim of understanding the Christian faith. They exerted considerable effort in the defence of that faith and of orthodox doctrine against actual or perceived threats. Scholastics of both ages were heavily Aristotelian, giving 'the Philosopher' a prominent place in matters philosophical, but relying on authoritative patristic and scriptural sources for their theological doctrines. Both ages followed or were concurrent with periods of translation during which newly discovered works written in other languages were rendered into Latin. The centre of activity in both cases was the university, and the literary forms of expression used were largely a result of curricular activity. Finally, most scholastics were members of religious orders and, thus, had a strong commitment to the goals of those orders.

In spite of these points of similarity, there are profound differences between the two periods. Although both periods had the same aim of understanding the Christian faith, the overall theological emphasis that inspired most activities of the earlier scholastics had decreased in the sixteenth century. In theory and in some aspects of practice, philosophy remained the servant of theology, but a progressive independence of reason, as demonstrated by its increasing use apart from faith, developed in the later period. The traditional scholastic format of argument, in which both theologically authoritative sources and arguments based on reason were given in support of the positions to be defended, ceased to be the norm in non-theological works, and a greater emphasis was put upon reason. Moreover, the political structure and ideological situation of Europe during the silver age and, in particular, the discovery of the New World raised new important philosophical and legal issues of a secular nature that encouraged speculation independent of theology. For example, matters that had to do with the rights of conquered peoples produced a body of literature largely purged of theological considerations. There were, of course, many issues discussed by masters of arts and others in the earlier period that had nothing or little to do with theology, and in the discussion of which theological authorities were largely ignored. But the number of these secular issues increased substantially in the later period.

With respect to the apologetic spirit of both periods, again there are substantial differences. In the golden age the defence of Christian doctrine was primarily directed against infidels, as illustrated by Thomas's *Summa contra Gentiles,* or against those who were thought to have accepted too much of the thought of pagan philosophers, as is evident from the list of doctrines officially condemned in Paris in 1277. Yet there was no overall sense of urgency in the Church, nor was there a unified and institutional effort to deal with the challenges to orthodoxy. During the silver age, however, the situation was different. The challenges to the Church came from two different sources within the Christian community and one of them had considerable political power. The first source was humanism. The discovery of new literary, philosophical and artistic works from the ancient world had given rise not only to a renewed interest in pagan ideas, but to a change of attitude in the intellectual community that seemed to many to pose a threat to the integrity of the Christian faith. The second source was the Reformation, a movement of rebellion against institutionalized Christianity that gained considerable political support. As a result, a sense of urgency among members of the hierarchy and an organized Church-wide effort to meet these challenges developed, culminating in the Council of Trent (1545-63). There was, therefore, much apologetic literature written during this time, and its tone appears more urgent and compelling than that produced in the golden age. Medieval scholastics were fighting ideas, but scholastics from the silver age were fighting not only ideas, but also worldly power.

There is, as noted, remarkable agreement in the sources of both periods, with the later period depending heavily on the first as well. By the sixteenth century, scholasticism had become parcelled out into three traditions according to the author followed by each of them: Thomism, Scotism and Ockhamism. Moreover, these traditions had become identified with certain religious orders that looked upon the founders of these traditions with proprietary interests. For example, Dominicans were generally Thomistic, while Franciscans tended to follow Scotus or Ockham. This sort of ideological alignment had already begun in the thirteenth century, but it was not as rigid as it eventually became during the silver age. Moreover, the influence of Thomas Aquinas became increasingly pervasive in the silver age, particularly in the Iberian peninsula, a fact which has led some scholars to speak of a school of Spanish Thomism.

The heavy use of Aristotelian and medieval scholastic sources by scholastics of the silver age points to another interesting difference between the silver age and the golden age. While both ages coincided with or followed periods of intense translation activity, in the golden age the resulting translations helped shape the thought of the period and were the immediate source of much of that thought. By contrast, scholastics of the silver age largely ignored the new translations. There may be many reasons for this relative neglect, but surely one of them was the heavily Aristotelian character of scholasticism, which must have found distasteful the overwhelmingly Platonic material being translated.

The activity in both periods was concentrated in the university, but again there is an important difference. In the golden age, Paris was the unchallenged centre of both scholasticism and the intellectual life of Europe; it was the 'new Athens'. There were other important universities such as Oxford, Cambridge, Bologna and Naples, but none rivalled Paris. Moreover, an intellectual axis developed along a line which went from Rome to Oxford, passing through Paris. By contrast, the scholasticism of the silver age was most concentrated in the universities of the Iberian peninsula: Coimbra, Alcala, and, above all, Salamanca. There were significant places of learning in Italy too, but they were much less influential than the Iberian universities. Intellectual communication now extended from Coimbra, through Salamanca, and ultimately to Rome. These are two other important points to note. First, as in the earlier period, these strongholds of silver-age scholasticism were not alone in promoting great intellectual ferment. Paris, Oxford and Cambridge, for example, were also important, and there was considerable work done in the Netherlands and Germany. Second, these centres of silver-age scholasticism did not hold a monopoly on the intellectual life of Europe. By the sixteenth century scholasticism had become a regional, albeit powerful intellectual force perhaps the most powerful at the time but it had ceased to be the only intellectual force in Europe, as it had been during the golden age.

The scholastic literary genres favoured in the golden age, namely, the *summa,* the *quaestio,* and the commentary, were also used in the silver age, but with an important new development in this later period. Iberian scholastics, particularly Fonseca and Suarez, helped develop a new genre that became the standard form of expression among scholastics after the sixteenth century: the systematic and comprehensive treatise. There are plenty of examples of systematic and comprehensive treatises produced in the Middle Ages. Indeed, medieval *summae* are both systematic and comprehensive. But there are some important differences between medieval *summae* and the treatises produced during the silver age and thereafter. First, medieval *summae* tended to follow the established arrangement of the discourse in whatever subject-matter they explored. These patterns were derived from textual traditions going back to original paradigmatic works or particular doctrines. Thus, for example, the pattern of theological *summae* generally reflected an order of progression from God to creatures and back to God, the Neoplatonic *exitus-reditus* theme.

Second, the new type of literature differed from the medieval *summae* in that it abandoned the *quaestio* format, which had been used very frequently by earlier scholastics, in favour of an unbroken exposition of topics. Finally, these treatises were put together and organized into complete courses *(cursus)* of study that extended beyond particular disciplines, and included logic, natural philosophy and other philosophical disciplines. Sometimes these 'courses' were the result of co-operative efforts, as was the case with the well-known *Cursus Conimbricensis,* the main author of which was Fonseca. At other times, they were the result of a single author's effort (or that of his editors), as was the case with John of St Thomas's *Cursus philosophicus.*

The didactic advantages of the new genre should be obvious, for it organized materials in a continuous, comprehensive and logical way which facilitated teaching and made these works ideal textbooks. On the other hand, it introduced an element of dogmatism that was lacking in most of the earlier literature, for it veered toward the expository and away from the polemical, losing the sense of the controversial character of the topics discussed. This was not the case with all the philosophical treatises of the period; some still presented the *status questionis* of the issues they discussed in a polemical or quasi-polemical manner, but it certainly applied to a considerable portion of the philosophical literature produced at the time. Moreover, the adoption of the systematic and comprehensive format contributed to the neglect of the commentary and, therefore, the further estrangement of scholasticism from humanism. Primary sources were read in conjunction with these secondary sources, resulting in the neglect of the original authors and the frequent misunderstanding of their views.

Finally, although the most prominent members of both periods belonged to religious orders, the leading order during the silver age was the Society of Jesus, which had been founded by Ignacio de Loyola in 1540 in response, first, to the challenges that the Reformation posed to the Catholic Church and, second, to the need to convert the heathen. The mission of the Jesuit order, then, was from the start an apologetic one; and the order was organized like an army a clear indication of its aim. By contrast, the Franciscan and Dominican orders, which had dominated the golden age, had less defined and militant missions. The aim of the Franciscans was one of service, and the aim of the Dominicans was instruction through preaching. The latter was in part a response to the need to defend the faith against infidels and heretics Domingo de Guzman was a Spaniard and was quite aware of the needs of a frontier church but the Dominican order was never intended to be an army for the Church.

Understanding the similarities and differences between the golden and silver ages of scholasticism should help us understand Suarez, for he eminently displayed most of the characteristics of the scholasticism of the silver age we have discussed. He pursued the medieval aim of understanding faith, but granted philosophy a sphere of operation separate from and largely independent of theology. As a theologian, he was at the forefront of the defence of Catholic doctrine and the Catholic Church against the attacks of the Reformation. He was aware of the rigid conceptual traditions associated with the medieval religious orders and moved easily within their frameworks, although he frequently tried to break down the barriers among them. His thought was strongly Aristotelian, ignoring to a great extent the recently produced translations of non-Aristotelian works, but he showed extensive and firsthand acquaintance with traditional Christian sources. Suarez spent his professional life almost entirely within the confines of the leading Iberian universities of the period. He never taught at Paris, and most of his exchanges took place with either Iberian or Italian authors. He was the first to apply a systematic approach to metaphysics, and finally, as a member of the Jesuit order, Suarez displayed some of the combative traits associated with that order in several of his more polemical works. In short, it would be hard to find among scholastics of his time one that displayed more clearly the traits that characterized the silver age.

Suarez's Life, Works and Influence

Suarez was born in Granada, Spain, on 5 January, 1548, at the height of Spanish imperial power. Under Isabella of Castile and Ferdinand of Aragon, known as *los Reyes Católicos* (the Catholic Kings), a large part of the Iberian peninsula had become unified (1479) and power consolidated after the final defeat of the Moors at Granada (1492). Also in 1492 America was discovered, opening up unheard-of resources to the newly united kingdom. In a matter of fifty years, Spain became the pre-eminent political and economic power in Europe. As a result, artists and intellectuals flocked to Madrid, stimulating the development of arts and letters. Indeed, the period that goes roughly from 1500 to 1650 is generally known as the *Siglo de Oro* of Spanish letters because of the abundance and extraordinary quality of the literature produced. Spain became an intellectual leader in Europe and the undisputed leader of the Counter-Reformation. The Spanish mystics of the time, Teresa of Avila, Juan de la Cruz and Fray Luis de León, were among the most renowned anywhere. Antonio de Nebrija composed the first grammar of any romance language in 1492. The music of Victoria, Cabezón and other Spanish composers was played all over

Europe. The theatre flourished under the pens of Lope de Vega and Calderón de la Barca. The novel reached new heights in the work of Cervantes. And Spanish painting achieved international acclaim with Ribera, Zurbaran and Velazquez.

Philosophy, of course, could not be left behind, and so we find a score of Iberian figures of high rank. Among the most celebrated are Juan Luis Vives (1492–1540), Francisco de Vitoria (1492/3–1546), Domingo de Soto (1494–1560), Alonso de Castro (1495–1558), Melchior Cano (1509–60), Pedro Fonseca (1528–99), Domingo Bañez (1528–1604), Francisco Toletus (1532–96), Luis de Molina (1535–1600), Juan de Mariana (1536–1624), Gabriel Vazquez (1549–1604) and Juan de Santo Tomas (1589–1644). The greatest of the philosophers, however, is Francisco Suarez (1548–1617). Indeed, his work surpasses in depth, originality and comprehensiveness that of any other of these, and his influence, both in modern philosophy and in subsequent scholastic thought, has been substantial.

Suarez decided early in life that he would pursue an ecclesiastical career. Accordingly, he went to Salamanca to study canon law. While engaged in his studies there, he requested admission into the Society of Jesus. At first he was refused admission for reasons of health and what was perceived as a lack of proper intellectual capacity. Insistence paid off, however, and he was allowed to join the order in 1564. After completing his studies, he began a teaching career that would last for over fifty years, taking him to some of the most renowned institutions of his time: Segovia, Valladolid, Rome, Alcala, Salamanca and Coimbra. Suarez died in Lisbon, at the age of 70, on 25 September, 1617.

Suarez did not publish early in his life. His first work, *De incarnatione verbi,* appeared in 1590 when he was 42. After this initial publication, however, a steady stream of works followed. Suarez's contributions are important in three areas in particular: philosophy, law and theology. From a philosophical standpoint his most important works are *De anima* (*On the Soul,* 1621), which contains his psychology, epistemology and philosophy of mind; *De gratia* (*On Grace*, 1619–51), which deals with issues of philosophical theology involving free will and determinism; and the monumental *Disputationes metaphysicae (Metaphysical Disputations,* 1597). The last is undoubtedly one of the great works of Western philosophy: the first systematic and comprehensive treatise on metaphysics composed in the West that is not a commentary on Aristotle's *Metaphysics*. Furthermore, it summarizes and evaluates medieval metaphysical thought and remains the most complete exposition of Aristotelian metaphysics ever produced.

De legibus (1612) is Suarez's most important work dealing with legal and political theory. In it he explores in detail the nature of law and of civil society. His views on *ius gentium* make him, together with Vitoria and other Spanish authors of the time, a founder of international law.

Suarez's contributions to theology are contained in his numerous books on the subject. He touched upon almost every aspect of sacred doctrine, from the Trinity to questions pertaining to the spiritual life. This has made his theological writings a standard source of Catholic theology. Moreover, his role in helping to shape the response of the Catholic Counter-Reformation to the rise of Protestantism guarantees him a place in history.

Suarez's position in the history of philosophy is frequently disputed. Some historians locate him firmly in the medieval tradition, claiming that he should be seen as perhaps the last world-class figure of that tradition, before modern philosophy changed the philosophical direction of the West. Others, however, see Suarez as providing the foundation for some of the views that came to form the core of subsequent developments, and thus as a precursor of modern philosophy.

There are bases for defending both of these interpretations. Indeed, if one looks at Suarez carefully, it becomes evident that he is both the last major medieval theologian and the first major modern philosopher. This can be best illustrated, perhaps, with reference to the stated intention and method of the *Disputationes metaphysicae*.

With respect to the intention of the work, we need to look no further than the Preface to see that Suarez follows the theological emphasis of the Middle Ages. His purpose is the same as that expressed by the Anselmian saying: *Fides quaerens intellectum* (Faith seeking understanding). Suarez tells us, first, that he deals with metaphysics precisely because his aim is theological, for the good theologian will set down the foundations of metaphysics before he goes on to theology. Accordingly, he postponed his theological commentaries on Aquinas until after he had finished the *Disputationes* in order to provide a proper foundation for theology. Moreover, like Aquinas and other medieval theologians before him, Suarez points out that he never loses sight of Christian doctrine while he philosophizes and, indeed, that he intends his philosophy to be both Christian and an instrument of theology. This end is what guides not only the way he deals with the issues he discusses, but also the very opinions and views he presents, leading him to favour those that appear to him more useful for piety and revealed doctrine. Finally, in strict medieval fashion, he closes the Preface by hoping that the work will lead to God's greater glory and be of use to the Catholic Church.

From this, it appears quite conclusively that Suarez's aim in the *Disputationes metaphysicae* is theological rather than philosophical, and that he fits squarely within the main medieval scholastic view in which philosophy is seen as a handmaiden of theology. However, in the very Preface to which reference has been made there are indications of a different attitude at play as well. First, Suarez speaks of giving back to metaphysics the place and position that rightly belongs to it, and that place and position are interpreted as being separate from and anterior to theology. Second, he states that his role as author of the *Disputationes* is not that of the theologian, but of the philosopher. And, third, he apologizes for the occasional digressions into theological matters found in the work, even though he does not discuss theological issues in depth.

All this indicates Suarez's rigorous view of the distinction between metaphysics and theology and of his role as philosopher and theologian. The fact that he calls himself a philosopher, that in philosophy he avoids arguments based on faith, and that he apologizes for dealing, even incidentally, with theological matters in a work of philosophy should be sufficient to make the point. Although many of the masters who taught liberal arts in the Middle Ages were not theologians and taught subjects independently of theology, the most famous scholastics of the age considered themselves theologians and their philosophical views were generally presented within theological works. Moreover, even though many scholastics distinguished between theology and philosophy, none of them would have apologized for the introduction of theological matter in a philosophical context, and most of them used both faith and reason to argue for both philosophical and theological views. But such a procedure is abandoned in Suarez's *Disputationes*. Occasionally, he does bring up a theological point, but in such cases the aim is to show the reader how to apply metaphysical principles to theology rather than to use theology to prove philosophy. This secular emphasis in metaphysics both sets Suarez apart from his medieval predecessors and situates him at the beginning of the modern tradition.

Another point that sets him apart from medieval scholasticism is the very structure and procedure he follows in the *Disputationes*. The work does not adopt the standard medieval scholastic literary genres used in works of metaphysics. Medieval authors generally presented their metaphysical views in commentaries on Aristotle, which were sometimes internally organized in *quaestiones;* or they presented them in the course of theological works, such as theological *summae* or commentaries on the *Sentences* of Peter Lombard. Occasionally, short didactic or polemical tracts *(opuscula)* such as Thomas's *De ente et essentia* or *De unitate intellectus contra Averroistas* were also composed. But no systematic and comprehensive metaphysical treatises were produced. Suarez, however, adopted precisely this format. Nor did he follow the popular custom of structuring works as *quaestiones* reflecting current controversies and polemics.

Rather, he adopted a logical procedure in which metaphysical issues are discussed according to their relation to overall topics. Suarez is the first to apply this procedure to metaphysics. His originality in this is what distinguishes him from his predecessors and points to modern philosophy.

In short, Suarez cannot be considered exclusively a medieval scholastic or a modern philosopher. He has to be seen in context, as restating the past and anticipating the future. His overall aims and views go back to the Middle Ages, but some of his procedures point toward the modern period. He should be seen as both a medieval scholastic and a modern philosopher.

Before concluding this section I should say something about Suarez's influence on the Catholic tradition, modern thought and Latin American scholasticism. Along with Augustine, Aquinas and other figures of similar stature, Suarez is one of the most influential figures in Catholicism. He played a major role in the response to the growing challenge of Protestantism and the secularizing impact of humanism. Many of his theological ideas were considered highly original at the time and have become part of the common stock of Catholic theology. His analogical understanding of the doctrine of the Trinity, his position concerning the motivation for the Incarnation, and his views on morality have all played important roles in Catholic teaching. But perhaps it is his doctrine of the relation between divine grace, merit and human freedom that has most firmly established his influence and most evidently contrasts him with the Protestant ideas of the time.

Suarez's influence, however, is not confined to the Catholic tradition. Most early modern philosophers learned metaphysics from his *Disputationes,* and many of their ideas can be traced to that work. Among those most clearly influenced by Suarez are Jungius, Descartes, Leibniz, Spinoza, Wolff, Berkeley, Schopenhauer and Vico, but echoes of his language and views can be seen in many others, including Locke. Indeed, Suarez is often blamed for contributing to the development of the mentalistic metaphysics characteristic of modern philosophy. Whether this attribution is correct is a matter of debate, but what is clear is that his terminology seeped into early modern philosophy and became a part of the common philosophical way of speaking. In addition to his metaphysics, moreover, his legal and political views had considerable impact on modern legal theorists such as Holdsworth and Grotius. Indeed, some consider Suarez's thought in these areas to be as influential and valuable as, if not more so than, his metaphysical views.

Finally, there is Suarez's impact on Latin American thought. The New World was discovered in 1492, and by the middle of the next century, schools and universities teaching scholastic thought were already functioning in Mexico and elsewhere. Thus, by the time Suarez's *Disputationes metaphysicae* was published in 1597, there was a ready audience available for them. The result was to be expected: his metaphysical and theological views established themselves as alternatives to the already popular views of Aquinas, Scotus and Ockham.

Suarez's Metaphysics

The core of Suarez's philosophical, theological and legal thought is his metaphysics. The rest of this essay will therefore be devoted to the exploration of two key elements of Suarez's metaphysical thought, which illustrate both the transitional role it played between medieval scholasticism and modern philosophy and the innovation within traditional parameters that is so characteristic of it. These elements are his conception of metaphysics and the doctrine of the transcendentals.

Suarez's Conception of Metaphysics

Most conceptions of metaphysics fall into one of two categories: views that regard metaphysics as concerned with the real as opposed to the mental, and views that conceive it as concerned with the mental rather than the real. Aristotle (*Metaphysics* 1, 1-3) and his medieval commentators are usually identified as proponents of the first view. Metaphysics in this context is conceived as a science not very different from other sciences, except for some peculiarities of the object it studies and the method it employs. Like other sciences its aim is to describe the world, noting its characteristics and the causal relationships that hold among the entities that are part of it. There is, then, nothing mental about the object that metaphysics studies; its object of study is extramental reality, not concepts or other mental entities.

In contrast, the mentalistic conception of metaphysics is a favourite in contemporary philosophical circles. According to it, metaphysics is not concerned with the description of the extramental world or the way it functions; it is concerned with our concepts about the world, rather than the world itself. In that sense, metaphysics is not realistic but mentalistic.

The mentalistic conception of metaphysics did not come about as a result of a single drastic change in the history of philosophy. Descartes, Hume, Kant and many others figure prominently in the slow process that produced a change from realism to mentalism. Among the figures that are often cited as having contributed to that process is Suarez.

Suarez conceives metaphysics as a perfect and a priori science. Something is perfect if it is complete, that is, if it lacks nothing for it to be the sort of thing it is. Thus a perfect science is a science that lacks none of the conditions required of sciences. Such conditions stipulate that sciences provide certain and evident knowledge of the objects they study through knowledge of the properties, principles, and causes of those objects. Moreover, since metaphysics is an a priori science, such knowledge is not based on experience.

A property, in the Aristotelian context within which Suarez works, is a feature of a thing which necessarily characterizes the members of the species to which the thing belongs but is not part of the essence of the thing in question and thus does not appear in its definition. The capacity to laugh, for example, is a property of human beings because it necessarily characterizes human beings, although it is not part of the definition of human being. A property, in contrast with an accident, always accompanies each member of a species. The task of science, and therefore of metaphysics, is twofold: first, to identify the properties of the object it studies and, second, to demonstrate the necessary connection of those properties to the object in question through an analysis of the principles and causes of that object.

The object of metaphysics was a matter of intense discussion in the Middle Ages. The origin of the debate can be traced back to Aristotle's *Metaphysics,* where he presents four different understandings of its object: being *qua* being, substance, divine entities, and primary causes and principles. Settling the issue was important, for most medievals believed that the unity of a science is derived from the unity of its object. Yet, the four objects that Aristotle identified as objects of metaphysics were not easily collapsed into one.

By the time Suarez was addressing this issue, the possible objects of metaphysics had grown in number and certain precisions had been introduced. Suarez considers and rejects six different opinions on the object of metaphysics: (1) being taken most abstractly and generally so that it includes not only all real beings, whether substantial or accidental, but also mental beings; (2) only real being, leaving out mental beings, so that its object includes both substantial and accidental beings; (3) the supreme, real being, namely God; (4) immaterial being or substance; (5) categorical being, namely, being as divided into the ten Aristotelian categories; and (6) substance *qua* substance, that is substance considered apart from whether it is material or immaterial, finite or infinite.

Suarez's view is that the object of metaphysics is 'being insofar as it is real being' *(ens in quantum ens reale).* As such, metaphysics includes the study of God, immaterial substances, and the real accidents of immaterial substances. It excludes, however, the study of purely mental beings *(entia rationis)* and the study of beings which are completely accidental, and abstracts from all matter.

If Suarez had said nothing else about the nature of metaphysics and its object than what I have presented in summary so far, he could have been interpreted only as having a realistic conception of metaphysics, albeit a somewhat different one from those of his predecessors. Moreover, it would have been very difficult to accuse him of having moved in the direction of mentalistic metaphysics. After all, he clearly states that metaphysics deals with real being and only real being, and argues against it having to do with mental being. However, Suarez did not stop there. He went on to discuss the nature of the object metaphysics studies. It is what he says on this matter in particular, coupled with how his views were used by later philosophers, that has given rise to speculation about his role in the history of metaphysics and its development toward mentalism.

The view that Suarez contributed substantially to the mentalization of metaphysics is based, first, on his conception of real being and, second, on his statement that the object of metaphysics is the objective concept of being. Real being for Suarez is not the same as actual being. Actual being is the kind of being existing things have. Real being need not be actual; it can be possible. Thus, real being encompasses both actual being (e.g. my existing cat Minina and the colour of her fur) and possible being (e.g. my non-existing cat Misifus and the colour of his fur). The difference between non-real beings and possible beings is that possible beings have an aptitude for existence, even though they do not exist, whereas non-real beings do not. A possible being like Misifus, has an aptitude such that it could exist even if it does not; but a non-real being like a goatstag, lacks such an aptitude and neither exists nor can exist.

Real being, then, includes possible, unactualized essences in addition to actualized ones. This means that the object of science, and thus of metaphysics, is not restricted to actually existing being, but extends to and includes possible being. This conception of metaphysics, as the study of not only actual essences but also possible essences, has been identified as one of the sources of the mentalism of modern philosophy; for possible being, so the argument goes, can be nothing but mental, and thus the door is open to a conception of metaphysics as a science of the mental.

This interpretation is disputable, however, for Suarez does not identify possible being with mental being. He understands mental being as 'what has objective being only in the intellect or as what is thought by the mind as a being, although it has no being in itself', that is, what has no being outside the mind. Blindness is a good example of a mental being, for blindness is a lack of something rather than having something and, as such, has no reality outside the mind.

From this it follows that possible beings for Suarez are not the same as mental beings. For possible beings, even though they do not exist, have an aptitude for existence. But it is impossible for mental beings ever to exist, so they cannot have an aptitude for existence. Consequently, that metaphysics includes the study of possible beings does not mean that it is concerned with mental entities.

The second source of the charge that Suarez's conception of metaphysics contributed substantially to the mentalization of the discipline is his claim that the object studied by metaphysics is the objective concept of being. This claim may be interpreted as implying mentalism because objective concepts, *qua* concepts, presumably cannot be anything but mental; therefore, it turns out that metaphysics studies something mental rather than something real.

The notion of objective concept is one of two members of a distinction widely used by later scholastics. The other member of the distinction is the formal concept. The formal concept, according to Suarez, is an act of our minds whereby we conceive something. As an act of the mind, it is a quality and thus an accident of the mind. The formal concept is called 'formal' because it informs the mind in the way any form informs its subject, and it is the end of the process of conception. Moreover, it is by means of the formal concept that the mind knows an object, for the formal concept represents the thing known to the mind.

The objective concept, on the other hand, is what is represented in the act, or quality, which is the formal concept. The objective concept is not a concept in the way a formal concept is, namely as a form that modifies the mind, determining its conception. Indeed, it is called a concept only derivatively because of the relation it has to the formal concept. It is objective in so far as it is the object with which the formal concept is concerned; it is not objective in the sense of being an image or representation of something else. On the contrary, the objective concept is what is represented by the formal concept and, as Suarez states elsewhere, 'the thing signified' by it.

In short, we might say that the distinction between the objective concept and the formal concept is the distinction between what I think about (objective) and that through which I think it (formal). So, whereas 'the formal concept cat', for example, is the mental act whereby someone thinks of 'cat', 'the objective concept cat' is whatever one thinks about when one thinks of 'cat', namely cat.

Put this way, it does not look as if objective concepts are mental in any way. As Suarez states, they are not concepts strictly speaking; they are not representations or images; and they are not mental acts or qualities. Instead, they are the objects of the (formal) concepts the mind forms. This would seem to indicate that they are not mental at all.

This inference is corroborated by the fact that the being and unity of objective concepts turn out to be the same being and unity of their objects and, thus, that objective concepts can be mental or real depending on those objects. Suarez makes quite clear that whereas the formal concept is real, always 'a true and positive thing', the objective concept need not always be something real; it can be mental or real, depending on the objective concept in question. If, for example, the objective concept in question is 'blindness', what we have is a mental being because blindness is not a real entity. If, on the other hand, the objective concept in question is 'humanity', what we have is a real being, namely an actual or possible substance (i.e. a human being). Indeed, Suarez says that this is the case with the objective concept of being.

From these considerations we must conclude that not all objective concepts have only a mental status; some objective concepts exist in reality. This entails, then, that to be an objective concept does not necessarily imply mental existence alone. Whether that is the case depends not on the nature of objective concepts as such, but on the particular objective concept involved. In the case of 'blindness', it does imply mental existence alone because blindness does not and cannot exist outside the mind; but in the case of 'humanity', it does not because human beings can and do exist outside the mind. This same point is corroborated when we look at the unity of objective concepts.

Do objective concepts, *qua* objective concepts, have universal or individual unity? Suarez's answer is unequivocal. The formal concept is always present in some mind that produces it and is, therefore, individual. With respect to the objective concept, however, the case is different, for an objective concept is universal or individual depending on the particular objective concept involved. If the objective concept in question is 'man' or 'substance', the objective concept is universal. If, on the other hand, the objective concept in question is something determinate, like 'Socrates', then the objective concept is individual. From this it also follows that only those objective concepts that are individual can exist extramentally and therefore be real, since for Suarez universals have no such existence.

The situation with respect to the unity of objective concepts, then, is quite similar to the one with respect to their being. Objective concepts can be individual or universal; therefore, they cannot, *qua* objective concepts, be one of these to the exclusion of the other. In cases where there is an exclusion, as it happens with 'blindness', the exclusion arises from the nature of the objective concept in question, not from the fact that it is an objective concept.

The implication of what Suarez says concerning the being and unity of objective concepts is that objective concepts have the ontological status, that is, the being and unity, of their objects. We know, for example, that the objective concept 'blindness' has the same ontological status as blindness, and that the same applies to the objective concepts 'humanity' and 'Minina'. The being and unity of the objective concept of Minina is the being (real) and unity (individual) of Minina; the being and unity of the objective concept of tree is the being (real) and unity (universal) of tree; and the being and unity of the objective concept of blindness is the being (mental) and unity (universal) of blindness. This seems quite clear. Now, since the objective concept that metaphysics studies is 'real being', the object of metaphysics cannot be anything but real, and Suarez's conception of metaphysics cannot be anything but realistic.

The Transcendentals

Suarez's conception of metaphysics prompts an interesting objection. The function of science, as already noted, is to identity the properties of its object, demonstrating their necessary connection with it through an analysis of principles and causes. It follows, then, that metaphysics, as a science of being *qua* being, must be concerned with identifying the properties of being and demonstrating how those properties are necessarily tied to being through an examination of the principles and causes of being. The difficulty posed by this view is that being *qua* being does not have any properties, for considered this abstractly, being is common to every being and its properties. Thus it does not appear that being *qua* being can have any properties which are peculiarly its own.

Suarez is aware of this difficulty and gives an explicit answer to it. The answer is important both philosophically and historically. It is philosophically important because it makes clear that, even though Suarez never explicitly says so, metaphysics for him turns out to be the science of the transcendentals; it is historically important because this conception of metaphysics may have served to prepare the way for the growth of transcendentalism in later European Continental philosophy.

Suarez's solution to the difficulty is to propose that, although being *qua* being has no properties that are really distinct from it, it does have properties that are conceptually distinct from it. These properties are unity, truth and goodness. They are coextensional with being because whatever is a being is also one, good and true, and whatever is one, good or true is also a being.

It is the coextension of these properties with being that makes them transcendental, for they are common to the ten categories into which being is divided. These properties are not cointensional with being, however, because their conceptual analyses do not coincide with that of being or with those of each other. In short, although whatever is a being is also one, good and true, to be and to be one, to be good, and to be true are not the same.

Metaphysics can be conceived as the study of being *qua* real being so long as it is understood that it deals with properties of being that are only intensionally distinct from it. Moreover, since what is coextensional but not cointensional with being are precisely its transcendental attributes (unity, truth, goodness), it turns out that what metaphysics studies as principles and what it studies as properties of being are the same. Under these circumstances, metaphysics turns out to be the science of the transcendentals.

Suarez's answer to the difficulty posed by the fact that being does not appear to have any properties is to argue that indeed being has properties even though they are not the same sort of property other things have. According to Suarez, properties must fulfil several conditions: they must be real, and really distinct from their subjects, and they must be coextensional with their subjects but not included in their essences. The capacity to laugh, for example, fulfils all these conditions with respect to human beings and thus is a property of them. But it is obvious that none of the transcendental properties of being Suarez accepts, namely, one, true, and good, fulfil all these conditions.

Suarez grants this conclusion, but he argues that being can still have properties because it has some 'attributes which are not mere products of the mind, but are truly and really predicated of it'. But how, then, are these attributes related to being? What kind of properties are they if they cannot be properties in the usual way? Suarez's answer is that these attributes add to being negations, privations, or real extrinsic denominations taken from real relations; unity adds a negation or privation, and truth and goodness add real extrinsic denominations.

For Suarez, both negations and privations are lacks, but there is an important difference between the two. Privations are lacks of what things ought to have by virtue of their natures. Thus, a privation is a lack or absence in a thing of what naturally belongs to it, such as blindness in a human being. A negation, by contrast, is an absence of what is not natural to a subject, such as the absence of wings in a human being. The issue of what is or is not natural to a thing is determined by a definition which specifies those features that make the thing what it is.

Strictly speaking, therefore, negations and privations are not real if by real one means, as Suarez often does, actual or possible being, for negations and privations are not beings at all, but lacks of being. Their only ontological status is as mental beings *(entia rationis)*.

Still, this does not entail that negations and privations are fictitious constructs of the mind. The mind may arrive at truth or falsity regarding reality through negations and privations, for 'negations and privations can be truly and absolutely predicated of a thing without involving any kind of intellectual fictions'. A person *X* who concludes that another person *Y* is blind has understood something true about *Y* if *Y* is in fact blind and something false about *Y* if *Y* is not blind, even though blindness is not something in the world. In either case, the truth or falsity arrived at by *X* is not dependent on *X's* understanding, but on *Y*, that is, on reality, even if the truth is that *Y* lacks sight.

From this we may gather that 'one', which is predicated of being as a negation of privation, is not real in the sense of being either an actual or possible entity. Its reality lies only in that it is not a fictitious product of the mind and thus can be truly predicated of being. Suarez is using two senses of 'real', then, which allow him to say that unity is both real (i.e. non-fictitious) and not real (i.e. neither actual nor possible) without contradiction.

The other properties of being, namely truth and goodness, are not conceived as negations and privations. Rather, they express real extrinsic denominations based on real relations. For Suarez, real extrinsic denominations have four terms: denomination, thing denominated, denominating form, and relation founding the denomination. In the case of a wall, for example, which is extrinsically denominated as 'seen', the terms of the denomination break down as follows:

denomination:	seen
thing denominated:	a wall
denominating form:	the act of seeing
founding relation:	relation of seeing the wall

Relations for Suarez also have four elements: relation, subject, term and foundation. Consider the case of the relation of similarity of *S*, a white "3×5" card, to *T*, another white "3×5" card. In this example, *S* is what Suarez calls the *subject; T* is the *term* of the relation, the white colour of *S* is the *foundation* of the relation; and the similarity of *S* to *T* is the *relation.*

In a real relation, the subject, the term, and the foundation of the relation must be, according to Suarez, real, and the term must also be actual and really or at least modally distinct from the foundation. (It must be remembered that for Suarez real being includes not only actual, but also possible being.) Thus, for the relation of similarity of *S* to *T* to be real, *S* and the white colour of *S* must be real, and *T* must actually exist. That does not entail, however, that the relation is something really distinct from its foundation; the relation and its foundation are only conceptually distinct. In the example given above, the white colour of *S*, a form in *S* which is the foundation of the relation, is not really distinct from the similarity of *S* to *T*.

If any of these conditions is not met, that is, if some of the elements of a relation are not real, or if the term is not actual, or if the distinction between the term and the foundation is not at least modal, then the relation is mental (54, 6, 2 and 47, 6-8; 26, 1039 and 808-18). The reason is that in none of these cases would the relation describe accurately the way things are, and thus would have to be considered, at least in part, a mental construct.

A key difference between a real extrinsic denomination founded on a relation and a real relation is that the real extrinsic denomination applies to the term of the real relation on which the denomination is founded and not to the subject of that relation. It could not be otherwise, for if it were, a real extrinsic denomination would posit in the thing it denominates, namely, in the subject of the relation, a form really distinct from it, which is impossible according to Suarez (54, 2, 9; 26, 1020). That the real extrinsic denomination applies to the term and not the subject of the real relation becomes clear if we use the real relation of similarity of *S* to *T* as the basis for a real extrinsic denomination. In this case, the thing denominated is not *S*, the subject of the relation, but *T*, its term. Thus:

denomination	**similar**
thing denominated:	*T* (the term of the relation)
denominating form:	the whiteness of *S*
founding relation:	similarity of *S* to *T*
subject of founding relation:	*S*
term of relation:	*T*

Now let us apply what has been established concerning real extrinsic denomination to being and its transcendental attributes true and good:

denomination:	true	Good
thing denominated:	being	being
denominating form:	act of intellect	act of will
founding relation:	understanding of being by intellect	desiring of being by will
subject of founding relation:	intellect	will
term of relation:	being	being

Thus, we see what Suarez means when he says that being, true and good are convertible in reality but not conceptually, for whatever is a being is capable also of being the term of a real relation between an intellect or a will and being itself. Such a relation does not affect being, nor do the transcendental attributes true and good refer to a form in being really distinct from it. True and good express extrinsic denominations of being founded on real relations between an intellect or a will and being. The subjects of the relations are intellects and wills, and the forms on which the relations are founded are the acts which modify those intellects and wills. As such, therefore, true and good are neither real properties of being, strictly speaking, nor real or mental relations of being to something else. If they were real properties or real relations, it would imply a kind of distinction between being and them, or their foundation (in the case of real relations), which would be impossible. If they were mental relations, it would imply that true and good are the result of mental activity and, therefore, fictitious.

Summary

Suarez is, without a doubt, one of the key figures in the transition from medieval thought to modern philosophy. He played a substantial role in this transition in so far as he worked within a scholastic tradition that went back to the thirteenth century and beyond but introduced modifications in it that anticipated and prepared the way for modern thought.

This is evident in his conception of metaphysics in so far as he still substantially adheres to the realistic conception of the discipline defended by such medieval scholastics as Aquinas. But the extension of the object of study of metaphysics to possible being and some of the mentalistic language he uses to refer to such an object anticipates and prepares the way for the mentalism so characteristic of modern philosophy.

In the doctrine of the transcendentals, Suarez again works within the parameters he inherits, but he introduces modifications in the doctrine by understanding two of the transcendental properties of being true and good as expressions of real extrinsic denominations of being rather than as mental relations, the popular view among scholastics. This understanding of the transcendentals opens the way to interpretations that, again, pave the way for future developments. In short, Suarez is a figure in whom both the scholastic past and the modern future of philosophy meet and interact in interesting and peculiar ways. From studying his works, one can learn much about both the Middle Ages and modern philosophy.

12

Epilogue in Medieval Philosophy

Introduction

At first, our attitude toward the systems we had picked out was "critical"; that is, for pure types, we thought that there could be no translation. *How* the different types originated we could not decide; perhaps someday genetics or sociology or developmental psychology would, we thought, have an answer (or answers, since each of these suggests plausible factors in explanation). That our fourfold scheme was comprehensive and its influence pervasive continued to seem true.

It had appeared to me that the scheme was system neutral. To my surprise, both friendly and hostile critics said it was Platonic. That would be all right if Platonism were accepted as the best and most comprehensive system of the four we had discovered. The others could then be ordered below it, matching the segments of Plato's Divided Line:

Formal direction	*NOESIS*	:	Platonism
		:	
	DIANOIA	:	Aristotelianism
	PISTIS	:	Atomism
Material		:	
direction	*EIKASIA*	:	Heracliteanism

The label Heracliteanism, suggesting that the most "literary" of the process philosophers represents *eikasia*, does less than justice to the more systematic Anaxagoras, just as picking Bergson as a modern paradigm would shortchange Whitehead. Also, the figure ignores the atomic theories' repeated [shrill] claim that they represent *more* metaphysically than the ubiquitous technology of *pistis*. Nor does this Divided Line representation argue the claim it presents: that forms are *actualities*, not just possibilities or incomplete "abstract ideas."

Here my wife and I parted company. She saw no reason to argue with people who could not see that Platonism was the best and most comprehensive system: Let them use trial and error, and they would find out that this was the best way. I had more subtle evangelical ambitions: I wanted to begin with some kind of proof that the four systems fitted together, without introducing an invidious hierarchy that in varying degrees discounted three out of the four. That drive toward synthesis is certainly "Platonic"; and it expresses the natural human propensity for metaphysics that Kant both recognized and knew he was unlikely to put an end to with his *Critiques*.

"Platonism" has overtones today, in current literature on ethics and education, of rigid and dogmatic application of absolute moral criteria. But that is because of two contemporary misunderstandings of Plato. The forms *are* absolute, but also absolutely general, so that they are never mere rules suited to the situations in books of etiquette. And, being general, the ideas are not the "mental pictures" of the British empiricist tradition. Descartes gives an excellent modern reformulation of Platonism on this point, as he criticizes "most people" for mistaking mental *images* for genuine *concepts* (for example, of a perfect being).

Correcting for these misunderstandings helps prepare the way for what I want. This is a method of using insights for cross-system appreciation and cooperation, without insisting on everyone's *prior* conversion to Platonism. Richard McKeon's claim, in his later essays, was that "the theory of four alternative systems can be formulated in each of the four." That did appeal to me and offered a challenge: If I could prove this thesis formally, our classification of systems could claim general validity. I would also have met one of Professor Plochmann's early objections to the enterprise, namely, that the supposed set of *alternative* systems was only the projection of *one* of them.

My project failed, however, because of an ambiguity in the first premise, that philosophic systems are "either *A* or *B* or *C* or *D*." That "or" is different in holoscopic and meroscopic frameworks and thus so are the "formulations" that are derived from the premise. Whatever we consider the pattern of the four systems to be, we can only state it correctly in two of the four cases and must transform it into something quite different in the other pair.

My wife has been satisfied with her own method of observation and comparison of life-styles and cultures. (In this, she has the precedent of Kierkegaard when he presented his ideas by imagined living within each of the ways of life: For him, these are the aesthete, the moralist, and the knight of faith.) Certainly feeling will count at least as much as formal logic in philosophic communication and appreciation. But there is still a place for explorations of the formal comparisons and transformations that reveal supporting structures beneath the textures of these alternative styles.

I remained convinced that our set of four, supported as it was both by philosophers and by nonphilosophic observers in other fields when they set up large-scale classifications, was correct and complete.

I went back to my early studies of a theorem of Plato's: "But the whole is necessarily one from many, of which the parts will be parts. If something should be part of a many in which it were itself included, then it would be a part of itself, which is impossible." This sounds very like Bertrand Russell's "a class and its members must differ in type," and it introduces Whitehead's thesis that "participation" must be an *asymmetrical* relation in its "internal" or "external" character. Given this combination of insights, I saw that my own discussion had been in a distinctive system of philosophy, a new "one" arising from the group of four taken as "many," *but not itself a fifth member of the group.*

This austere scheme of systems on a level different from that of its members is too abstract to be a concrete philosophy. It is like an outlined handbook of foreign culture for the traveler setting out. For travel in modern Greece, we may read about proper conversational distance, proper serious expressions as greeting, avoidance of "the five" gesture; but that is a long way from having any feeling for them. Language teachers, in our age of amplified migration and travel, find that a fluently spoken language brings gesture, personality, and a whole culture with it. Before, they usually settled for an abstract reading knowledge, adequate for concepts, hopeless for concrete communication.

Whatever formal transsystematic scheme I may present, I now recognize more than ever that we have to be at home in each of the systems just as we would with any four cultures we were comparing. This means not only speaking the language but sharing the feeling and style. The formal scheme of transformation rules is like an ethnographic map: It shows the boundaries, sharp or gradual, of regions different in texture, and where we can make border crossings. Only here the cultures are the worlds of systematic philosophers, each able, somehow, to act through logical space and cross borders to reach the others.

So my final map is an abstraction from full philosophies, each of which has a feeling and a texture of its own. But there are transformation routes that show to each of us that there are assumptions, gaps, and positive entities in our own familiar systems, which we would not have noticed without the intruding contrast. And consider what would happen if we wholly destroyed one quadrant of the set of alternative system families. We live mixed lives, and the mixture needs all four of the cardinal virtues: Justice should hold each to its proper function, temperance bringing a harmonizing friendship, courage and wisdom serving as ideals of all.

Philosophy deserves better than the scattered skirmishing of factions, the unity of each faction depending primarily on its shared hostilities against other factions. We can surely, by this stage of evolution, keep a common ideal in sight while we venture in alternative experiments to pursue it. We can evaluate without destroying, though destruction has, along the evolutionary way, been the past's mode of evaluation.

Plato gives four explanations of his Form of the Good in the *Republic.* Each matches one level of the kind of knowledge ordered on his Divided Line. The most vivid is a myth, comparing us to prisoners in a cave. There we mistake the excitement on a picture screen for the real world that lies outside. The pictures are devised and manipulated by "leaders," but they, too, are unaware of the reality beyond their projection apparatus.

The formal, mathematical, account of the Good, on the line's third level, is summarized in the figure of the Divided Line itself. All knowledge is treated as evaluation, increasing in precision of abstraction and application, with truth, rightness, and beauty the respective reflections on the three lower levels. The line itself is a clear case of *dianoetic* abstract geometrical representation.

The practical, "technological," account of the Good, distinct from the allegorical and algebraic and lying between, on the line's second level, appears as an ideal curriculum. Through three institutions, selected students master, in turn, music, mathematics, and philosophy (the third of these figures in the curriculum as a five-year course in "theoretical dialectic"). This whole study is to be followed by fifteen years of philosophy practiced in application. But even with that 3:1 ratio, Plato seems to have greatly underestimated the relative difficulty and time required for reaching a rightly applied, as opposed to pure, philosophy.

The first account that Socrates offers Glaucon of the Form of the Good is the direct vision of something neither object nor thought, but beyond and ordering both. Throughout the curriculum (and indeed throughout the contextual *Republic* as a whole) the repeating theme of *synoptic vision* calls attention to the way this image of illumination figures in this account of the line on its own highest level. The Good on that level is the criterion of "perfection" a "completeness" with no part or level lacking.

Plato's Socrates does not want to entangle himself and Glaucon in the distinction between "hypothetical" and "nonhypothetical" forms as respective ontological referents of *dianoia* and *noesis*. The Good, however, *is* characterized as "nonhypothetical." And I take this to hold because any challenge to this thesis would have to claim to be a "good" one. This is not a play on words, but a fact about the normative foundations of logic. For discursive purposes, Aristotle translated "good" into "consistently rational" and made its "form" the "law of contradiction." He argues that *this* is *anhypotheton* (appropriating Plato's coined technical term), because without it no one can meaningfully argue against it.

In any case, the final criterion for a comparative study and design of lifestyles, cultures, or philosophies is that each has a synoptic overview. From the standpoint of the philosopher comparing systems, we see what the contrasting components are that a *good* philosophy must harmonize. The final question is whether my transformations and imagined dialogues are a guide toward the resolution of the contrasts of system families, their thoughts and feelings, in some more inclusive harmony. And, though it is inspired by Plato, this is not a parochially Platonic final question and ideal. The requirement of *synopticity*, including *sympathy*, remains invariant beyond any specific system.

Bibliography

Armstrong, A. H., ed. [1970]. *The Cambridge History of Later Greek & Early Medieval Philosophy*. Cambridge: Cambridge University Press.

Augustine [1992]. *Confessions*. James J. O'Donnell, ed. 3 vols. Oxford: Clarendon Press. Vol. 1 = Latin text. Vols. 2–3 = commentary.

Baird, Forrest E., and Kaufmann, Walter [1997]. *Medieval Philosophy*. 2nd ed. Philosophic Classics, vol. 2. Upper Skaddle River, N. J.: Prentice-Hall.

Bocheński, I. M. [1961]. *A History of Formal Logic*. Ivo Thomas, trans. Notre Dame, Ind.: University of Notre Dame Press. A translation of the author's *Formale Logik* [1955]. Freiburg/München: Verlag Karl Alber.

Boethius [1880]. *Anicii Manlii Severini Boethii Commentarii in librum ÐåñéÌ 'åñìçíéìáò pars posterior secundam editionem et indices continens*. Carolus Meiser, ed. Leipzig: B. G. Teubner.

Bosley, Richard N., and Tweedale, Martin [1997]. *Basic Issues in Medieval Philosophy: Selected Readings Presenting the Interactive Discourses among the Major Figures*. Peterborough, Ont.: Broadview Press.

Chadwick, Henry [1981]. *Boethius: The Consolations of Music, Logic, Theology and Philosophy*. Oxford: Clarendon Press.

Copleston, Frederick Copleston [1950]. *A History of Philosophy*. Vol. II: *Medieval Philosophy: From Augustine to Duns Scotus*. Westminster, Md.: The Newman Press.

(Many subsequent reprintings by various presses.)

Dod, Bernard G. [1982]. "Aristoteles latinus." In Kretzmann, *et al.* [1982], Chap. 2 (pp. 45–79).

Dronke, Peter, ed. [1988]. *A History of Twelfth-Century Western Philosophy.* Cambridge: Cambridge University Press.

Ebbesen, Sten [1973]. "Manlius Boethius on Aristotle's *Analytica Posteriora.*" *Cahiers de l'institut du moyen-âge grec et latin (University of Copenhagen)*, 9, pp. 68–73.

Gersh, Stephen [1986]. *Middle Platonism and Neoplatonism: The Latin Tradition.* 2 vols. Publications in Medieval Studies, vol. 23. Notre Dame, Ind.: University of Notre Dame Press.

Gibson, Margaret, ed. [1981]. *Boethius: His Life, Thought and Influence.* Oxford: Basil Blackwell.

Haskins, Charles Homer [1957]. *The Renaissance of the 12th Century.* Cleveland: Meridian Books. Originally published Cambridge, Mass.: Harvard University Press, 1927.

Henry, Desmond Paul [1967]. "Medieval Philosophy." *The Encyclopedia of Philosophy.* New York: Macmillan. Vol. 5, pp. 253–58.

Inglis, John, ed. [2002] *Medieval Philosophy and the Classical Tradition: In Islam, Judaism, and Christianity.* London-New York: Routledge.

John of Salisbury [1955]. *The Metalogicon of John of Salisbury: A Twelfth-Century Defense of the Verbal and Logical Arts of the Trivium.* D. D. McGarry, trans. Berkeley, Cal.: University of California Press.

Klima, Gyula, ed. & trans., with Allhof, Fritz and Vaidya, Anand Jaiprakash [2007]. *Medieval Philosophy: Essential Readings with Commentary.* Oxford: Blackwell Publishers.

Knowles, David [1964]. *The Evolution of Medieval Thought.* New York: Vintage Books.

Koterski, Joseph W., S.J. *An Introduction to Medieval Philosophy: Basic Concepts.* Chichester: Wiley-Blackwell, 2009.

Kretzmann, Norman, and Stump, Eleonore, ed. & trans.

[1988]. *The Cambridge Translations of Medieval Philosophical Texts.* Vol. 1: *Logic and the Philosophy of Language.* Cambridge: Cambridge University Press.

Kretzmann, Norman, *et al.*, ed. [1982]. *The Cambridge History of Later Medieval Philosophy: From the Rediscovery of Aristotle to the Disintegration of Scholasticism, 1100–1600.* Cambridge: Cambridge University Press.

Leff, Gordon [1958]. *Medieval Thought: St. Augustine to Ockham.* Harmondsworth: Penguin Books.

Luscombe, D. E. [1997]. *Medieval Thought.* History of Western Philosophy, vol. 2. Oxford: Oxford University Press.

MacDonald, Scott, and Kretzmann, Norman [1998]. "Medieval Philosophy." *Routledge Encyclopedia of Philosophy.* London: Routledge. Vol. 6, pp. 269–77.

Marenbon, John, ed. [1998]. *The Routledge History of Philosophy,* vol. III: "The Middle Ages." London: Routledge.

Maurer, Armand A. [1982]. *Medieval Philosophy.* 2nd ed. Toronto: Pontifical Institute of Mediaeval Studies.

McGrade, A. S., ed. [2003]. *The Cambridge Companion to Medieval Philosophy.* Cambridge: Cambridge University Press.

McGrade, Arthur Stephen, Kilcullen, John, and Kempshall, Matthew, ed. & trans. [2001]. *The Cambridge Translations of Medieval Philosophical Texts.* Vol. 2: *Ethics and Political Philosophy.* Cambridge: Cambridge University Press.

McInerny, Ralph [1970]. *Philosophy from St. Augustine to Ockham.* A History of Western Philosophy, vol. 2; Notre Dame, Ind: University of Notre Dame Press.

McKeon, Richard, ed. and trans. [1929]. *Selections from Medieval Philosophers.* 2 vols. New York: Charles Scribner's Sons. (Vol. 1: *Augustine to Albert the Great.* Vol. 2: *Roger Bacon to William of Ockham.*)

Migne, Jacques-Paul, ed. [1844–64]. *Patrologiae cursus completus ... series latina.* 221 vols. Paris: J.-P. Migne. (Commonly cited as "PL.")

Obertello, Luca [1974]. *Severino Boezio.* 2 vols. Collana di Monografie, I. Genoa: Accademica ligure di scienze e lettere.

Pasnau, Robert, ed. & trans. [2002]. *The Cambridge Translations of Medieval Philosophical Texts.* Vol. 3: *Mind and Knowledge.* Cambridge: Cambridge University Press.

Quasten, Johannes [1950–86]. *Patrology.* 4 vols. Vols. 1–3, Utrecht: Speculum, and Westminster, Md.: The Newman Press, 1950–60. Vol. 4, Westminster, Md.: Christian Classics. 1986.

Robinson, Fred. C. [1984]. *"Medieval: the Middle Ages."* *Speculum* 59, pp. 745–56. (Presidential address to the annual meeting of the Medieval Academy of America, 1984.)

Schoedinger, Andrew B., ed. [1996]. *Readings in Medieval Philosophy.* New York: Oxford University Press.

Shapiro, Herman, ed. [1964]. *Medieval Philosophy: Selected Readings from Augustine to Buridan.* New York: The Modern Library.

Spade, Paul Vincent [1994]. "Medieval Philosophy." In Anthony Kenny, ed. *The Oxford Illustrated History of Philosophy.* Oxford: Oxford University Press. Chap. 2, pp. 55–105.

Verbeke, Gerard [1983]. *The Presence of Stoicism in Medieval Thought.* Washington, D. C.: The Catholic University of America Press.

Weinberg, Julius R. [1964]. *A Short History of Medieval Philosophy.* Princeton, N. J.: Princeton University Press.

Wippel, John F., and Wolter, Allan, ed. [1969]. *Medieval Philosophy: From St. Augustine to Nicholas of Cusa.* New York: The Free Press.

Index

R

S

T

U

V

W